Praise for *Talk, Inc.*

"This great book shows the importance of harnessing the power of real conversations to drive real change."

— Ian Cheshire, Group Chief Executive, Kingfisher PLC

"Effective communications are the lifeblood of an effective organization. *Talk, Inc.*, shows how companies are replacing an outdated, top-down, command-and-control communications model with a model based on authentic, give-and-take conversation. The result is a workplace where intelligent, motivated employees are engaged, trusted, and empowered—where they are treated as adults rather than as passive spectators of a drama beyond their control."

— William J. Teuber Jr., Vice Chairman, EMC Corporation

"Business thinking today is preoccupied with rising processor speeds that run ever more sophisticated financial models. *Talk, Inc.*, however, appropriately draws attention back to the power of conversation. The points raised in this book about the value of conversation—whether it involves loyal customers, engaged employees, or critical suppliers—are well worth heeding."

— Steve Voigt, CEO, King Arthur Flour Company

"In the new economy, work *is* conversation. It's how you make connections, issue challenges, create culture—and stay competitive. If you want to know how to have truly strategic conversations, read this book!"

— Alan M. Webber, Cofounder, *Fast Company*; author, *Rules of Thumb: 52 Truths for Winning at Business Without Losing Your Self*

"Drawing on the experiences and perspectives of a diverse group of global experts, *Talk, Inc.*, argues convincingly that organizational communication must move from 'command and control' to *conversation*. Through examples and extended case studies, the authors offer practical guidance on how to implement this new approach. This book also provides communicators with the ammunition that they need to persuade senior leadership that everyone in an organization must engage in authentic communication. Thoroughly readable, *Talk, Inc.*, will be an essential resource for business leaders."

— Julie Freeman, former President, International Association of Business Communicators

Talk,
Inc.

HOW
TRUSTED
LEADERS
USE
CONVERSATION
TO POWER
THEIR
ORGANIZATIONS

Talk, Inc.

BORIS GROYSBERG

MICHAEL SLIND

Harvard Business Review Press • Boston, Massachusetts

Copyright 2012 Harvard Business School Publishing

Printed in the United States of America

10 9 8 7 6 5 4

Library of Congress Cataloging-in-Publication Data

Groysberg, Boris.
    Talk, Inc. : how trusted leaders use conversation to power their organizations / Boris Groysberg, Michael Slind.
        p. cm.
    ISBN 978-1-4221-7333-6 (alk. paper)
    1. Communication in management.   2. Communication in organizations.
3. Organizational behavior.   4. Leadership.   I. Slind, Michael.   II. Title.
    HD30.3.G768 2012
    658.4'5—dc23

                                                                        2011053282

The paper used in this publication meets the requirements of the American National Standard for Permanence of Paper for Publications and Documents in Libraries and Archives Z39.48-1992.

To our wives, Liliya Groysberg and Bina Patel,

who allowed us to talk and talk and talk about this book

and who showed infinite understanding and patience

when we had to stop talking and start writing

CONTENTS

Introduction

Not Just Talk

NOT SO LONG AGO, power within organizations emanated from the commands of top executives. Those leaders drove organizational performance by devising strategic objectives, which they translated into directives that passed down through a hierarchy before reaching employees, whose job was merely to take orders and to act on those orders. Today, that model of organizational life has essentially fallen apart. At more and more companies in more and more industries, leaders recognize that driving their company in a traditional command-and-control manner doesn't work anymore. To an ever-increasing degree, people—and the energies and capabilities that lie inside them—are the ultimate source of optimal performance and sustainable competitive advantage. Yet the kind of value that people now deliver to an organization isn't the kind of value that leaders can leverage simply by issuing orders from the executive suite. In an environment where employees have that much power to determine the success or failure of an organization, the ability of leaders to command grows weak and their sense of control grows weaker still.

For most leaders, that story will have considerable resonance. Even those who retain a firm grip on the main levers of activity within their organization will sense, deep down, that their ability to harness the creative and operational energy of their people has grown more tenuous over the years. Yet, as familiar as the loss-of-command story has become, leaders continue to grapple with the question of where that story ends—or, more pertinently, the question of what comes next. Now that the model of driving a company from its commanding heights has become obsolete, what will take its place? How, in this new era, should leaders seek to power their organization?

In *Talk, Inc.,* we argue that a new source of organizational power has come to the fore. Our term for that power source is *organizational conversation*. Instead of handing down commands or imposing formal controls, many leaders today are interacting with their workforce in ways that call to mind an ordinary conversation between two people. What's more, they are fostering and facilitating conversation-like practices throughout their company—practices that enable a company to achieve higher degrees of trust, improved operational efficiency, greater motivation and commitment among employees, and better coordination between top-level strategy and frontline execution. The power of organizational conversation isn't the kind of power that manifests itself as control over a person or a process. Rather, it's the kind of power that makes a person or a process *go*. It's energy, in other words. It's fuel. In organizational terms, conversation is what keeps the engine of value creation firing on all cylinders.

Simply put, organizational conversation isn't "just talk." To understand why, think about the way that start-ups and other small companies have come to embody an ideal of organizational excellence. Then consider that one hallmark of a high-performing small company is the eminently *conversational* mode in which its people operate. In the old business world, organizational success was largely a function of organizational size. As companies grew bigger, their leaders were able to issue orders that reached ever-larger workforces, and employees in turn were able to generate more and more products for a wider and wider share of a given market. Nowadays, by contrast, it's small companies that often demonstrate a superior ability to mobilize resources optimally and to target fresh markets quickly. What accounts for the relative success of relatively compact organizations?

It's a matter of *scale*. In a small company, leaders remain close to employees—close not just in terms of space, but also in terms of spirit—and employees trust them as a result.

It's a matter of *structure*. In a small company, physical proximity and an open culture allow people to share key insights and crucial data, and information moves freely and efficiently in multiple directions.

It's a matter of *participation*. In a small company, cumbersome divisions of labor are rare, and a wide range of employees are able to play a part in accomplishing major tasks.

It's a matter of *focus*. In a small company, all employees enjoy a clear line of sight on the guiding plans and priorities that their leaders have developed.

Look closely at those elements of small-company success, and you'll note that they correspond to elements of a good person-to-person conversation. When two people talk with each other, and when that talk is at its most robust, the scale of their conversation is typically small and, indeed, intimate; the structure of their conversation is dynamic and interactive; their participation in the conversation is equal and inclusive; and their approach to the conversation is focused and intentional. Those qualities (as we will explain more fully in a moment) also correspond to the defining elements of organizational conversation.

Through conversation, we contend, a big or growing organization can retain or recapture much of the nimbleness, the cohesiveness, and the raw, productive energy of a well-oiled small company. That, at bottom, is the core promise of this book—that leaders, drawing upon the ideas and practices that we present in the pages that follow, can tap into this new form of organizational power.

The *I*'s Have It

Organizational conversation, in our use of the term, applies to the full range of patterns and processes by which information circulates through a company—all of the ways in which ideas, images, and other forms of organizational content pass between leaders and employees, or from one employee (or group of employees) to another. It occupies roughly the same space that "corporate communication" has traditionally occupied in organizational life. Yet, both in spirit and in practice, organizational conversation is quite different from corporate communication. The latter function grew naturally out of the command-and-control model.

Top-down and one-way in its orientation, corporate communication aptly suited the needs of large, hierarchy-driven companies by serving as a central organ for distributing news of corporate activity to internal as well as external audiences. In effect, it served as a vehicle for making human conversation all but unnecessary, at least from an organizational perspective. Departments of corporate communication remain in place, of course, and that legacy term remains in common usage. No company (to our knowledge) has yet created an "organizational conversation department" or hired a "chief conversation officer." Nonetheless, those phrases hint at the new approach that many leaders at many organizations are beginning to take.

Where organizational conversation flourishes, it involves up to four elements. These elements reflect the essential attributes of interpersonal conversation, and likewise they reflect the classic distinguishing features of a high-flying small company. In developing our model of organizational conversation, we have attached to each element a word that begins with the letter *I*.

Intimacy: Conversation between two people both requires and enables its participants to stay close to one another, figuratively as well as literally. Only through intimacy of that kind can they achieve a true meeting of minds. In organizational conversation, similarly, leaders reduce the distance—institutional as well as spatial—that would normally separate them from their employees. They do so by cultivating the art of listening to people at all levels of their organization, and by learning to talk with those people in ways that are personal, honest, and authentic. Conversational intimacy equips leaders to manage change within their company, and it helps them to solidify buy-in among employees for new strategic initiatives. In short, it allows them to build trust through talk.

Interactivity: Talk is a two-way affair—an exchange of comments and questions, of musings and mutterings. The sound of one person talking, whatever else it may be, is not a conversation. Following that same logic, organizational conversation replaces the traditional one-way structure of corporate communication with a dynamic process in which leaders talk *with* employees and not just *to* them. Changes in the technology of communication, especially those that incorporate emerging forms of social media, support that shift. Equally important, though, is the emergence of cultural norms that favor dialogue over monologue. The benefits that accrue from conversational interactivity include lower transaction costs, an easing of the pressure caused by information overload, and an increase in employees' ability to respond readily to customer needs.

Inclusion: At its best, interpersonal conversation is an equal-opportunity proposition. It invites all participants to put their own ideas, and indeed their heart and soul, into the conversational mix. Organizational conversation, by the same token, calls upon employees to participate eagerly in the work of generating the content through which a company tells its story, both internally and externally. People in frontline and midlevel posts act as semiofficial company bloggers, for example, or as trained brand ambassadors. By empowering employees to communicate in that way, leaders relinquish much of the control that they formerly exerted over organizational messaging. But they gain a great deal in return. Through conversational inclusion, leaders are able to boost employee engagement, to spur innovation and creativity, and to improve the branding and reputation of their organization.

Intentionality: Even in the most casual two-person chat, the two people in question will each have some sense of where they want the conversation to go. Talk that's truly rewarding is never truly "idle." So it is with organizational conversation, which puts a premium on developing and following an agenda that aligns with the strategic objectives of a company. Over time, the many voices that contribute to conversation within an organization must converge in a single vision for that organization—a single understanding of its mission in the world and its place in the marketplace. While the elements of intimacy, interactivity, and inclusion serve to open up that conversation, the element of intentionality serves to "close the loop" on it. Among the outcomes that conversational intentionality helps to promote are a keen focus on driving business value and a more effective approach to strategic alignment.

Leaders who power their organization through conversation-based practices will not always "dot" all four of these I's. But as we've discovered in our research, these elements tend to reinforce each other. In many instances, they overlap with each other significantly. As we address each element in turn, it will be apparent that our model of organizational conversation is (like conversation itself) highly iterative: Some ideas will recur, in slightly or more-than-slightly altered form, as we move from one element to the next. In the end, these four elements coalesce to form a single integrated process—a single source of organizational power.

Talking About *Talk, Inc.*

When we began the project that led to this book, the focus of our research was fairly narrow. One of us, Boris Groysberg, is a business scholar and an educator with a background in studying organizational dynamics. The other, Michael Slind, is a professional communicator with an interest in organizational strategy. Together, we fastened on the idea of investigating how people in organizations communicate internally in the twenty-first century. Our initial guiding questions were straightforward enough: What are the current activities and norms, the prevailing aims and objectives, that characterize the way that companies manage the flow of information to, from, and among employees? How have those activities and aims changed in recent years? Are there developments in this area that qualify as being particularly innovative? Our research consisted chiefly of interviews with communication professionals at all manner of organizations—large and small, blue-chip and start-up, for-profit and nonprofit, U.S. and international. (We spoke, in all, with nearly 150 people at more than one hundred organizations.) Before long, we discovered that something greater was afoot than what our original research design had allowed for. The field known as "communication," which had long been a discrete institutional function, was evolving at many companies into a constellation of practices that extends across the entirety of organizational life.

We had hit upon a development that goes beyond the traditional scope of what communication leaders do, and we therefore widened our research to encompass interviews with other organizational leaders, including senior executives with general-management responsibility. Those interviews crystallized what we had begun to see earlier. Certain recurring themes had become apparent, and they now coalesced into the overarching theme of *conversation*. More and more leaders today, we found, place a high value on forms of discourse and styles of interaction that have far more in common with the model of two people talking than they do with standard-issue corporate communication. In implicit as well as explicit terms, the leaders whom we interviewed spoke of their efforts to "have a conversation" with their people, or their ambition to "advance the conversation" within their organization. They described steps that they had taken to make that conversation (as we would now put it) more intimate, more interactive, more inclusive, and more intentional. They suggested that maintaining organizational conversation is a task that top executives must adopt as their own—that delegating it to professional communicators is no longer a viable option.

Our findings also revealed that the shift from corporate communication to organizational conversation has occurred because of several long-term changes that have affected the business world profoundly.

First, there is *economic* change. As service industries become more economically significant than manufacturing industries, and as knowledge work supplants other kinds of labor, the need for sophisticated ways to process and share information grows more acute.

Second, there is *organizational* change. As companies become flatter and less hierarchical in structure, and as frontline employees become more pivotally involved in value-creating work, lateral and bottom-up communication comes to be no less important than top-down communication.

Third, there is *global* change. As workforces become more diverse and more widely dispersed, the challenge of navigating across lines of cultural and geographic division entails modes of interaction that are fluid and complex.

Fourth, there is *generational* change. As millennials and other younger workers gain a foothold in organizations, they bring an expectation that peers and authority figures alike will communicate with them in a dynamic, two-way fashion.

Fifth, there is *technological* change. As digital networks make instant connectivity the norm of business life, and as social media platforms grow more powerful and more ubiquitous, a reliance on older, less conversational channels of organizational communication ceases to be tenable.

Finally, there is the brute fact that all of these changes have steeply accelerated the pace at which business gets done today. As the time available for decision making becomes shorter and shorter, a commitment to engaging employees in that process becomes a make-or-break imperative for leaders.

One of those changes in particular—the rapid adoption of social media technology among both consumers and businesspeople—has received a lot of attention in recent years. There are, indeed, several books that deal centrally with that topic. *Talk, Inc.*, is different. It's not about social media. Instead, it's about (among other things) what leaders and their employees *do* with social media. It's about the increasing tendency among people in organizations to put conversation at the center of their work lives. And it's about the way that conversation-based practices both generate and release organizational energy.

We've divided the book into four parts, with one part for each of the four elements that make up our model of organizational conversation. Each part includes a series of three chapters, and those chapters conform to a simple template. The orientation of the first chapter in each part is *analytical*: We define one of the four elements, outline some of its key dynamics, and delve into a few broad topics that reflect the conversational turn that many leaders are now taking. (In a couple of instances, we stop to take an "In Depth" look at a relevant practice that the leaders of a particular organization have adopted.) In the second chapter of each part, we shift toward a *descriptive* orientation. Under the banner of "Walking the Talk," we present a discussion of one company—a full-dress case study that not only highlights one element of our model, but also illustrates how multiple elements gel into the unified pursuit of organizational conversation. The last chapter in each part offers a *prescriptive* coda to the preceding chapters. Called "Talk, Inc., Points" (or TIPs), this chapter provides brief take-away ideas for you to keep in mind as you explore our model. Think of these TIPs as conversation starters— as practical insights on how to set in motion a vibrant conversation within your own organization.

Throughout the book, we draw extensively from the conversations that we have had with people who took part in our research. Unless otherwise indicated by an endnote, every quotation in the pages that follow comes from one of those interviews. Some of the people quoted here, as it happens, no longer work at the organization whose communication practices were the focus of our interview with them. Nonetheless, in discussing their views and experiences, we follow the same approach that we use elsewhere—an approach that treats all such material as being relevant, and relevant *now*, to our model of organizational conversation. (In other words, even though each of our interviews with organizational leaders clearly took place in the past, we refer to their comments in the present tense.) We should also note that in preparing the book for publication, we took care to confirm with each interview subject the accuracy and current relevance of the comments that he or she shared with us.

We end here with one last thought: There is a conversation that takes place within every company—whether company leaders know it or not, and whether they like it or not. At the nearest water cooler or at the virtual rumor mill, employees chat about the state of their organization, and that chatter has a bearing on the company's operational performance. Is the company doing well? Does it treat its people well? Is it heading in the right direction? What people say when they talk about those issues, and how they say it, will affect the capacity of leaders to drive their organization forward. Smart leaders understand that they can't avoid that conversation for very long. Nor can they fully control it. But if they engage with it in the right way, they have the potential to unleash organizational energy of a sort that no leader could ever command.

PART I

Intimacy

CHAPTER ONE

Up and Down

The Promise of Trust-Based Leadership

DISTANCE IS A DISEASE that cripples true conversation. Frequently, the distance that exists between conversational participants is spatial: Good talk rarely occurs when people have to yell at each other. Yet physical proximity, while it's often a vital ingredient in the success of a conversation, isn't essential. The telephone can mediate an emotionally charged dialogue or a heartfelt meeting of minds, if people choose to use it that way, and the same point applies to instant messaging and phone-based texting. What *is* essential to the conduct of interpersonal conversation is mental or emotional proximity. Our term for that quality is conversational *intimacy*.

Organizational conversation, no less than the kind of conversation that takes place between friends, depends upon this element of intimacy. In an organizational context, conversational intimacy is a function of leadership. It refers to a mode of human relations in which those with decision-making authority seek and earn the trust (and hence the careful attention) of those who work under that authority. It thrives when the leaders of a company succeed in *getting close* to employees—when senior executives, in particular, shrink the gaps that would otherwise separate them from employees. Sometimes those gaps are, indeed, spatial. (As we'll see, one aspect of effective conversational leadership involves getting close to employees in a straightforwardly literal way.) More profound than any challenge caused by physical distance, however, are the institutional and psychological gaps that typically open up between leaders and employees in organizations that feature a sharply delineated hierarchy. Even in a small company, the functional distance between top executives and lower-level employees can grow quite large quite fast. To counteract that tendency, many leaders today have begun to change the way that conversation unfolds between the "up" and "down" parts of their organization.

The four elements of organizational conversation that we describe in this book are all salient to our model of high-performance internal communication. Still, our decision to begin the book with an account of conversational intimacy isn't random. Intimacy creates the foundation upon which the other building blocks of this model either stand or fall. Without a commitment by top executives to making the distance between themselves and their employees as narrow as possible, neither they nor those employees will be able to tap the full power of organizational conversation.

Intimacy merits a prime spot in our model for another reason: Over the past few decades, as we noted in our introduction, the top-down approach to organizational management has yielded to an approach that encourages a more complex and fluid interaction between the upper and lower levels of an organization. Companies and their leaders have gravitated toward a managerial system that's less about command and control than it is about collaboration and coordination—less about issuing and taking orders than about asking and answering questions. Communication has become less top-down in structure and more bottom-up, less corporate in tone and more casual. For leaders, commanding assent and being "right" matter less than talking straight and listening well. In relating to employees, they adopt a stance that has less to do with projecting an aura of authority than it does with carving out opportunities for dialogue. Forging a relationship with employees, in fact, has become a prominent goal of organizational communication.

"Internal communications is now becoming a C-suite opportunity," says Gary F. Grates, a PR consultant. The increasingly acute challenge of attracting and retaining talented people has spurred senior executives to take employee communication more seriously than they did in earlier eras. "As we went through the nineties, we began to realize that the workforce is not a captive audience; it's a constituency. So we began to see a focus on having a relationship with employees: What are we doing as leaders to manage that relationship effectively—to engage in it?" Grates says. A "new management model" has emerged in which "the premise is really about conversation and connection," and adapting to that model "is going to be difficult for people who were brought up in the traditional form of management, which is more top-down," he argues.

Which isn't to say that bottom-up communication has altogether replaced the top-down model of old. Leaders still must lead, and still do lead. They haven't turned the basic structure of employee communication upside-down. But they have, in many cases, turned their approach to employee communication inside-out. How they conceive of their own role in that endeavor has changed considerably, for example. If employees are now a "constituency," as Grates suggests, then executives who lead them must apply energy, attention, and ingenuity to the task of winning their vote of confidence. "In the old days, senior executives would care a little bit about public relations: Make sure that the press release is right; make sure that the investor-relations guys get it. But increasingly, it became apparent that they had to be internal politicians and to communicate better within their world," says Peter McKillop, who directed communication for Bank of America's retail division from 2004 to 2008. (Today, he is chief communications officer for the Americas at UBS AG.) "At Bank of America, the president of the consumer and small-business bank division spent a big percentage of his time focused on internal communication, whether it was visiting retail branches or doing a town-hall broadcast—all of the different ways that a top executive communicates to his troops."

Time spent by leaders on communicating internally is another indicator of how their approach to that task has evolved in recent decades. "Twenty years ago, a senior executive might think about engaging in employee communications once every week, every two weeks, every three weeks. Most of the time, they were focused on customers or running operations," says Larry Solomon, senior vice president of corporate communications at AT&T. "Now, not a day goes by when we're not talking about how we need to post a blog on this topic, we need to record a video on that topic—'Let's make sure that employees understand this'—et cetera." David Liu, cofounder and CEO of XO Group, Inc. (formerly The Knot), a media company that specializes in wedding and other life-stage content, flatly states that communicating with employees commands a big share of his attention span: "It is fifty percent of my job."

Ultimately, the quality of a leader's practice of employee communication outweighs the sheer quantity of time that he or she devotes to it. To appreciate how the element of intimacy plays out within an organization, consider again the features that distinguish interpersonal conversation. When two friends talk with each other, their conversation is open, honest, direct, and informal. They speak together on the basis of mutual respect and with a sense of reciprocity. Their chatter is not stilted and bureaucratic, but lively and full of personality. So it is with organizational conversation. For leaders, the pursuit of intimacy in communication means stepping down from their corporate perch and then stepping up to the challenge of speaking with employees in ways that are personal, authentic, and transparent. It's partly a matter of style and partly a state of mind. Where conversational intimacy prevails in an organization, bottom-up communication supplements and coexists with top-down communication: Employees at all levels are comfortable with speaking directly to top managers, and leaders are at ease with revealing to employees not only their thoughts about strategy and operations, but also a glimpse of themselves.

Getting close to employees is easiest when leaders make an effort to meet with them in close quarters. Although physical proximity isn't an absolute prerequisite to achieving conversational intimacy, it certainly helps. The face-to-face, in-person meeting with employees, in fact, remains a kind of gold standard for executive communication. "That face-to-face component is now being done at a very strategic level," says Grates, who has counseled leaders at high-profile companies such as Dell, General Motors, and Visa International. "That's why you see a lot of CEOs, when they first join a company, spending several months on the road. They're meeting as many employees and customers as they can." Advances in other forms of communication, including those that exploit digital media, have hardly diminished the value of direct contact between senior leaders and those who work in their organization.

Seen from one vantage point, organizational conversation unfolds on two basic levels. On the first level, leaders get close to employees only in a figurative sense; on the other level, they engage with employees in a fully here-and-now sense. "There's Big C and Little C," says Judith Rossi, director of global communications for Smiths Medical, a medical-device provider based in St. Paul, Minnesota. "Big C is mass communication. It's the newsletters, it's the intranet, it's the all-hands meeting. It's the form of communication that everybody receives and that everybody generally sees, and it's the easier one to manage. Little C is the lunches, the one-on-one meetings. It's face-to-face, but on a more intimate scale than, say, a town-hall meeting with a large group. It's the most difficult kind of communication to do." That kind of communication is difficult for reasons of time and scale—"How do you get executives as close to their people as possible, given everything else that they have to do?" Rossi asks—and because not every leader has the proper temperament for it. Even so, Rossi contends, executives and those who support them should make a big push on the "Little C" front: "The best practice is to get the president or the CEO out talking to people directly, in as intimate a setting as you can provide, so that people feel comfortable enough to speak up."

Here we run into a paradox. On the one hand, the shift away from a strictly top-down approach to communication fundamentally alters the patterns by which ideas and information move up and down the structure of an organization. It overturns long-standing norms that once empowered a select few to talk and allowed everyone else merely to listen. It brings leaders down to the level of their employees, and it brings employees up to their level. On the other hand, the impetus behind any push to close the gap between leaders and employees must originate at the top of an organizational hierarchy. "You have to start with a leader who wants to do it and who believes in it," Rossi argues. "You cannot build good internal communications from the ground up. You have to build it from the top down." In other words, even as leaders give others license to speak, they cannot cede responsibility for setting that process in motion, or for setting a tone that others will emulate in the conversation that follows.

Gaining Trust—and Giving Trust

Where there is no trust, there can be no intimacy. And for all practical purposes, the reverse is true as well. No one will dive into a heartfelt exchange of views with someone who seems to have a hidden agenda or a hostile manner, and any discussion that does unfold between two people will be rewarding and substantive only to the extent that each person can take the other at face value. The need for trust within organizational conversation is no less strong. Indeed, it might well be stronger, since group dynamics and institutional complexity by their very nature increase the risk that cynicism and feelings of alienation will fester among would-be conversational participants. A habit of tuning out whenever executives try to speak, or of shutting up whenever executives offer to listen, can take hold among employees all too easily. To counter that tendency, leaders must learn to be givers—to be generous with their own reserves of trust. Before they can achieve conversational intimacy, they need to "put some skin in the game." They must be willing to impart information to their workforce that they might otherwise, out of strategic caution or simple prudence, keep to themselves. Trust begets trust, in other words, and to earn the good faith of their employees, those in charge of an organization often must prove their capacity to show a little faith in those whom they lead.

Trust has become a hot topic among organizational leaders, if only because maintaining it has become so difficult. "CEOs are trusted by seventeen percent of people now. It's pathetic," says Richard Edelman, president and CEO of Edelman, a public-relations firm. Every year, his firm conducts survey research to find out which groups in society and in business have high or low levels of credibility, and it issues a Trust Barometer report to publicize its findings. "The Trust Barometer shows that an average employee is as much as three times more credible than a CEO as a source of information about a company," Edelman says, citing the firm's 2009 report. Employees have achieved that ranking in just the past few years, he adds, and in that time they have effectively become the "new credible source." A company's top leaders, therefore, must show genuine respect for members of that population—and vest genuine trust in them. When a leader communicates with employees, the goal should not be simply to "talk at" them, Edelman argues: "It's allowing them to 'talk out.' You talk to them, and then you allow them to speak more broadly. And then you benefit as well." His point applies mainly to the value of empowering employees to "talk out" to the world at large, and thereby to serve as public advocates for their company. But the idea, and the data behind it, have broad implications.

Making it easy for employees to "talk out" within their organization, for example, makes it easier for them to trust not only their senior leaders but also one another. Thus, one upshot of generating trust through talk is improved operational effectiveness. Ken Bagan has seen this dynamic at work in organizations that he has helped to lead. "I try to engender an atmosphere of trust, so that everybody feels that they share in the common vision of the place," says Bagan, who over the past decade has held the post of CEO at two Canadian energy companies (including, most recently, Enerchem International, an oil-marketing concern based in Calgary). "If everybody is involved and knows what's going on, then nobody feels marginalized and everybody contributes in a superior way. If people are marginalized, they begin to feel distrust, and if they feel distrust, then you start to experience a breakdown in your ability to manage the company's efforts." He recalls an episode at one company where he worked in which the trust factor (or, to be precise, the distrust factor) operated counterproductively: "There were silos, and within those silos, there was a rumor mill. The silos competed with each other, or they kept secrets from each other, and certainly they didn't cooperate with each other. And that led to suboptimal performance. Once the silos were broken down, communication was established between those groups and they began to work together. It starts with better communication."

The art of enhancing organizational trust through "better communication" requires executives to display two key leadership behaviors: an openness to hearing what employees have to say, and a willingness to talk straight about matters that senior leaders often prefer *not* to talk about. (Those behaviors, not coincidentally, align with the practice of listening to employees and that of speaking with them authentically.) Trust flourishes when it operates like a two-way street. After all, people aren't apt to trust a leader who doesn't trust them enough to let them speak out. Meanwhile, when it comes to addressing topics that might otherwise be off-limits—in particular, topics that involve sensitive financial data—many leaders find that the value of entrusting that data to employees outweighs the risks that come with doing so. "We share high-level financial information with everybody," says Scott Huennekens, president and CEO of Volcano Corporation, a medical-device vendor based in San Diego. "A lot of companies don't share financial information to a great degree. But we'd rather overcommunicate than undercommunicate."

In Depth: An Inside Story

Talking about financial matters, in fact, puts the ideal of conversational intimacy to the ultimate test. One company that has pushed the boundary on that front is Athenahealth, a medical-records technology provider. In 2007, when the leaders of Athenahealth took the company public, they adopted a highly venturesome form of placing trust in their employees. As they prepared for an initial public offering (IPO), cofounders Jonathan Bush and Todd Park decided to treat every last one of those employees as an *insider* under the strict, legal meaning of that term. At the time, Athenahealth had a head count of about six hundred, and the prospect of including that number of people in what is normally a rather select group raised serious qualms among certain people—investors, lawyers—who would play a pivotal role in determining the company's future.

An insider, as defined in securities law, is any employee whom a public company has entrusted with strategic and financial information that could materially affect its business prospects, and hence its stock price. As a rule, a company's insiders include only its top-tier officers; very rarely does a company declare that every member of its workforce will be privy to essential "inside" data. Understandably and inevitably, high-powered experts from the firms that would help float the Athenahealth offering (including lead underwriters Goldman Sachs and Merrill Lynch) argued against the cofounders' everyone-is-an-insider plan. "We were sitting at big tables with the bankers and all their attorneys and all our attorneys," says John Hallock, director of global corporate communications at Athenahealth. "Every risk and concern that they aired was absolutely valid."

The dangers posed by a commitment to sharing information broadly within the Athenahealth organization were quite evident. Giving inside data to hundreds of employees would greatly complicate the task of managing the flow of company information during the highly sensitive "quiet period" that precedes an IPO. In general, moreover, regulators at the Securities and Exchange Commission and elsewhere do not look kindly on companies that create a large pool of people who could be suspects in an insider-trading investigation. A policy of entrusting all employees with strategically critical information also opens the possibility that such information might fall into the hands of competitors. Alongside those universal risks to its legal and financial position, meanwhile, Athenahealth must contend with challenges that are specific to its industry. It competes in the brisk market for electronic medical records (EMR) technology, and it brings to that industry an innovative service model that adds an extra layer of information-security risk.

Beyond merely providing software to clients, Athenahealth operates a network-driven platform for managing data on behalf of medical professionals. "We put a lot of trust in our employees. We have thirty million patient records—live—on AthenaNet," Hallock notes, referring to the company's proprietary Web-based network. In handling those records, Athenahealth must follow stringent rules, including the privacy provisions of the federal Health Insurance Portability and Accountability Act (known as HIPAA), and a commitment to internal transparency entails a risk to successful compliance with such regulations.

Equally clear to Athenahealth leaders, however, were the risks associated with *not* trusting employees enough to share data with them. Founded in 1997, Athenahealth in its first decade had developed a spirit of conversational intimacy—and a practice of vesting considerable trust in its workforce—that its leaders had no intention of relinquishing. Company executives, starting with Bush and Park, insisted on the need to retain their ability to talk freely and fully with all employees. (Bush, a cousin of former president George W. Bush and a nephew of former president George H. W. Bush, has an MBA from Harvard Business School. Park, who has a background in high-tech consulting, left Athenahealth in August 2009 to join the Obama administration as chief technology officer in the Department of Health and Human Services.) Hallock summarizes the message that Bush, Park, and their leadership team conveyed to the company's investment bankers: "The number one asset that we have is our culture, our people. If we lose it, then you guys might as well not even take us out." Despite the qualms of advisers, Bush and Park proceeded with an all-insider policy. That decision had no discernible adverse effect on the company as it went public. The Athenahealth IPO, launched in September 2007, registered the largest one-day share-price increase of any new offering that year.

Today, Athenahealth employs about a thousand people at its headquarters in Watertown, Massachusetts, and at separate locations in Georgia and Maine, as well as in Chennai, India. With allowance for practical safeguards, the policy of organizational transparency remains in place. And it applies to all employees. "They know information, in some cases, days or weeks before we disseminate it to the world in a formal fashion. They know the bookings. They know key financial metrics that we do not disclose to investors," Hallock explains. "Everybody in the company is an insider straight-up, under what the SEC would consider an insider. We take that designation very seriously."

Day by day, quarter after quarter, Athenahealth continues to incur a high degree of risk because of this policy. "But we embrace that risk, and the responsibility that comes with it. It's core to our internal communications strategy," Hallock says. Certain tactical adaptations arise from that strategy. Town-hall meetings, for instance, take place under a specially designed protocol. "Our various facilities have to be shut down," Hallock explains. "There can't be any outsiders in the room or in the building who might hear things. The chief compliance officer reads a long insider disclaimer and reviews our various communications rules." As cumbersome as those procedures might be, the leaders of Athenahealth take such difficulties in stride. To them, trusting employees is not a nicety; it's a necessity—a decisive factor in how the company does business. Only by including employees in all aspects of organizational conversation can Athenahealth "continue its quest to be a disrupter in health care," Hallock says.

The world that Athenahealth seeks to disrupt encompasses thousands of medical practices and all of the data that flows into and out of them. The company has developed sophisticated software tools for managing the many kinds of documents that proliferate in every doctor's office—bills and insurance claims, prescriptions and patient records. But the 22,000-plus medical providers who belong to the company's client base don't pay for those tools. The software comes tightly bundled with various EMR services (billing, chart management, and so forth) that Athenahealth offers through its AthenaNet platform. Yet clients don't pay directly for those services, either. Rather, in exchange for the right to use that software and those services, customers allow Athenahealth to take a cut of the billings that they recoup as a result. In 2008, collections posted by clients on the Athenahealth network came to $3.7 billion. (That year, Athenahealth's own revenues totaled nearly $140 million.) Through AthenaNet, providers connect not only to Athenahealth and its services, but also to other links in the medical value chain, including insurers, laboratories, and pharmacies. "The company's claim to fame, its key differentiator," Hallock says, is that "it's the only company in America that runs one centralized platform for doctors to do their business on."

To build and maintain AthenaNet, and to support the company's network-based business model, Athenahealth leaders must ensure that communication among employees occurs in a fast and fluid manner. "Internally, the culture has to be one of not being siloed, of open and transparent communication, because if you have information on how a health insurer is billing in New Mexico and you don't share it with me over in another department, then I can't get that intelligence into AthenaNet for clients in New Mexico, so that they can bill correctly," Hallock explains. The growth plan for Athenahealth puts an additional premium on organizational transparency and trust. It calls for spotting and pursuing opportunities to offer extra back-end services to medical providers—opportunities that emerge from information that travels over AthenaNet. If employees couldn't easily track that information and then discuss it with one another, the company wouldn't be able to expand into new lines of business. "We run a national network, which plays a huge role in how we communicate," Hallock says. "To think that we can't be networked ourselves is ridiculous. Of course we have to be. If we couldn't communicate what's going on operationally in real time, then we wouldn't be able to deliver information in real time. It would be impossible."

At Athenahealth, top leaders want employees to become insiders not just in the regulatory sense of the term, but also in the sense of involving themselves in the company—and in its conversation—no less thoroughly than top executives do. Each quarter, when Athenahealth issues its earnings announcement to investors, Jonathan Bush uses the occasion to highlight the level of employee engagement within the company. "We tell Wall Street," Hallock says. "They didn't always understand why we issued this metric, or why we focused so much on it." Bush persists in addressing the topic, anyway. The reason, according to Hallock, is simple: "The culture is core to our service. If employees are unhappy, or if they don't understand the mission, that's going to damage the level of service that we deliver."

In speaking to employees, meanwhile, Athenahealth leaders seek to convey a similar point about the value of conversational intimacy. Before the IPO, for example, they talked up their plan to designate everyone in the newly public company as an official insider. "It is management's commitment to preserving the culture and expanding the culture," Hallock explains. "And we communicated that: 'What we are giving you, many people told us not to give you. We're giving it to you because we need you to believe in our mission to be the medical profession's most trusted business service.' That is a huge show of confidence and trust in employees."

Listening—and Learning

Leaders who take organizational conversation seriously know when to stop talking and to start listening. Few types of behavior enhance conversational intimacy as robustly as the practice of attending to what other people say. Real attentiveness to others' questions and concerns, particularly when senior managers exhibit that quality in dealing with lower-level employees, carries great symbolic weight. It signals a feeling of respect for people of all ranks and roles, a sense of curiosity, even a degree of humility. It tells employees that their views matter within the organization—and that *they* matter. Yet the habit of listening when rank-and-file employees take the opportunity to speak carries more tangible benefits as well. By attuning themselves to the contributions that employees make to organizational conversation, leaders gain access to new information and critical insights that might otherwise escape their notice. They learn about what's happening, both for better and for worse, at the front lines of their company.

For many top leaders, quite understandably, the task of closing one's mouth and opening one's ears doesn't come easy. "Sometimes, people at that level are used to presenting their strategies, so their natural inclination is to create another presentation," notes James Harkness, a partner at Harkness Kennett, a London-based internal-communication consultancy. "But often the most important thing that they can do is to create opportunities to listen to people. They need to get into a room with a cross-section of staff and have a conversation." The habits of executive communication tilt strongly in favor of conveying thoroughly processed, carefully vetted information—facts and figures, decisions and deadlines—and leave very little scope for eliciting novel ideas and unexpected observations. Leaders too often focus on demonstrating mastery of a certain domain of knowledge, rather than on adding to their overall store of knowledge. "People use PowerPoint as a total crutch," Harkness argues. "It's fine if they've got to do a big set-piece presentation. But we should be trying to build people's conversation skills, and not necessarily their presentation skills."

When a leader starts to treat listening to employees as no less important than speaking to them, the lines of communication between the top and the bottom of an organization become a set of arrows that point up as well as down. Leaders can work toward that ideal in any number of ways—by establishing an open-door policy, for example, or by creating an open e-mail account through which employees can submit comments and queries. "That kind of two-way communication is much more successful at creating trust and at creating a sense that this leader is a human being. It creates a feeling that senior management is real and is listening to them," says Julie Freeman, former president of the International Association of Business Communicators. The most effective method of listening to employees involves meeting with them in person and without regard to intervening levels of organizational hierarchy. Whether it's through casual get-togethers or through a more formal and structured process, more and more leaders today are closing organizational gaps by opening up ways for people to speak to them directly and intimately.

"People don't like to be talked *to*; they like to be talked *with*," says William Hickey, president and CEO of Sealed Air Corporation, a global packaging manufacturer based in Elmwood Park, New Jersey. In

Hickey's view, listening to employees helps him to forge a close, productive relationship with them. "The only way to engage employees is through communication, and engaged employees are a very powerful resource," he says. Using communication to build engagement, he adds, is only partly a matter of conveying information *to* employees: "I count communication *from* employees as part of that overall effort." To gather input from Sealed Air employees—there are nearly seventeen thousand of them, spread across facilities in more than fifty countries—Hickey meets regularly with people at various company sites. Every month, on average, he visits one or two factories. On each visit, he typically conducts a plant tour, chatting with employees along the way, and then he holds a group meeting. After talking about the current state of the company for five to ten minutes, he opens up an opportunity for employees to speak to him.

Hickey doesn't approach the listening portion of this event passively. On the contrary, he takes concrete steps to make sure that employees are comfortable enough to speak their mind. First, he acts to remove an element that might interfere with his ability to hear what employees want to say. "I generally dismiss all of the supervisors and managers, so that everyone feels somewhat protected," he says. Then, instead of simply allowing employees to put questions to him, Hickey puts questions to *them*. "I'll start the dialogue, usually by picking up on something that I saw on the plant tour: 'Gee, I was looking at this particular machine. Is there a way to do this better?' No one wants to be the first to speak. No one wants to raise their hand and ask the boss a question that might embarrass them. So I find that if I throw a couple of softballs out there, I can get them engaged," Hickey explains.

Ricardo Madureira, a managing director at Genes, a Brazilian company that develops sustainable-energy projects, also views the practice of regular site visits as a crucial way to hear from employees. "People really love to be listened to. They really want to have the opportunity to challenge you, to make comments. So I make sure that I have the appropriate time and tools to listen to people. It's fundamental. It's a strategic thing," he says. Previously, Madureira worked at Monsanto, where he was director of the company's South American crop protection division, and in that role he deployed one tool in particular to help keep an ear to the ground within that highly dispersed organization. Roughly once per quarter, he traveled to each Monsanto facility in his region, and there he would meet with employees in a town-hall setting. Going a step further, he made a point of meeting not only with the seven executives who reported to him directly, but also with the managers who reported to each of those executives. (Madureira reports that he pursues a similar approach to communication in his current position.) The point of this exercise is to create a sense of "fresh air for people in the field," Madureira says. "I schedule time to talk to them one-to-one, to be engaged with them, and to listen to them."

That kind of top-level interest in listening to employees is a new development in many quarters. "There has been a big change since I joined my family business twenty years ago," says Sunshik Min, president of YBM, an education and publishing company based in Seoul. "Back then, information always flowed top-down. It was like a military organization. But these days, communication is pretty much two-way. If you do not listen to what your employees are talking about, you will be isolated, and maybe you will end up making the wrong decisions." Because of the increasing pace and growing complexity of business today, the best way—and sometimes the only way—for senior leaders to stay close to their customers is to stay close to the employees who interact with customers on a regular basis. Min, in that spirit, views members of his workforce as an indispensable early-warning system; he counts on them to send out an alarm if his company is failing to meet the needs of those who buy its products and services. "The market is crowded with many competitors, so I hope that my employees will inform me of what is going on in the marketplace," he says.

As communication at YBM has become less top-down in orientation over the past two decades, it has become less formal, too. "If you put too much emphasis on formal communication, then people will always try to guess what is going on," Min says. In addition, he notes, they "will be afraid to speak out." Although he and his colleagues still rely heavily on practices that distribute messages to employees through official channels, they now also look for ways to promote conversational intimacy. "I ask people to report to me directly if something is wrong. They can just call me anytime," he explains. Min also solicits comments from employees in a more active fashion by having lunch with them occasionally, or by making impromptu visits to the schools that his company operates. "I need to maintain some kind of informal channel in order to stay informed about what is happening at the working level," he says. In his view, though, merely taking in whatever an employee might say to him isn't sufficient. "When you listen to your employees, it matters whether you act or do not act on what you hear," Min argues. "You have to act, so that employees will realize that they have contributed to the organization."

Many leaders, to ensure that they're hearing from the right people in the right time and in the right way, have developed carefully structured procedures for listening to employees. Instead of talking with employees during one-off occasions or on an ad hoc basis, these leaders establish recurring events that put them in touch with specific members of their workforce. At Smiths Medical, for example, an institution called the Executive Sales Council supports key senior leaders in the company. Through meetings with this council, top sales and marketing executives keep up-to-date on issues and problems that customer-facing employees encounter while navigating the medical-device marketplace. The council consists of twelve people, all of them drawn from the company's sales force. "Field reps only, no managers," says Judith Rossi, who helps manage the council. "It can be anybody, from a very experienced rep to a rookie." While all salespeople are eligible to join the group, those who sit on the council have undergone a formal selection process based on nomination by their peers. "For the average sales rep, it's an honor to be on the council. It's a résumé builder," Rossi says. A clearly defined framework is essential to the success of the council: Members serve fixed two-year terms, and their meetings with executives follow a regular schedule. (The group convenes in person about four times annually and by teleconference several other times per year.) Council members, rather than executives, set the agenda for each meeting.

Understandably, some leaders in some organizations are wary of meeting with frontline employees in this way. "They're concerned about the action that they might be expected to take," Rossi notes. But at Smiths Medical, the Executive Sales Council has become a reliable tool for narrowing the conversational distance between top leaders and members of the company's marketing infantry. "It is a way for the feet-on-the-street foot soldier to have a direct line of communication to the top of the house. No filter," Rossi says. "If we've got a supply-chain

issue, if we've got a quality problem with a product, that issue or problem gets raised directly with the senior leadership team and with the
people who can fix it, as opposed to going up the organizational chain of
command." Through the council, salespeople out in the field are able to
bend the ears of company leaders back in the home office. "Think of it
like the House of Representatives. Its members each have a constituency base, and their job is to represent that constituency," Rossi
explains. "From the sales-rep perspective, it's a chance to hear firsthand
from the senior executives about what is really important." For Smiths
Medical leaders, using the council as a receiver for tuning in to the voice
of employees carries benefits that extend beyond the boundaries of the
company proper. "It brings the voice of the customer directly to the senior executives of the company," Rossi says. "It's a preview of where
potential risks and opportunities are going to come from, and how big
each risk or opportunity might end up becoming." So useful has the
Executive Sales Council proven to be, according to Rossi, that Smiths
Medical has recently created similar groups to support regional sales
executives.

Jim Rogers, now the president and CEO of Duke Energy, has followed
a slightly different—but no less effective—model of formalizing the business of listening to employees. In 2004, when he was CEO and chairman
of Cinergy (which later merged with Duke), Rogers initiated a series of
"listening sessions," as he called them. It was a way for frontline supervisors and other company managers to engage him in direct, open, and
uninhibited conversation. Meeting with groups of ninety to one
hundred managers in sessions that each lasted three hours, he invited
participants to talk about issues of pressing concern to them. Topics
ranged from "any burr under their saddle in terms of HR policy, all the
away to the grand visions of the future," Rogers says.[1] Through these
discussions, he gleaned information about Cinergy, its people, and its
day-to-day operations that would otherwise have escaped his attention.

At one session, for example, he heard from a group of supervisors
about a problem related to uneven compensation. "You know how long
it would have taken for that to bubble up in the organization and to fix
that?" Rogers says. In this case, having heard about the problem straight
from those affected by it, he was able to instruct the company's HR
department to implement a solution right away. Getting things done for

employees in that way helps Rogers to get closer to them—and closer to the work that they do. Holding sessions in which he can speak intimately with people throughout his company brings other advantages as well. "It allows me to get smarter about what's really going on in the company," he observes. "And as I go up the food chain, I go, 'Well, you know, supervisors are worried about this. What's your answer to that?' So it allows me to move the ideas back and forth across the organization."[2]

Getting Personal—and Getting Real

Rogers, in his listening sessions at Cinergy, did more than merely listen to employees. He turned those sessions into a forum where employees could put *him* on the spot. He put himself on the line, in other words, allowing participants in these conversations to address the strengths and weaknesses of his own leadership performance. He listened, and learned, as people at Cinergy subjected his managerial decisions and his management style to an open and honest critique. True listening, after all, involves taking in the bad with the good. It means absorbing criticism, even when the criticism is direct and personal—and even when those who deliver critical remarks happen to work for you.

That next phase of Rogers's story began during a second annual round of listening sessions. At one session, a Cinergy supervisor suggested to Rogers that he ask employees to grade him as a CEO—to mark him on a scale of A through F, as if he were a student and they were his instructors. Rogers took up the challenge. At the very next session, he invited each attendee to enter a grade for him on an electronic voting device. The results, which the voting devices recorded anonymously, appeared on a screen for Rogers and everyone else to see. Over the course of three sessions in the spring of 2005, nearly four hundred Cinergy managers registered their marks for him, and he announced the totals in a memo: 39 percent of listening-session participants awarded him an A (the highest grade), 52 percent gave him a B, and most of the remainder assigned him a C. (There was one D.) At first, Rogers recalls, he "had some trepidation" about this form of listening to employees. Soon enough, though, the value of overcoming such doubts became evident. "I really do believe that trust is built when you are unafraid to be vulnerable," he says. "When you put yourself at risk, you and they [employees] find out what kind of person you are."[3]

Employees at Cinergy found out that Rogers was an apt pupil, eager to learn from the grades that they had given him. And Rogers discovered that while employees generally awarded high marks to him, they also believed that he had room for improvement in certain managerial disciplines. Along with asking listening-session participants to grade him, Rogers put an open-ended question to them: "What's the one thing I need to do better as CEO?" Later, in a memo, he analyzed their written answers and grouped those answers into a few broad categories— *Strategy, Vetting of Major Decisions,* and so on. Tellingly, the category into which the largest number of responses fell was one that Rogers labeled *Internal Communications.* Some 20 percent of respondents, he noted in the memo, voiced a wish that he and other senior executives would "visit the field more and . . . share more 'bad news' when appropriate." Thus, even as he sought to get close to employees by way of organizational conversation, Rogers learned that many of them were urging him to get closer still. Another lesson that he took from this exercise concerned the need to follow up on what employees had told him. "My challenge is how to use this data," he says. "Has it changed me as a person? What will I behaviorally do as a consequence of knowing this? If I do nothing, I know I have lost an opportunity to be a better CEO."[4]

This focus on a leader's status *as a person,* with a personal stake in the work of organizational communication and with personal qualities that bear on that work, is another signature feature of conversational intimacy. Senior leaders who find occasions to get personal in their interaction with employees—to reveal themselves fully, even when (as Rogers suggests) doing so means revealing a vulnerable side of themselves— send out an intangible message that transcends any particular thing that they say. In face-to-face meetings such as the listening sessions at Cinergy or the Executive Sales Council gatherings at Smiths Medical, leaders come across to their people less as abstract figureheads than as real figures with real personalities. "It makes the senior executive team more personal," Judith Rossi says, referring to the Executive Sales Council. "And to employees, that's really important. They get to see that these are people who laugh, who like red wine versus white wine, who joke around. It allows the senior executive team to look like people you would want to work with, as opposed to just an isolated group of people who sit in an ivory tower, making decisions. It humanizes the executive team for people." Rossi advises leaders to devote as much as 25 percent of their time to meeting with employees in small, preferably cross-functional groups. "Senior executives learn immeasurably valuable things by having breakfast with people who they don't see every day," she says. "Most importantly, they start to win hearts and minds."

What ultimately enables top leaders to capture the allegiance of employees, Rossi adds, is their ability to be "seen as intimately involved and caring" in their approach to organizational conversation. Along with letting employees view them in a personal light, leaders should strive to see their employees as people, too—as individual human beings, with names as well as roles and with thoughts as well as responsibilities. Intimacy, in short, calls for reciprocity. "The best way to communicate on a day-to-day level with your employees is face-to-face: Talk to them. Know their names. If possible, know their wives' or girlfriends' names," says Daniel Harris, former CEO of Alba PLC (now called Harvard PLC), a U.K.-based consumer-electronics distributor. (Harris's point, of course, extends to knowing the names of spouses and partners in general.) "It's too easy to send things out and to assume that everybody understands what you're saying. If you don't explain it, or if they don't 'see the whites of your eyes,' they won't necessarily understand where you're coming from." Ken Bagan, a former CEO, offers this advice to others who attain that top spot: "If you feel that people aren't hearing what you have to say, get in your car and go talk to them. Get interested in them. Find out who they are personally, and get to know them a little bit. It will improve the quality of your conversation. They'll start to see you as a person, not as a talking head who spouts the company line."

Getting real—doing whatever it takes not to "spout the company line"—is a necessary complement to getting personal. "Messaging is most successful when you pay attention to developing relationships and to developing trust," Julie Freeman says. "What you don't want is to start talking to employees and have them roll their eyes and think, 'Okay, here we go with the corporate-speak.' You know how the adults in *Peanuts* talk: 'Wah-wah-wah.' Sometimes, that's the way that senior managers sound to employees if they're not making an effort to have some kind of relationship with people." The watchword, in this context, is *authenticity*. While that term can too easily devolve into a mere buzzword, behind it there lies an abiding truth: We know authentic leadership, and likewise authentic communication, when we see it. The closer leaders in an organization get to their employees, the harder it becomes for them to hide behind a false corporate front or behind canned corporate language. In a conversation that's "real," whether it's a chat between friends or a dialogue that extends across an entire company, participants must themselves be real. They must let down their guard, set aside the roles that they otherwise play in life, and talk straight with each other.

Avoiding the stilted and impersonal tones of corporate-speak is a starting point to engaging in authentic communication. But the pursuit of conversational authenticity also has broad conceptual implications. "Companies make a mistake when they use a marketing lens or a marketing approach in dealing with employee communication," Gary F. Grates argues. Organizational conversation, to the extent that it aims to generate buy-in and enthusiasm among employees, does arguably qualify as a form of internal marketing. The analogy between external marketing and internal communication goes only so far, however. "You can't sell to employees," Grates says. "You can sell to customers because they don't see what's behind the curtain. They just see the end product, and they base their relationship with a brand on what that end product does or doesn't do. When you're an employee, you see the warts. You see under the rug. Inside a company, people have to discover on their own—through conversation, through dissent, through debate—what the reality is." For an organizational leader, the point of communicating authentically isn't to adopt the verbal equivalent of Casual Friday. (Employees will see through a starched khaki facade every time.) Nor should leaders try to conjure up an air of chummy camaraderie. Instead, they should do their best to treat employees as real people with whom they can have a real conversation.

At Exelon Corporation, a utility holding company headquartered in Chicago, a keenly "real" form of organizational conversation emerged from a somewhat unlikely source—namely, a project aimed at making a statement of corporate values come alive for Exelon's seventeen thousand employees. Statements of that kind, of course, rarely serve as promising ground on which to demonstrate authenticity. On the contrary, that territory is strewn with officially generated verbiage of the sort that gives all talk about "mission" and "values" a bad name. Employees, when they hear those words, are apt to reach for their noise-canceling headphones. According to Howard N. Karesh, though, Exelon has made its set of six core values (safety, integrity, diversity, respect, accountability, and continuous improvement) a vital element of company life. "These are not things that we just print up every year, and everybody just tacks them on a bulletin board. We talk about them constantly. We try to model them. We make them real," says Karesh, director of internal communications. One way that Exelon communicates its matrix of values is through a glossy, magazine-style newsletter that all employees receive. It comes out six times per year, and each issue has a theme that aligns explicitly with one of the half dozen items on the company's statement of values. "We want to make sure, in no uncertain terms, that we have an employee population that is truly engaged in our vision, that gets it at a strategic level, that understands their role in it," Karesh says.

Yet Exelon leaders have also found ways to convey the company's values to employees in a less conventional, and decidedly more intimate, manner. Take the value of diversity. In the fall of 2008, Exelon launched a major initiative called Diversity and Inclusion, or D&I. "Diversity has been a priority at this company forever. We've won awards for our diversity effort," Karesh says. "The problem was, it didn't stick culturally. It was a topic to discuss at certain times of the year." (He cites Black History Month as an example of this tendency.) To alter that pattern, and to support the D&I initiative, Karesh and his team developed a simple practice that proved to be remarkably effective: They created a series of short video clips in which top Exelon leaders—without fuss or pretense, and without relying on "high-production values"—discuss their own experience of confronting issues related to difference and discrimination. Those clips then appeared on a dedicated D&I section of Exelon's intranet site.

The videos, called D&I Discussions, are each about two to three minutes long. Although they use Web-based video technology, they are fundamentally an old-fashioned, low-tech affair. They show Exelon's "senior-most executives talking unscripted, very personally, about what diversity means to them," Karesh explains. Producers on the project made the videos in-house and shot them in black-and-white. Their decision not to use color stemmed from a purely practical motive: They wanted to avoid the need for makeup. (No doubt the participating executives did, too.) But the black-and-white look confers an aura of authenticity on the final product. In Karesh's words, it has a "very normalizing, equalizing" effect, enabling the executives who appear in the series to come across as approachable and trustworthy. Partly because of the video series, the D&I initiative made a strong impact on the culture of Exelon. "We're talking about diversity differently," Karesh says. "We're much more open about it. We're willing to talk about sexual orientation. We're willing to talk about race."

One D&I Discussion video demonstrates what can happen when an executive commits to bringing a measure of personal authenticity to employee communication. It features Ian McLean, who at that time held the lofty position of executive vice president of finance and markets at Exelon. But McLean grew up in Manchester, England, where he was the son of a working-class family, and in the video he vividly remembers the sting of class prejudice that he endured in his youth. Responding to one of a set of standard questions—"How did you deal with a time when you felt different from those around you?"— McLean talks about going to work in a bank where most of his colleagues clearly had an upper-class background. "My accent was different. My background was different . . . ," he says in the video. "I wasn't included, I wasn't invited, and I was made to think I wasn't quite as smart as they were. And I didn't like that, so I never want anyone else to feel that [way] around me."[5] For those who see him tell it, McLean's unadorned personal story leaves an impression that is as real as the story itself. "That's a very personal, very private moment that a senior executive shares with employees," Karesh says. "Let me tell you, it is very, very powerful."

TWO OF THE COMPANIES that we've featured in this chapter, Cinergy (now part of Duke) and Exelon, happen to be in the business of producing and distributing energy. Those organizations, along with a few others that we've mentioned thus far, show by their example that a new spirit of conversational intimacy can arise even in an old-line industrial setting. Leaders in any industry, we contend, can draw upon this element of intimacy to energize their people and to improve the way that information flows up and down their organization. That point applies with particular force to another energy company, Hindustan Petroleum—an organization that we will discuss at length in the next chapter.

CHAPTER TWO

Walking the Talk

Hindustan Petroleum Corporation Ltd.

IN THE FIRST YEARS of the twenty-first century, the leaders of Hindustan Petroleum Corporation Ltd. (HPCL) launched an effort to develop a new statement of vision for the company. For an organization like HPCL— it's the third-largest oil company based in India, with more than eleven thousand employees and with revenues that came to more than $23 billion in 2010—endeavors of that kind have traditionally taken place wholly or primarily in the upper ranks of management. In this case, however, those at the top of the HPCL organizational ladder decided to include people on lower rungs of the ladder in the work of envisioning a new future for the company. Starting in 2003, under the auspices of an elaborate series of workshops called Vision 2006, HPCL employees met in small groups and talked about their company. Instead of simply hearing what top executives had to say about HPCL's competitive strategy, for example, they had a chance to offer their own thoughts on that subject. They also heard what their colleagues had to say about it, and they tested their own and others' ideas in spirited back-and-forth discussions. Not least, they took part in those discussions with the knowledge that top HPCL leaders would take seriously what they said.

These "vision workshops," as people at HPCL called them, were both extensive and intensive. Thousands of employees took part in hundreds of such events over the course of several years. Each workshop included about twenty participants, and a typical workshop lasted three days. During that three-day period, employees would systematically discuss the company—its strengths and weaknesses, its purpose and prospects—along several dimensions of analysis. HPCL divides its operations into nine strategic business units (SBUs), and it further divides some SBUs into regional units. In many instances, workshop participants would conclude their work by producing one vision document that applied to their regional office, another that applied to their SBU, and another that applied to HPCL as a whole. Each document took the form of a vision statement that featured five bulleted items, and those items corresponded to certain key categories: *Customer Orientation, Work Environment, Core Values,* and so forth. Vision statements developed at the regional or SBU level often featured specific targets for growth, profitability, and market share, while the statements that applied to the company as a whole offered ambitious views of what HPCL might achieve strategically by the year 2006, and beyond.

For senior leaders at HPCL, the vision workshop process entailed considerable risk. If leading an organization means anything, then surely it means owning the task of creating a vision for that organization. In opting to share that prerogative with legions of people at multiple organizational levels, executives not only risked undermining their own authority, but also raised the possibility of discovering (and highlighting) a lack of alignment between their idea of HPCL's future direction and that of rank-and-file employees. Yet, as the Vision 2006 project unfolded, company leaders began to see a remarkable convergence among the ideas and aspirations that emerged from the workshops conducted by various groups within HPCL. "It was amazing to see that irrespective of the level in the hierarchy, the vision statements that were coming out were almost the same, from the senior management down to the unionized staff—*especially* the unionized staff," says Arun Balakrishnan, who served as chairman and managing director (CMD) from 2007 to 2010. (At HPCL, as at many similar companies in India, the CMD functions in a CEO-like role.) As director of human resources from 2002 to 2007, Balakrishnan helped to oversee the vision workshop initiative. Senior executives, he explains, had prepared a five-bullet vision statement of their own, and he compared that statement point-by-point with the five items on a statement that came out of a workshop held for union members. "Four of them were the same, and only one of them was different," Balakrishnan says. "This did come as a surprise, because we'd thought that this would be so for the senior level, but not for the junior level, the younger recruits, or the unionized staff."

But the statements generated by workshop participants didn't merely reinforce a preexisting top-down vision; they also charted new territory for HPCL executives to explore in finalizing a new strategic vision for the company. "The most telling point was when our union leaders said, 'We want our company to be global.' And they were surprised that the top management did not include the word *global* in their vision statement. These people made a better vision than the top management people!" says Ashis Sen, deputy general manager of HPCL's Balanced Scorecard initiative, who belonged to a select group of coaches who led the Vision 2006 workshops. "There were other recurring patterns. People at large wanted the vision to be more broad-based: 'Instead of being a *petroleum* company, we should think of ourselves as an *energy* company.' That kind of attitude was so powerful. People started feeling, 'This is *my* vision.' And changes in the vision did come about, because people wanted these things."

The final, official version of the company's stated vision reflects those changes. A document called "Our Vision," posted on its corporate Web site, begins by affirming that HPCL aspires "to be a World Class Energy Company"—that is, not just a petroleum company. Complementing that document is a statement called "Our Mission," which announces HPCL's aim to "attain scale dimensions by diversifying into other energy related fields and by taking up transnational operations"; the latter phrase, clearly, signals the company's intent to achieve a global scope that extends beyond the boundaries of India.[1] In sum, the organization still known as Hindustan Petroleum now aspires to transcend both the "Hindustan" part and the "Petroleum" part of its corporate legacy, and its leaders arrived at that far-reaching vision with the help of decisive input from their employees.

Oil Change

The Vision 2006 workshops marked a notable departure for HPCL. "That is the first time that we emphasized communication in the forefront of our organization," says S. Roy Choudhury, who joined HPCL in 1982 and who assumed the CMD post in mid-2010. (Previously, he served as director of HPCL's marketing division, the largest unit in the company.) Along with other practices that HPCL leaders have introduced over the past decade, vision workshops have come to embody a new mode of interaction between the company's senior executives and its lower-level employees. "Communication must reach the bottom of the pyramid," Choudhury argues. "Otherwise, people today would not know what the strategy of top management is. If we have made the strategy only at the topmost level, people will not have to own it. And the important thing is that *everybody* has to own it. If the ownership is not there at every level, people will not take it seriously." In giving employees partial ownership of the conversation through which HPCL develops its strategy, its leaders have shortened the distance that once kept company executives at a far remove from much of their workforce. They have (to use our term) made that conversation more *intimate*. In place of what had been a traditional system of corporate communication, HPCL has instituted a form of organizational conversation in which visions and viewpoints migrate up as well as down the company's organizational structure. As a result, rank-and-file employees now enjoy a closer relationship to HPCL's ultimate decision-makers, and the latter are now in closer touch with people who work at the company's front lines.

The push to reinvent the way that HPCL leaders communicate with employees grew out of a larger push to reinvent the company in light of sharply changed circumstances. HPCL, a *Fortune* Global 500 company, has product lines that range from industrial lubricants to jet fuel. It operates two major refineries, and its distribution facilities span the Indian subcontinent. Until somewhat recently, however, the core defining fact about HPCL was this: It was a wholly state-owned enterprise within a wholly state-controlled market. Then, in the 1990s, the government of India began to subject the company to new competitive pressures—and in response, the leaders of HPCL undertook a major organizational transformation effort.

HPCL traces its roots to 1952, but it dates in its current form to 1974, when the Indian government nationalized two companies, ESSO of India and Lube India, and combined them into a new entity called Hindustan Petroleum. Two decades later, the government reversed course and moved to liberalize the Indian economy. By 1995, officials had sold 49 percent of HPCL to private investors. During the same period, the government sold off large stakes in India's two other state-owned petroleum companies, Bharat Petroleum and Indian Oil; it pared back much of the regulatory structure that had limited competition among the three state-owned enterprises; and it began to allow wholly private concerns to enter certain energy markets on an equal footing with those companies. At the start of the new century, the government was taking steps to sell off its majority stake in HPCL, along with its remaining stake in each of the other two state-controlled companies. In 2003, a court ruling blocked that move, thereby forestalling complete privatization of HPCL, and that's essentially where the matter stands today.

That ruling, however, didn't weaken the conviction among HPCL executives that they had to adapt to a fundamentally altered environment. "The company realized that we ought to change, and change drastically, so that we are able to compete with the private sector within the country," says Balakrishnan. "Culturally, there was a lot that needed to change. People still had what you'd call a public-system mentality, and they really didn't focus on the customer. For a long time, we were used to the customer coming to us, rather than our going to the customer." The best way to "go to the customer," Balakrishnan and his fellow executives decided, was to go first to the employees of HPCL. That decision was by no means intuitive. Since the pressures that HPCL now faced were external in origin, the obvious tack for its leaders to follow was to direct their attention outside the company—to focus on the strengths and weaknesses of existing and potential competitors, or to channel resources toward one customer segment or another. And, to be sure, getting close to customers would be a pivotal element of HPCL strategy as the company pursued its change initiative. Yet, before HPCL executives turned outward, they turned inward. Before they delved wholeheartedly into the task of narrowing the distance between the company and its customers, they made a concerted effort to close the gap between themselves and their employees.

Like many established institutions in India, both in the public sector and in the private sector, HPCL had traditionally organized its operations along the lines of a clear-cut hierarchy. Relations between people at different levels of that hierarchy, and especially between those at the executive level and those at or near the customer-facing levels of the business, were remote and formal. The means by which leaders conveyed messages to their workforce, and by which they elicited information from that workforce, were likewise detached and impersonal. Faced with the need to overhaul the company's "public-system mentality," HPCL leaders moved to overhaul the top-down mentality that went with it. The key to changing that top-down orientation, they recognized, was to embark on a new approach to communicating with employees. "It is a participative kind of management that we have started," Choudhury says. "This exercise is not done by a top-down approach. It is a bottom-up approach, based on total participation of each and every employee." Today, an investment in conversational intimacy both allows and requires HPCL leaders to hear what's on the minds of their employees. It encourages HPCL employees to have greater trust in their leaders, and it calls upon those leaders to trust employees enough to grant them a meaningful role in charting their company's future. For leaders and employees alike, it makes organizational communication at HPCL a personal matter and not just a corporate endeavor.

Vision Test

Enabling employees to invest personally in organizational conversation at HPCL was a hallmark of the vision workshops that began in 2003. Although not every HPCL employee was able to take part in one of those workshops, the Vision 2006 initiative drew in employees of all ranks and from every business unit. Employees, many of them accustomed primarily to taking orders from others, could now offer their own opinions and insights on the current state and future course of the company. Talk for the mere sake of talking wasn't the point of these workshops, of course. Partly for that reason, HPCL leaders carefully selected a team of fourteen workshop coaches and trained them to impose a clear structure on each phase of discussion. And yet, as these coaches discovered, it was often participants themselves who kept a workshop conversation on track. "We had a workshop for union people, and one of them said that there was some problem that they had on a local basis," Sen recalls. "Others said, 'We are discussing an important issue about the company's future. Let us not talk of small and trivial things here.' That's when we knew that the vision workshop concept worked. If you are involved in creating the vision, then it makes sense to you personally and you get hooked into it."

In the view of HPCL leaders, the Vision 2006 project achieved all that they had hoped for it. There was a certain "magic," Sen believes, in how employees began to claim partial ownership of HPCL's future. That process, moreover, had the effect of shrinking the distances that otherwise separated people within the organization. "Almost every employee was involved in arriving at this vision for the company," Balakrishnan says. "That was a very earth-shaking experience. It brought the company together, with everyone working for the same cause. The heart of it is that there is no real difference between levels of employees at this company." So successful was the Vision 2006 initiative that company leaders have made the practice of employee workshops an ongoing part of the HPCL's organizational conversation. In 2010, for instance, the company rolled out a new promotion policy that applied to a broad swath of its office and clerical staff. Instead of merely issuing an announcement of that change, human resource officers put on workshops in which employees could comment on the new policy. HPCL leaders also sponsor follow-up vision workshops that focus on refining, updating, and implementing the vision statements and planning documents that came out of earlier workshop sessions.

One aspect of the workshop format used at HPCL illustrates the enduring power of this practice. During the first segment of a typical workshop, coaches invite participants to discuss goals that they (the participating employees) harbor for themselves and their families. In other words, as Sen explains, employees begin by setting their sights not on an organizational vision, but on a *personal* vision: "We ask people, 'What do you want out of life? What is the future that you would like to create for yourself?' And they say, 'I want to feel success in my work life, I want to become a chief manager, I want to have a great work environment.' Then we talk about what they want for their family, in their relationships with their children, and so on. So they build a rich vision, and then we tell them to share it with one person in the group." That approach helps to promote trust and collegiality among workshop participants, and it familiarizes them with the speculative, aspiration-driven style of thinking that vision creation requires. Not least, it sets up a dynamic in which employees start to perceive a close link between their personal vision and any vision that they help to develop for HPCL as a whole. "The realization that has to happen is, 'If the corporation grows, I can meet my personal aspirations.' There has to be a tight integration between personal aspirations and the organization's growth and development plans," says Pushp Joshi, general manager for human resources in HPCL's marketing division. In short, employees who hope to become managers must come to understand that opportunities for promotion will expand only to the degree that HPCL can increase its operational scope or its market share.

HPCL executives, for their part, have come to understand that increasing the degree of conversational intimacy in their company—by shifting away from an older, more impersonal mode of internal communication—increases employee engagement. Joshi frames the matter this way: "It has to be a more informal conversation, rather than a single, top-down, one-way channel. It *has* to be. Feedback is now a necessity if the corporation is to survive, if it is to grow. If the employee is to get involved, he has to see what's in it for him. If he's not able to communicate, if he's not able to share, then you can't get one hundred percent of his engagement. And it can't be only a few representatives of your employees who participate. There has to be more grassroots-level participation." Or, to phrase it in a way that well suits HPCL and its core business, intimacy releases *energy*. It helps drive the people of HPCL as they navigate a newly competitive environment and an increasingly complex business climate. As Sen observes, referring to employees who took part in the Vision 2006 sessions: "They were energized because they built the vision."

Pumped Up

In the aftermath of the first sequence of Vision 2006 workshops, HPCL leaders initiated a campaign to see how the company could implement key ideas that were emerging from those discussions. Having turned inward to engage employees in planning for the HPCL's future, they now sent groups of those employees out into the marketplace. "Building a vision to be a world-class company is fine, but how do we go about reaching it? That was the question," Balakrishnan recalls. He and his colleagues formed about twenty cross-functional teams, drawing their membership from the ranks of young employees who had been at HPCL for less than ten years, and assigned each team to a specific market segment—gasoline and diesel fuel in one instance, cooking gas in another, and so forth. "We sent them into the field and asked them to find out where the customer is," Balakrishnan says. "They went and lived where the market was, for about two or three weeks. They developed a good understanding of the views of the customer toward our company as against competing companies. For these young men and women, it was an eye-opener."

Opening the eyes of employees—and, ultimately, the eyes of their leaders as well—to the needs and attitudes of customers went a long way toward counteracting some of the problematic tendencies that had arisen during the period when HPCL was an entirely state-owned enterprise. The field research done by teams of employees, for example, produced critical insights into how the company could improve its retail performance by improving its retail *presence*. Drawing upon those insights, HPCL began to modernize a large portion of the roadside gas stations that it operates. (By 2011, the company had more than eighty-five hundred retail outlets nationwide.) In particular, it upgraded signs, canopies, and other physical structures in order to give HPCL stations greater visibility and a more unified look. "There was a lot of deviation from place to place," says Rakesh Misri, general manager for North Zone Retail. (HPCL divides the Indian retail market into seven zones.) "We spent a lot of money as part of a branding exercise, so that we could have a standardized visual identity across all retail outlets, all across the country—so that this identity will remain embedded in the mind of the customer."

Another set of findings to emerge from grassroots investigation dealt with the opportunity to serve rural markets. Traditionally, HPCL and other fuel vendors have placed their retail outlets only along major highways or in relatively urban areas. When members of the cross-functional teams ventured into outlying areas, they heard complaints from farmers and villagers about needing to travel long distances to buy fuel at such outlets. In response to those concerns, team members developed a plan for installing stations along secondary highways and near the villages where rural customers lived. It was a proposal that met with some resistance. "When people from the front line came up with this concept of retail outlets in those places, everybody at the senior level said that it could not work, because the investment is so high: 'How do we get a decent return?'" Sen recalls. But team members had an idea for surmounting that obstacle. They envisioned a smaller-scale outlet that would be much cheaper to build and operate than a standard retail facility. Called Hamara Pumps (*hamara* means "ours" in Hindi), stations on this new model would not only boost sales for HPCL, but also increase its brand presence in rural districts. Company leaders agreed to pursue that idea, and HPCL began to open small rural outlets in 2004. Each Hamara Pump station requires an up-front investment that's about one-tenth as high as the cost of building a full-scale urban outlet, and the sales volume at the new stations has proved to be higher than planners' original estimates—twice as high, in some cases. According to Sen, HPCL recouped its investment on many Hamara Pump projects within just three years. "Those outlets have given us continuous increases," he says. "We really found value at the bottom of the pyramid. It happened because employees at the front line had talked to so many people in those regions. They felt that they needed to do it for those people. So they felt a personal sense of satisfaction and achievement."

A major factor in the success of HPCL's cross-functional market-research teams is that they were, in fact, cross-functional. Created with the goal of breaking down barriers between the company and its customers, these teams featured a diverse composition that also served to break down barriers within the company. "We brought in people who normally don't have anything to do with marketing, people from the legal department or the secretaries department," Sen explains. "That helped in two ways. Not only did they give us input, but they also remained committed to the strategy." Making these teams cross-functional opened up new opportunities for people from diverse parts of the company to talk with each other—and to talk about issues that lay outside their official areas of responsibility.

Sen cites a separate but related example in which input from a rank-and-file employee proved to be especially valuable. About a decade ago, when HPCL was in the throes of its change initiative, the Indian government was building a vast nationwide highway system known as the Golden Quadrilateral (so called because it connects the four cities of New Delhi, Calcutta, Chennai, and Mumbai). "One of the ladies in the finance office was traveling at that time, and she said that as more and more tourists would be traveling with family members, there would be a need to have clean washrooms for ladies in our retail outlets," Sen recalls. "That's where we now have a competitive edge: Our major outlets have the best washrooms for men and women. That developed from the front lines."

Open Pipeline

To keep ideas of that kind flowing from one end of HPCL to another, company leaders have moved to make the company's communication channels more open and more interactive than they were previously. The vision workshops represent an especially powerful example of that development, but other examples—several of them involving the use of digital technology—stand out as well.

In designing and deploying vehicles through which to communicate with employees, HPCL leaders first consider the *purpose* behind any given communication effort. "We distinguish between transactional communication, which is the plain sharing of information, and transformational communication, where we talk about our aspirations, where we talk about integrating employees' aspirations with the company," Joshi says. When it comes to conveying basic company information—about the comings and goings of people within the organization, for example—Joshi and his colleagues use traditional channels: a printed memo, an e-mail bulletin, an announcement posted on the HPCL intranet portal. By necessity, such "transactions" entail a certain distance between the officials who issue a message and the employees who receive it.

When the purpose of communication is to change the company by changing the way that people engage with it, however, HPCL leaders opt for channels that are truly conversational in nature. "Our belief is that there's no substitute for interactive communication," Joshi says. "Communication that is top-down, that is one-way, can be useful for sharing facts and figures. But when we want to share an idea, when we want to share the rationale behind a policy, or when we want to get feedback, communication has to be two-way." Channels that operate in two directions offer another advantage, he adds: "If we are communicating only one way, there will be questions and there will be apprehensions in the minds of people. If we can't clarify the point right away, then people will make their own assumptions. They will get information through the grapevine. And by the time we clarify it, they will have gotten other input, which may be negative. So we always try to provide ways for the employee to have his say on matters that affect him."

One venue for two-way communication at HPCL is the company's intranet portal, MyHPCL, which gives employees access to tools that enable them to reach up, over, and across the HPCL bureaucracy. Through the portal's eCare section, for instance, they can take advantage of a program called ICS, which stands for Internal Customer Service. ICS allows any employee at any level to file a service request or a grievance with the company. In the marketing division, Joshi explains, a dedicated team of ICS officers aims to respond to each submission within three days. Following that period, the matter escalates to a higher level; Joshi himself handles any complaint or request that remains open after ten days. The name of the program signals a commitment to retaining a tight connection with employees. "That is my philosophy—that employees *are* my internal customers," Joshi says. "And my objective is to take care of those internal customers, because if we take care of them, they will be willing to take care of customers of the corporation." Another program, called Coin Your Idea, uses an intranet-based tool to let employees submit ideas on how to improve HPCL's internal operations or external performance. The name of the program, in this case, is a play on words: Employees can coin an idea in the sense of inventing it, but they also have a chance to convert their idea into coinage of a literal, monetary sort. "We have a system to acknowledge every idea," Choudhury says. "If we find that an idea is really good, we try to implement it, and we reward the employee as well."

Another feature on the HPCL portal uses blogging capability to promote interactive communication. Two main blogs, both launched in early 2009, now reside on the site: one that the CMD and other directors use to present ideas and announcements, and one that any HPCL employee can use to post a message. Each blog includes a comments function that turns it into a channel for two-way communication. A few rules limit usage (contributors must use language that shows respect for other employees, and their comments must be relevant to HPCL as a business), but otherwise the two blogs are broadly open to participation by all employees. "We provide the employee with a kind of free platform. If he wants to criticize a particular policy, he can do that," Joshi says. Top executives, moreover, pay attention to the views that employees express through this channel; they use it, in effect, as another means of "listening" to the HPCL workforce. "Today, the senior management makes sure that they read the blog regularly," Balakrishnan says, referring to the blog used by all members of the HPCL community. "It is a very popular way for people to write about any problem they have with a new policy."

Up Close and Personnel

Despite the allure and the increasing reach of digital technology, HPCL executives strongly prefer a lower-tech approach to employee communication. "It is individual, one-to-one conversation that we encourage," Choudhury says. "People like the intranet system that we have, and we use it regularly. But I always feel more comfortable when I'm talking to people who are in the office. Sometimes, I call my engineers, my officers in the field, and I ask them, 'What is happening?' My door is open to people. Anybody can ring me up. Anybody can talk to me." For Choudhury and his colleagues, the mainstay of organizational conversation involves visiting employees out in the field. "I and my team visit our locations at least once a month," he says, referring to a practice that he followed during his tenure as director of HPCL's marketing division. "Wherever we go, we make it a practice to call every individual officer there, and we share everything—the good things that have happened, the bad things that have happened, the challenges that we have in the future. That communication, I think, has resulted in huge enthusiasm among people. One-to-one conversation, we find, is much more beneficial than sending a newsletter or an e-mail." While serving in the marketing-director role, Choudhury met personally with nearly eight thousand HPCL officers and staff members, and he came to know a great many of them by name. "It is a not a monologue. It becomes a dialogue," he says of the practice of "one-to-one" conversation. "And you see a positive result. It really transforms a person. He finds out that somebody cares about him, and I think that has a tremendous impact."

That outlook extends beyond the top executive ranks, encompassing HPCL leaders at all organizational levels. Misri, for example, has responsibility for roughly two hundred employees, and he keeps in touch with them by visiting each of the eight regions in his zone on a monthly basis. "I make it a point to meet everybody—management and nonmanagement, even workers in the depot," he says. "They should have an outlet to express themselves, so I go out there and basically listen to them, rather than just telling them what is going on." The benefits of engaging in one-to-one communication with employees are widely applicable. As Joshi notes, though, that approach has particular salience in the context of Indian society. Indians, he explains, tend to put a high premium on nonverbal expression: "For us, a lot of communication takes place without speaking. In a meeting with twenty-five union leaders, say, a lot depends on my mannerisms. A lot depends on how I project myself and whether I make them comfortable. If I want to involve them, then my body language—even the way I use my hands— that has to be different."

At a company as large as HPCL, of course, top executives can't rely too extensively on one-to-one communication. Leaders at HPCL, therefore, have opened up other channels that help to close conversational gaps between themselves and rank-and-file employees. Using specially created telephone numbers and e-mail addresses, anyone at HPCL can now address comments and questions directly to the company's senior-most leaders, including the CMD. "Anybody can send me an e-mail about any problem that they have," says Balakrishnan, referring to the period when he served as CMD. "I get about 150 e-mails a day, and I do reply. People, by appointment, can walk into my room and meet with me. These are the kinds of informalities that are now in place." HPCL executives also see value in holding traditional town-hall meetings, and they often travel from the company's headquarters in Mumbai to conduct such gatherings in outposts all across India. Although the town-hall format doesn't lend itself to direct, one-to-one communication, it does give leaders an efficient yet relatively personal way to reach people in far-flung regional offices. "People can actually shake hands and touch you, and ask questions, and enter a conversation," Balakrishnan says of that format.

The use within HPCL of practices that hinge on one-to-one conversation predates the transformation initiative that began in 2003. Yet the emphasis by company leaders on getting closer to employees in that way has only grown stronger in subsequent years, and such practices have had a notable cumulative effect both on the logistics of communication at HPCL and on its organizational culture. "We were a formal company once upon a time, but that formality has really diluted quite a bit," Balakrishnan says. "People are more at ease with each other. We have become much more informal than we were ten years ago, without in any way damaging the formal organization structure: A boss is a boss here. But at the same time, the way he behaves to his subordinates—the quality of that relationship—has changed. It's more nurturing now than the top-down kind of thing which was there before."

"Full Steam"

HPCL operates in an environment that's hardly known for enjoying a high degree of labor peace. The Indian oil industry and the Indian public sector alike are prone to strikes and other labor actions. Yet, in a sign that its transformation effort has achieved a measure of success, HPCL has done relatively well on that front during the past decade. It is, Joshi notes, "one of the few organizations in India that have not had any major industrial unrest" over that period. "Now, to my mind, we have been able to achieve that on the strength of communication." HPCL executives meet regularly with union leaders, both in structured negotiation sessions and in more informal settings. "Because we give them an opportunity to be heard, and because we engage in two-way communication with them, we can clarify a lot of apprehensions that they have,"

Joshi says. Company leaders, according to Sen, have built a foundation of "friendship, trust, camaraderie, and communication" in their relations with employees at every level: "They [HPCL's top leaders] are frequently talking to people, meeting with frontline people, discussing with them what the company is doing. All of those things paid off—not immediately, but after six and a half years of this work."

That payoff came in January 2009, when a strike by salaried officers at public-sector companies swept across the Indian oil industry. Despite substantial moves toward privatization, the government still set pay levels at those companies, and members of the Oil Sector Officers Association (which covers employees at fourteen state-owned organizations) deemed the latest round of government-approved salary increases to be too low. After the officers went on strike, refineries throughout India shut down or reduced production, and gas pumps went dry in many parts of the country. But HPCL, alone among the major state-owned oil companies, kept all of its officers on the job. "It was a huge strike," Sen says. "Everything came almost to a standstill. But our company went full steam." The strike lasted only two days. However, Sen adds, "those two days were hell for our officers, hell for our people in the retail outlets." Over that period, many HPCL employees ended up working twenty-hour days, so that the company could accommodate the sudden, immense boost in demand for its products.

Robust communication between senior leaders and strike-ready officers played a pivotal role in helping HPCL to stand apart from its peer companies. As the strike deadline neared, executives directed appeals to members of the officers' association via e-mail and through the HPCL intranet. Balakrishnan also talked personally with many officers, urging them not to join the planned work stoppage. "We told the officers that all of us need more money, no question about it," he recalls. "But I said, 'We are not going to hold the country ransom for our personal benefit.' I said that we, as top management, will go to the government and say that we're looking for a better deal. I said, 'Look, there's no need for all of you to go on strike and to stop the functioning of the company.'" That appeal worked. "I was surprised that all of them listened to us," Balakrishnan says. "That's the proof in the pudding, really." HPCL officers no doubt listened to their leaders in part because those leaders had made a habit of listening to *them*. By way of further "proof," an Indian government official later told Balakrishnan that "HPCL [had] saved the country"—thanks to the efforts of HPCL employees who stayed on the job during the strike.

HPCL leaders, refusing to rest on such laurels, proceeded to launch a new stage in the company's organizational conversation. In April 2009, Balakrishnan posted an entry on the CMD blog titled "Time to Be No. 1: A Call to Colleagues in Retail SBU." In the Indian retail petroleum sector, HPCL has long vied with Bharat Petroleum for the number two spot, and both companies have lagged far behind Indian Oil, which controls roughly half of the market. But conditions inside the company and in the marketplace have changed markedly in recent years, Balakrishnan noted in his post. "So why are we not No. 1 in Retail?" he asked. "The answer is very simple. We have never really aspired for it." Employees, he suggested, should use the blog as a place to debate a "strategy to reach the pole position, as the advertising jargon goes." In effect, he invited them to conduct an online vision workshop: "We would be happy to hear from Sales Officers and Regional Managers. They are closer to the ground realities than I am. Tell us what help you need to be No. 1." That summons to aim for the top came as a shock to many employees who read it. But initial shock soon gave way to real engagement with the idea. "We had never thought in those terms," Misri recalls. "The number one scenario, in our context, was just too far away. But as we started thinking about it, we started to have a kind of vision. It took some time to sink in, and then I posted my comments. By that time, you could devise a few points of an action plan: Maybe slowly, in some pockets, we *can* become number one."

IN THE DECADE SINCE THE leaders of HPCL launched their company-wide change initiative, they have adopted or at least explored each of the elements that figure in our model of organizational conversation. By analyzing communication channels in light of whether they have a transactional or a transformational purpose, HPCL demonstrates conversational *intentionality*. Through its Coin Your Idea tool, along with other features on its intranet site, HPCL practices conversational *inclusion*. (The practice of sending cross-functional teams out into the marketplace, where they help to develop new branding ideas and new retailing opportunities, also reflects an inclusive sensibility.) The two blogs that reside on the HPCL intranet, which top executives and frontline employees alike use to discuss changes at the company, show a commitment to conversational *interactivity*—as does the culture of one-to-one communication that HPCL leaders have worked to build.

Then there are the vision workshops that have become central to business life at HPCL since the turn of the last century. That practice, we believe, taps into all four elements of the organizational conversation model. It calls upon employees, as well as executives, to take an intentional approach to talking about the future of HPCL. It includes employees from all ranks and divisions of the company in an ongoing discussion about that future. It allows employees to interact with one another in a robust, back-and-forth manner. Above all, though, vision workshops have enabled HPCL leaders and employees to close the organizational gaps that had long existed between them. Together with the emphasis that HPCL executives place on direct, face-to-face communication, the vision workshop practice illustrates the energy that a company can generate when its leaders promote conversational *intimacy*.

CHAPTER THREE

Talk, Inc., Points (TIPs)

Close Encounters

TWO PARTIES TO A CONVERSATION might or might not be close to each other in space, but talk between them will sputter or even stop if they aren't close to each other in spirit. That idea applies at least as much to people in organizations as it does to people in other settings. As a consequence, more and more leaders are pursuing forms of communication that allow them to get closer—closer in spirit, and sometimes closer in space as well—to the people who make up their workforce. Underlying that big, simple idea is a profusion of smaller-scale ideas that companies have sought to implement in recent years. Here, drawn from a sampling of those ideas, are a few practical steps that leaders can take to promote conversational intimacy.

Be the First

Few factors disrupt organizational conversation more sharply than the intrusion of an outside party into that process. Too often, in an age of instantaneous Internet-driven communication, people learn about key events at their company from media reports. Whether the news is good, bad, or neutral, hearing about it in that way can lead to a fraying of trust. For that reason, conversationally adept leaders treat employees as the primary audience for big company announcements.

When Hindustan Petroleum Corporation Ltd. (HPCL) revamped its approach to interacting with employees, at the start of a change initiative that began in 2002, its leaders put a premium on sharing information in a timely fashion. "We brought a tremendous level of communication to employees. 'Whatever we do in the company, whatever happens in the company,' we told employees, 'you will hear it from the senior management first, before you read it in a newspaper,'" says Arun Balakrishnan, formerly the chairman and managing director (CMD) of HPCL. "That was a tall promise that we made."

Today, HPCL leaders fight speed with speed. Use of e-mail and the company intranet enables them to head off most assaults from outside news sources. "Everything is flashed immediately through the intranet— all successes, all failures, everything. So people really know what is happening in the organization," says S. Roy Choudhury, the company's current CMD. He and his colleagues stay close to employees in part by helping employees to stay in tune with major developments at HPCL— from turnover in the leadership ranks to new long-range investment plans. "They hear from us first," Balakrishnan says. "And I think that has great power."

Break Rank

Effective organizational conversation occurs only where leaders are able to get close to *all* employees—not just to their direct reports. One way that leaders do so is to initiate regularly scheduled meetings in which they can talk with employees whose jobs are two, three, or more levels below theirs on a formal organization chart. By reaching around the intermediate boxes on that org chart, they break down some of the barriers that stymie communication at very large companies in particular.

At General Motors, for instance, a practice known as a "diagonal slice" meeting brings together a senior leader and a small cross-section of employees (typically, between six and fifteen of them) from various departments and at various levels within a functional area. In effect, it lets the leader *slice* across divisional lines and corporate hierarchies, with the aim of creating alternative pathways of feedback and trust. "What makes it a powerful tool is that you start to see the world through other people's eyes," says Kim Carpenter, communications manager for global quality and engineering at GM.

A similar practice takes place on the GM intranet. It's a semiregular online chat between a top executive and a group of employees from various parts of the company. Offering another boundary-crossing opportunity for leaders, it follows a slightly different format from that of the diagonal-slice meeting. "Instead of employees asking a question for the leader to answer, the leader is asking a question and getting employees' perspective," Carpenter says. "So a leader might pose a question like, 'What can we do to improve our quality?' It's an opportunity for a leader to see what messages are resonating and where there are disconnects in the organization."

Talk Small

There's a fundamental tension between organizational bulk and conversational intimacy. Which is why smart leaders work to preserve a small-group sensibility even as their organization undergoes otherwise desirable growth. Often the best way to do so is to communicate with employees through the vehicle of, well, small groups.

Leaders at Dewey & LeBoeuf LLP, an international corporate law firm, arrived at that conclusion not long after the 2007 merger of its two parent firms, Dewey Ballantine and LeBoeuf Lamb. Mergers, of course, often bring trouble—and even turmoil. In one instance, though, this merger led to a useful innovation. As the firm grew in size, its managers decided to reduce the size of certain meetings that they use to communicate with employees. And in that context, they discovered, small is definitely beneficial. At its New York City office, for example, the firm moved away from hosting big, all-hands events for the six hundred staff members who work at that site. (The term *staff* applies to all employees who aren't attorneys.) Instead, leaders began to convene a series of floor-by-floor meetings that gather thirty to forty people per session. "We like the intimacy," says Jason S. Dinwoodie, who formerly served as the firm's former chief human resource officer. (Dinwoodie is now U.S. executive director at another law firm, Withers Bergman LLP.) "We think it gives people the opportunity to feel more connected to us as management than if they were to sit in a gigantic auditorium. It becomes more of a conversation and less of a lecture."

Shifting the scale of organizational conversation from "the firm" to "the floor" takes a logistical toll on Dewey & LeBoeuf. But firm leaders highlight the advantages of this practice. "We get a more accurate assessment of where the organization is, collectively, than if we had a big meeting where people don't feel free to speak," Dinwoodie says. In larger gatherings, he points out, people too often worry about asking questions that others might perceive as dumb. Small, relatively intimate meetings help to engender trust in employees as well, Dinwoodie observes: "People want to look you in the eye and see that you're being sincere."

Tough It Out

In an intimate setting, people can smell fear. No less acutely, they can sense authenticity. The worst thing that leaders can do in organizational conversation is to let fear—or any other strong emotion—seep into the discussion without being fully honest about it. When the going is good *and* when the going gets tough, leaders therefore must be open, direct, and "real" in their communication with employees.

"That is what people expect," says Anne Mulcahy, former CEO and chairwoman of Xerox. "They expect a leader to have a vision, to be authentic in communication—to *walk the talk*, for lack of a better term—and to hear the tough questions and respond honestly to them." Mulcahy, thinking back on a challenging, tumultuous period at Xerox, outlines a few lessons that she learned along the way. "I instinctively knew that in troubled times, you'd better build support one person at a time," she recalls. "I was amazed at the impact you can have when you give people a clear perspective on what the problems are and you don't try to give them a lot of corporate bull: You actually talk about the business in ways that are very understandable. You talk about what needs to be done."

To show her commitment to getting real during meetings with Xerox employees, Mulcahy occasionally did something that might seem para-doxical: She solicited questions that were, in fact, not quite real. "I remem-ber at times *planting* some of the ugliest and toughest questions, so that people would get a sense that it was okay to confront the reality of what was going on," she says. Her goal was to offer answers to those questions that were "honest but also hopeful about the future," she explains. "There are lots of ways of communicating these days, all of which can be incred-ibly effective and efficient. But there's nothing that takes the place of touch—the personal aspect of having people understand your fear and, hopefully, the integrity of what you believe in."

Step Outside

One pitfall of organizational conversation is that employees have perfectly good reasons not to say what's really on their minds. It can be dangerous, after all, to stick your neck out. In the interest of conversational intimacy, though, a capable leader will draw people out of their protective shell. Doing so requires a measure of empathy and a little ingenuity.

Executives at HPCL have hit upon a couple of useful techniques in that regard. During regional site visits, for example, Choudhury likes to step beyond the light of a daytime, workplace setting. "People don't open up sometimes," he notes. "But when you meet them informally, in the evening, you will find that there are lots of issues which are normally kept hidden." Rakesh Misri, general manager for North Zone Retail, suggests a tack to follow during group meetings. "The hierarchical structure is still there in the public-sector organizations. Out of respect for the boss, or not to offend anybody, people have a tendency to keep their views to themselves," he says. When a new issue arises in a meeting with subordinates, therefore, he tends to hold off on voicing his own opinion until other participants have had a chance to voice theirs. "Let them express their views first, so that they can state very clearly how they feel about the subject," Misri advises.

Take the Leap

To develop the kind of trust that makes for conversational intimacy, someone must take the first step—the initial, and inevitably uncertain, step of trusting someone else. To be sure, trust can beget trust. But that process has to start somewhere, and frequently it starts with leaders who understand that bold risk-taking has value not only in the marketplace, but also in the workplace. Ultimately, the only way to show that trust is worth the risk is to take the risk, come what may.

The leaders of Athenahealth knew the risks that came with making each of their employees an official insider—an insider, that is, under the terms of U.S. securities law—and they faced those risks squarely. In advance of the company's 2007 IPO, they outlined a course of action to follow if any of the company's several hundred insiders were to release proprietary data. "If someone were to go out and disclose information, or tell it to 'Uncle Bill,' and people could determine that a trade was made as a result, we'd have to take action against that person, and we wouldn't want to do that," says John Hallock, director of global corporate communications. Thus far, nothing of that kind has occurred. "If it ever did, that wouldn't stop us," he says. "We can't change an entire process because of one bad action. It goes back to the fundamentals of trusting people, and trusting them to believe in our culture and our mission."

Even the prospect of tough times doesn't necessarily undermine the logic of a trust-based model of organizational conversation. "It comes full circle," Hallock says. "If you've kept them on the outside the whole time, and then something really difficult does happen, such as layoffs, they're going to be angry. And no wonder. But if you've kept them inside and you say, 'Guys, here's where we are, and here's what we're trying to do,' people are still going to be angry, but they also know that the company is being as open and forthright as it possibly can be." And thus, while anger might fester, employees might also think twice before disclosing information entrusted to them. In any event, the relevant risk calculation operates in two directions. What would happen if Athenahealth leaders were to cease treating employees as trusted insiders? In that case, Hallock says, "the damage that could be done to the culture, and inevitably to the level of service that Athena delivers, would outweigh any risk associated with somebody posting a number on a Yahoo! message board."

PART II

Interactivity

CHAPTER FOUR

Back and Forth

The Emergence of Social Technology

IT TAKES AT LEAST TWO people to sustain a conversation. More to the point, both of them (or all of them) must take part in sustaining it. If one party monopolizes the conversation, then it's not really a conversation. That's obviously true of a person-to-person chat of the low-tech or no-tech variety. But it's equally true of organizational conversation—even, and perhaps especially, when an organization deploys sophisticated technology to extend that conversation through the ranks of a large employee base, or across great distances. Too easily, the media that a company uses to achieve scale and efficiency in its communication can devolve into one-way channels that accommodate only one voice.

For executives and managers, the temptation to treat every medium at their disposal as if it were a megaphone can be hard to resist. For that reason, conversationally adept leaders have come to value and to promote *interactivity* in the forms of communication that unfold at their organizations. The element of interactivity, in fact, reinforces and builds upon the element of intimacy: Efforts to get closer to employees, to listen to them, and to display trust in them will founder if employees don't have both the tools and the institutional support that they need to speak up and to talk back.

By definition, a conversation *is* an interaction. It's a bilateral or multi-lateral exchange of comments and ideas, a back-and-forth process in which the *inter* part (from the Latin word for "between") carries as much significance as the *act* part. Devoting a whole chapter to the inter-active component of organizational conversation, therefore, might seem like overkill—on a par with launching a discussion about the wet-ness of water. And yet, the phenomenon of interactivity is pivotal to understanding the shift toward a conversational model of organiza-tional communication. Here's why: A chief attribute of traditional com-munication practices has been their very lack of interactivity. The nature of existing communication technology has long made it difficult or impossible to enable true back-and-forth interaction within organiza-tions of any appreciable size. The prevailing culture within most organ-izations, meanwhile, has often worked against any attempt to treat corporate communication as a two-way affair. And each of those condi-tions has reinforced the other.

For decades, the chief media of communication—both within organizations and in society at large—encompassed print newsletters, magazines, brochures, and posters; broadcast television and radio pro-grams; and recorded film and sound productions. All of them were unidirectional: The flow of information moved in one way only. By necessity, one set of people produced content for those media, and another set of people consumed that content. The world of print was a world set in type, a world of fixed information; beyond letters to the editor and the like, it allowed practically no scope for back-and-forth communication. Early forms of electronic media were scarcely more apt to support interactivity. The very term *broadcast* embodied that fact. Deriving from an old word for the process by which a single farmer could disperse thousands of seeds across a field, that term cap-tured perfectly the way that radio and TV networks (for example) enabled the few to send out messages to the many. In organizational life, "the few" typically included senior executives and the corporate communication professionals who assisted them, while "the many" gathered in everyone else.

Today, though, new technologies and new ways of using technology have disrupted that structure. Grouped under the term *social media,* these technologies use network connectivity to replace a pure "push" mode of communication with the push-and-pull dynamics of vigorous conversation. "Communication was always *meant* to be two-way. But it never was. It was always pushed out," says Jacqueline Taggart, a vice president in the communication practice at Aon Hewitt, a human resource consulting firm. "To get information back from employees, there was always a set, formal structure. Back in the eighties, there were quality circles. In the fifties and sixties, there were employee suggestion boxes. But now it really *is* two-way. You see companies putting up things like wikis and blogs for employees."

Not so long ago, the words *wiki* and *blog* didn't exist. Today, they're part of the working vocabulary of every professional communicator, and wikis and blogs proper—along with other manifestations of social technology—are fast becoming commonplace at organizations throughout the world. Trends in this field move as rapidly as the digital technology that underlies them, and the specific twists and turns of this development are less consequential than its overall thrust. Here, though, is a quick overview of the basic landscape.

- BLOGS: text- or video-based Web logs that feature an immediate, casual style of conveying news and opinion, along with an interactive comments function

- WIKIS: online databases—including, most prominently, *Wikipedia*—that allow multiple users to create and edit content in a dynamic, collaborative fashion

- ONLINE COMMUNITIES: open forums where people can post comments of interest to a specific group

- TWITTER: a micro-blogging platform that lets users feed to subscribers a stream of messages (called "tweets") that are no longer than 140 characters each

- SOCIAL NETWORKS: services, such as Facebook and LinkedIn, that allow users to create a personal profile page that then becomes a platform through which they can interact with one another

- WEB-ENABLED VIDEO CHAT: a technology, offered most prominently by the Internet-telephony provider Skype, that creates a direct video link between users

- VIDEO SHARING: the practice, enabled by services such as YouTube, of creating video clips (usually short, often homemade or made with low production values) and posting them online

Behind all of the hoopla that has attended the emergence of social media, there's an irreducible truth: People now have access to media channels that are indeed more social than the dominant channels of an earlier era. And in this context, *social* means "conversational"; it entails a commitment to interactivity. "It's a conversation now and not a broadcast, and companies are being called upon to engage in that conversation," says Ronna Lichtenberg, president of Clear Peak Communications, a consulting firm. She describes a once-typical practice that illustrates how companies have long handled available channels of communication: "There would be a statement from the chairman. You'd draft it, and you'd redraft it, and lawyers would go over it. You'd labor over it for days, and you'd try to say as little as possible. That's not happening in a Twitter world. It doesn't work. Now it's, 'Let's be in the conversation.' It's about participating in conversations in the way that you would with anyone with whom you have a real relationship."

Interpersonal conversation, at its ideal best, entails collegiality and mutual respect between its participants. It thrives, as Lichtenberg suggests, to the degree that participants *relate* to each other. Shunning the simplicity of monologue in favor of the unpredictable vitality of dialogue, it is open and fluid, rather than closed and directive. Newly available channels create the potential for importing that spirit into an organizational setting. "The premise of social media is the ability to create, nurture, and maintain conversation," says PR consultant Gary F. Grates. "It's not *telling* people what the strategy is. It's giving them an opportunity to engage in the strategy through conversation. This level of communications is now necessary for an organization's survival and success." All the same, a communication channel is ultimately nothing more than what the term *channel* implies. It's a pathway or a passageway, a means of transmitting information from one point to another. Likewise, the much-talked-about tools that fall into the category of social media are merely that: tools, available for use by people who know how to integrate them into their organizational conversation.

Opening a Channel

Nora Denzel, a senior vice president at Intuit Software, has a broad portfolio. She's in charge of "big data, social design, and marketing," and in that role she must communicate with a wide array of employees about a wide range of topics. Maintaining an open conversation with people throughout Intuit, therefore, is among her top priorities. "I take communication really seriously. It's a very deliberate function for me," says Denzel, who heads an initiative that focuses on using large sets of data, while also managing Intuit's entire communication operation. (Previously, Denzel oversaw a large business unit at Intuit called Employee Management Solutions, or EMS.) "We don't simply try to inform people in a nonnegotiable way. It's a two-way communication. I have a blog, and anyone can post comments to it. We have roundtables where anyone can speak. It's all about creating a dialogue to foster engagement in support of our business strategy." Among the principal channels that she uses to interact with employees, and thereby to support company strategy, is that blog. Intuit as a whole plays host to hundreds of blogs that managers and lower-level employees alike have set up in recent years, and the company often syndicates individual posts to all of its 8,000-plus employees on its intranet site, called Snap. As of 2010, Denzel notes, her blog feed was the most widely read such feed in the entire organization.

Keeping a blog enables Denzel to reach people at Intuit directly and efficiently—and to do so in a mode that shows respect for their time, their attention, and their way of working. "Instead of pushing out e-mails, we just have a blog," she says (referring, in this case, to her efforts within the EMS unit). "People can pull it whenever they want. They can also append their questions, so that we can have a conversation within the division. It's almost like a personalized e-mail, rather than a memo with very corporate-like wording. It's an informal way of keeping up a relationship with employees. But it's on their terms." Denzel writes each blog entry herself (relying on Intuit editors only to correct occasional spelling and grammar errors), and she generally posts a new entry every week or so. Unlike the medium of a print memo, or even that of e-mail, blogging technology makes it easy for Denzel to track the number of people who actually read what she writes. Through the blog's built-in comments function, moreover, her readers are able to register feedback right away. "Some topics just evoke a more visceral reaction, and people really want to chime in. And then other topics, they're quiet about," she notes. One post about what she learned at an Intuit investors' conference garnered no substantive response, for example, while posts that feature career advice routinely generate a half dozen or more comments. Now and again, the comments on her blog become contentious. "It's very open and honest, and you have to accept that," Denzel says.

Before leaders can open an organizational conversation, they first must open a channel for it. That's one way in which organizational conversation tends to differ from interpersonal conversation: A difference in scale translates into different requirements for supporting back-and-forth communication. Today, digital technology offers a range of options for meeting those requirements. At one end of that spectrum are simple online Q&A devices that let employees put questions to company leaders. Such tools—they often appear under labels such as Ask the CEO—offer a rudimentary and yet potentially valuable way for an organization to ensure that its lines of internal communication are indeed open. At the other end of the spectrum are elaborate intranet platforms that support dynamic collaboration across voice, video, and other media. Somewhere in between those poles is the social media staple known as blogging. Denzel, with her text-based blog at Intuit, presents one model of what a leader can achieve through this channel. Other executives, going one technological step further, have taken up video blogging as a means to boost the degree and the quality of interactivity within their organization.

Blogging doesn't suits all leaders. Several years ago, when this medium first became popular, a buzz arose around the idea that CEOs might become bloggers. The buzz was eventually followed by a bust. "There are certainly some CEOs who are doing it, but probably fewer than there were three or four years ago," says communication consultant James Harkness. For several reasons, he notes, initial enthusiasm often gave way to a reluctance to keep up an executive blog: "There was always a skepticism as to whether the thing was actually written by the CEO, and there was the danger that it would get out into the media. Some CEOs got burnt by the experience." These days, most executives who maintain an internal blog do so because they enjoy interacting with employees in that way—and because they have a clear goal in mind. "Social media represents a great democratization of ideas and information," argues Mike Clement, a former director of corporate communications at Bank of America and the founder of Strait Insights, a communication-strategy firm. "But you've really got to understand what your business purpose is: What outcome do you want? It's like any other business problem. A blog isn't necessarily the answer to every problem, and you have to work through that."

At the media company XO Group, blogging helps to forge an ongoing connection between top leaders and members of a fast-growing staff. In the company's early days, when its head count was low, one of the main channels of open communication between executives and employees was the proverbial open door. But now that there are more than 550 people in the organization, fewer and fewer of them are comfortable with just walking into the office of, say, CEO and cofounder David Liu. "The idea of the blog was to give people an opportunity to gain a level of familiarity with senior managers," Liu says. "As managers, we have only so much visibility on a day-to-day basis, and if we don't create an environment where people will communicate with us, we'll wind up shielding ourselves from bad news until it's too late." He urges all senior leaders—from chief financial officer to chief content officer—to keep a blog and to post on it at least once per month. "It's a good opportunity for the staff to hear about ideas or strategies as they're forming," Liu says. He also emphasizes the difference between a blog entry and a "formal PowerPoint presentation, where it's all a fait accompli." The blog platform, he says, "engages people at a more creative and introspective level. It lets them understand how the management team is thinking."

Blogging by executives, then, can be another tool for fostering intimacy. But here, as in other cases, intimacy flourishes in combination with interactivity. Michael Croton, a communication professional who has worked at U.K.-based companies such as Barclays Bank and British Petroleum, recalls joining one of those organizations during the initial boom in executive blogging. That boom had made an impact on his new colleagues. "They were really upbeat about the fact that they had a CEO blog," he says. "But it wasn't a CEO blog. It was just a series of announcements and short diary entries by the CEO. It invited no comments and engaged nobody at all. By opening it up and making it more two-way and more transparent, we created a sense of engagement."

Along with his colleagues, Croton encouraged the CEO to solicit employees' views on several specific issues that the company then confronted, externally as well as internally. "What we managed to do was to make it a multiway conversation," he says. "Instead of seeing one or two comments on a piece, we'd see hundreds of comments on a piece over a twenty-four- or forty-eight-hour period. You could see comment threads emerging." Croton, who today works with clients as an independent consultant (he owns a firm called Albion Communication), summarizes a key lesson that he and his colleagues at the time took from this episode: "Previously, they had been doing an early example of social media. But it wasn't really a use of social *thinking*."

Going Social

To illustrate further what he means by "social thinking," Croton offers the example of a client company that sought to engage its employees in a new strategy based on environmental sustainability. The classic approach to that challenge would be to fashion a set of messages and then to broadcast those messages through internal channels as part of a communication "campaign." It would be, in short, a one-way process. In this instance, the company launched a competition in which employees could put forth their own ideas about the issue at hand. "People were proposing their ideals of sustainability," Croton says. "They debated those ideas online. There were blogs running, and chat rooms, and people could vote on the best ideas." The leaders of the client company began with a broad strategy, and eventually they developed "standard communication products" to spread the word about that strategy, Croton notes. In between, however, they created an interactive experience for employees. "As the world becomes more social, as brands become platforms for interaction and engagement, companies have to move in the same direction. They're in danger of sounding off the pace if they continue to assume that a message sent is a message understood," Croton argues. The emergence of social media technology, he says, doesn't "change the fundamentals, which are about involving people in a conversation that leads to action. Where you have the software without the thinking, you just get old wine in new bottles."

The "new bottle" into which organizations now pour an ever-larger share of their communication efforts—including both social media ventures and other, older practices—is the corporate intranet. That's where people in most organizations today go to find information about company policies, or to track updates on quarterly results, or to see video clips that feature their CEO, or to read internal blogs, or to take part in discussion forums with faraway colleagues. "The intranet is becoming a hub," Gary F. Grates says. "It's becoming a place where employees can experience their company at any given point during the day."

At this late date, in fact, the intranet is also becoming a rather old medium. Companies began to launch intranet sites during the mid- to late 1990s, not long after the public Internet began its rapid expansion. Even so, a close look at recent developments in the design and use of intranets shows that the medium has undergone considerable evolution in recent years. The overall trajectory of that evolution, moreover, reflects a growing commitment to social thinking. Roughly speaking, this transition toward greater interactivity has come in four stages, each with its own design principle. Each stage builds on what comes before it, and any actual intranet site is likely to incorporate features from multiple stages. For that reason, we'll refer to them here in the present tense.

SHARED DATABASE. In its initial manifestation, the corporate intranet is a repository of data—a collection of documents, accessible through a firewall-protected internal network. Such an intranet changes only when those who are in charge of it upload new documents to the company server. In that sense, it's a static medium, and it essentially involves no interaction with users or among users.

NEWS SERVICE. The next stage of intranet development shifts the focus from inert bodies of data to a fluid process of information delivery. In this model, communication leaders use an intranet to convey news about their organization—news that formerly went out in a press release or a newsletter. While not all organizations have dispensed with distributing news through traditional print vehicles, quite a few of them have taken that leap. "We do nothing with paper. Everything is driven through our intranet. We have a very robust online news package that we update daily," says Donna C. Peterman, executive vice president and chief communications officer at the PNC Financial Services Group.

At many organizations, as an intranet site evolves into an internal news service, it comes to resemble the Web site of a mainstream media outlet. Take the example of AT&T. In 2008, when AT&T relaunched its intranet, the company dubbed the new site AT&T Insider. Yet the creators of AT&T Insider, in designing the site, drew extensively on *outside* sources of inspiration. Company leaders had given site designers a simple mandate: Build an intranet that employees will visit just as readily as they might visit a popular Internet destination. "We're competing for their time and attention," says Larry Solomon, senior vice president of corporate communications. "So content is king, and it can't be all 'corporate.' It has to be fun, it has to be relevant, it has to be engaging." The Insider site, he notes, is "essentially modeled after WallStreetJournal.com or NewYorkTimes.com." On its front page, employees find a steadily updated stream of news about the company, and that content appears in a format that bears comparison to the look and feel of leading general interest sites. Along with standard written articles, there are photos, slide shows, and video features. In addition, the site offers feeds that deliver the latest business, technology, and world news, courtesy of the Associated Press and other external providers. A sizable investment of resources went into building all of those capabilities. Yet behind that investment lies a solid business logic, as Solomon explains: "Much as the *New York Times* and *USA Today* want to capture everybody's eyeballs so that they can sell more advertising, we want to capture everybody's eyeballs so that we can help employees understand the mission of the company."

The corporate intranet, recast in the mold of a traditional news site, remains a fundamentally one-way medium. It's more dynamic than a database-only intranet, but it's not necessarily more interactive. Nonetheless, by emphasizing the need to catch and hold employees' interest in the site, company leaders signal a move toward social thinking: Merely distributing information to employees isn't enough, they acknowledge; an organization, through its intranet, must also engage its people.

INTERACTIVE TOOL. The crucial next step in the evolution of intranet design arrives when site managers introduce elements that let employees engage directly with site content—and with one another. At this stage, the intranet begins to take a definitively social turn. In practice, the addition of basic interactive features to a site often happens in conjunction with the adoption of a dynamic news-driven model. Attached to each news item on AT&T Insider, for example, are options that allow users to enter a comment on that piece, to share it with a colleague via e-mail, or to rate it on a scale of greater or lesser appeal. "Employees, if they think a story is great, will give it five stars." Solomon says. "You can see 'Highest Rated' stories, 'Most Viewed' stories, et cetera."

Beyond adding functionality that enables site users to rate, share, and comment on standard news content, an increasing number of organizations have given over swaths of their intranet space to pure social media channels—to blogs, discussion communities, and other forums that exist solely to facilitate interaction among employees. By "going social" in this way, a company provides a venue both for structured dialogue and for the kind of informal chatter that takes place in every organization. "Through the blogs on our site, what used to happen around the water cooler or in the break room is now online," says Kris Gopalkrishnan, cofounder and executive co-chairman of Infosys, an information-technology services firm based in India. As he and other leaders have discovered, there are notable benefits to making that facet of organizational conversation open and visible.

A case in point occurred at Bank of America. In a bank of that size, the distance from the executive suite to the teller window can seem as large as the vastness of outer space. "We had this kind of black hole between the banking centers and senior managers at the bank," recalls Peter McKillop, who directed communication within the bank's retail division for four years, starting in 2004. In late 2007, as part of a broad effort to fill that "hole," McKillop and his team launched a new social media platform. They called it, simply, the Water Cooler, and its purpose was to allow people at all levels of the company—but those on the consumer-facing front lines, in particular—to make their voices heard. "The community instantly formed," McKillop says. "The feedback was very strong, very open, very honest. Suddenly, senior leaders were able to drop two, three, four levels down and to listen to the conversations that were going on, and to participate in those conversations. You had people at the teller level coming up with incredibly interesting feedback that we had not seen before."

The Water Cooler drew participants from the ranks of employees throughout Bank of America's network of more than six thousand retail branches, as well as from the bank's corporate-level retail group. It combined elements of a blog with elements of an online discussion board. At the bank's intranet home page, employees would see an icon that looked like a classic office water cooler. "You click on that hot link, and you would go right in to the conversations," McKillop says. "And they were *conversations*—different kinds of conversations that you could join and be part of." Issues addressed in discussion threads ranged from customer service to new products to bank policy. Any employee could post a comment or a question, or respond to someone else's post.

Creating an online community space did more than help Bank of America to address the goal of improving communication "from that middle level of the pyramid down," as McKillop puts it. The Water Cooler also helped the company to improve morale within the "army of associates who were delivering core consumer-banking services," and to do so in a way that suited that population. "We knew that people who worked in the banks really wanted to be part of a broader community," McKillop says. Opening up an opportunity for broad-based two-way communication, meanwhile, was no small thing for this very large organization. (Bank of America employs more than 280,000 people altogether.) "To accept feedback from the bottom up, in an organized fashion—versus just over drinks, or through the community suggestion box—was a big change for the company," McKillop notes. "It took us a long time to sort out the issues. But once we did, we were gobsmacked by the power of what we had done."

PROFESSIONAL NETWORK. In its latest and potentially most transformative iteration, the intranet relinquishes its primary identity as a place from which to retrieve information and becomes instead a place to find people, to interact with them, and to work with them. Inspired by both the popularity and the functionality of services such as Facebook and LinkedIn, leaders are reinventing all or part of their company's intranet site as a social network that functions as a *professional* network. This new kind of intranet is a full-fledged collaboration platform—a quintessentially conversational medium that blurs the line between talk and work, between gathering information and getting things done.

"We're seeing consumers drive social-networking technologies and collaborative behaviors beyond their personal lives into their work lives," says John Chambers, CEO of the networking giant Cisco Systems. "In response, global businesses are adding collaborative structures and processes to social-networking technologies and are beginning to reap large productivity benefits."[1] Defining features of an internal professional network include a directory that lets employees search for colleagues not only according to name, location, and position, but also according to domains of specialized knowledge; the ability to generate customized profile pages, through which employees can share a rich variety of information about themselves and their interests; and multiple tools that enable employees to make and maintain connections with people all across their organization.

"We have two internal social-networking systems," says Steven Rice, executive vice president of human resources at Juniper Networks, a technology company based in Sunnyvale, California. (Like Cisco, Juniper provides networking solutions.) "Both systems are designed to build communities for collaboration and information sharing." The first system, called Matrix, originated in Juniper's engineering department, but it subsequently spread throughout the company. It has become "a vital platform for candid discussions, news, and content management," Rice explains. The second system, called Chatter, is a Twitter-like platform that gives employees an easy way to share brief comments and updates with their colleagues. Juniper's sales and marketing professionals, in particular, have become active Chatter users. "Our executives are visible on both platforms," Rice notes.

At McKesson Corporation, meanwhile, leaders have opted for a collaboration platform provided by an external vendor. "It's a packaged solution that lets employees network with other employees all across the company, regardless of where they sit or what their role is," says Andy Burtis, vice president of corporate marketing and communications at McKesson, a health-care services and technology company based in San Francisco. In addition, employees can "very easily and organically create communities of interest," he says. "These can be communities of interest built around customer segments, or around actual customer accounts." Like Facebook or LinkedIn, Burtis notes, the platform "allows you to shrink the universe dramatically: You're able to find how many degrees of separation you are from other employees. It essentially allows you to navigate the world of McKesson in a far more effective way."

Seeing the Future

In 2007, a senior designer named Damien Vizcarra decided to move from the Boston area, where he worked at a product-design and innovation firm called Continuum, to Southern California. He was relocating mainly for family reasons, and he had secured a position at a design concern in the Los Angeles area. But his colleagues at Continuum didn't want to see him leave the firm. So they found a way that he could move to L.A., stay at Continuum, *and* remain a fixture of daily life at the firm's main offices in Newton, Massachusetts. To be precise, though, he became not so much a "fixture" in the Newton facility as a rolling presence. Network-enabled video technology is what made that presence possible: On a wheeled cart of the kind that nurses in a hospital use to transport equipment from one room to another, the IT crew at Continuum set up a laptop, a large LCD screen, and a video camera, and then linked the whole unit through a high-speed Internet connection to a similar configuration that Vizcarra set up at a desk in his new office in L.A. "We created this thing called the Damien Bot—*bot* as in 'robot'—so that he could stay with us," says Kory Kolligian, who served as the firm's chief operating officer at the time.

By wheeling the Damian Bot from one studio or meeting space to another, designers in Newton could remain in steady contact with their West Coast colleague. Through a real-time audiovisual link, members of his team were able to interact with him as a full partner on shared projects. (The firm also had Vizcarra fly back east for several days each month, so that he could meet with team members in person.) "If you're in a room, white-boarding, he's in there. He's watching everything on his screen. He can see what's going on," Kolligian explains. Working with a colleague who loomed in their presence as a face on an electronic device was an occasionally strange, often amusing experience for Continuum professionals in Newton, but it was also a fundamentally *human* experience. "On any given day, you walk by the Damien Bot, and you see Damien sitting at his desk," Kolligian says. "He can control his camera and control what he sees. I'll walk by, and he'll say, 'Hey, Kory, how are you doing?'"

For leaders at Continuum, the Damien Bot wasn't just a toy or a gee-whiz in-house science project. It grew out of a serious effort to reckon with the nature of collaboration in an expanding, globally oriented company. Kolligian, as he recalls, said to his fellow executives: "We work with clients all over the world. Why is it not possible for us to have a certain level and consistency of interaction with someone living in L.A.? We're moving into an age when we're going to open more offices, and we're going to get this right." As it happens, Continuum opened an office in L.A. a year after Vizcarra had relocated to the region. At that point, he moved his work space to the new facility—and significantly, the Damien Bot moved with him. "It ended up being a very useful device," Vizcarra says. "The best thing about it is that it's mobile." The Damien Bot, Vizcarra notes, was steadily in use during a "two-year buffer period" that began when he moved to the West Coast. Subsequently, Continuum has acquired more-advanced videoconferencing capability, but people at the firm still rely on mobile video bots (they no longer use the term Damien Bot) to facilitate transcontinental collaboration.

The Damien Bot amounted to little more than a portable, always-on videoconferencing system. Despite the degree of contrivance that went into its creation, it was a rather simple device. All the same, the example of that device points toward a simple fact about human interaction: Seeing truly is believing, and visual contact between people who work together remains a critical element of *how* they work together. The example of the Damien Bot also points to a simple fact about the current state of communication technology: "Seeing" of this kind is now much easier than it used to be, even in situations where organizational size or physical separation makes firsthand contact practically impossible. If the typical medium of corporate communication in the last century was the interoffice memo or the employee newsletter, then the typical medium of organizational conversation in the current century is the video chat between colleagues or the video clip that features a CEO talking directly into a camera—and directly to dozens or hundreds or thousands of employees. As video tools and video content have become embedded in more and more intranet sites, the experience of making and watching video messages has become more and more central to the way that people in organizations gather and exchange information. Network-enabled video communication, in sum, has become an increasingly prevalent capability that addresses the interactive needs and aspirations of top leaders and frontline employees alike.

Not all forms of video communication have a two-way structure; some operate in one direction only. A videoconferencing platform offers its users a rich back-and-forth experience, for example, whereas a produced video-on-demand segment—like a YouTube clip or a video blog post—emulates the pattern of traditional one-way media. In either case, though, the see-it-now quality of video generates a conversational dynamic that no other medium can match. All else being equal, for example, a message delivered through a video channel will be more expressive, more empathy-driven, and more effective than a message conveyed through print, e-mail, or any other text-based channel.

"Text is really limited as a communications tool," Ronna Lichtenberg says. "I say this with great respect, as a writer, for the written word. But text doesn't work as efficiently as video if you're trying to build trust and rapport." Or consider the standard audio teleconference. The ability to connect a face to a voice, or to observe the nuances of facial expression and body movement in a speaker, places video communication on a different plane from that of its voice-only counterpart. As Lichtenberg notes, the core purpose of deploying any communication technology is "to come as close as you can to a person-to-person experience."

Video capability can make a big company feel small again, and it can make the distances inherent in long-distance communication seem not so long. "It's a way of connecting without having to travel," says Julie Freeman, former president of the International Association of Business Communicators. To an increasing degree, business travel in recent years has become personally inconvenient, logistically difficult, and financially prohibitive. "People want to have live meetings, but they don't necessarily want to get on an airplane to fly across the world. So you're seeing people use Skype and Web cameras in order to have face-to-face meetings," Freeman notes.

Equally commonplace is a practice that replaces the traditional large-scale company gathering with a video-enabled virtual meeting. At Infosys, leaders use an intranet-based service called InfyTV to communicate with the company's highly dispersed workforce. Through that service, as many as 115,000 employees in more than forty countries can watch as executives discuss financial results at quarterly town-hall meetings. "It's not a physical town hall; it's using technology," Kris Gopalkrishnan says. The video component of that technology forms the basis of its power, he adds: "Seeing makes it more personal. It definitely increases the closeness."

Variations on the idea of meeting virtually with the help of video technology continue to emerge. Managers at AT&T, for example, have adopted a hybrid model. Each quarter, several hundred of the company's top executives gather physically in about a dozen major cities across the United States, and at each site they view a live video webcast that originates in Dallas. That practice began in 2009. "Previously, we had all six hundred people fly once a year to Dallas and spend two and a half to three days in meetings," Larry Solomon says. "That's crazy in today's economy, and it's crazy to wait a year before you do that, because the speed of business is now so fast." Under the new practice, senior leaders convene regularly as a group, and each meeting provides an opportunity for back-and-forth engagement. "They watch the webcast, and afterward they spend an hour and a half or two hours just socializing, face to face, with other officers and senior managers in their location," Solomon explains. For AT&T—the original long-distance company—that model serves to bring far-flung colleagues together in a way that strikes a balance between efficiency and interactivity. Participants can "reach out and touch someone" (to quote an old company catchphrase) without needing to venture far from their home base.

The chief benefit of any video tool comes down to the quality of the connection that it helps people to form. At Intuit, leaders record brief YouTube-like clips to connect with employees in a manner that blends professionalism with personality. "We're very crisp and very informal," Nora Denzel says of the style that she and her fellow executives bring to those video messages. By way of example, she cites the process of communicating with employees in the aftermath of a major acquisition that took place in 2010, during her tenure as head of the EMS unit at Intuit. "It was a huge shock to the system in our division," she recalls. "There were a plethora of questions, a lot of uncertainty and fear. We were assimilating two hundred new employees into the division on a single day. So we did a lot of videos." Employees could send questions about the acquisition to a dedicated e-mail address, and leaders such as Denzel then replied to those questions in a series of video segments. Each segment was just a few minutes long, and employees could view it—at their convenience—on the company intranet. "They can see the emotion in the leader's eyes," Denzel says. "They can see the leader talking about thorny issues: 'Are you going to downsize?' 'What about jobs?' We couldn't meet with each of them individually, so using a medium where they could pull the video on demand was one of the more effective ways to reach them." On-demand video, to be sure, doesn't afford a high degree of interactivity. In this case, though, it enabled Intuit leaders to achieve conversational intimacy on a scale that otherwise wouldn't have been attainable.

Videoconferencing, meanwhile, allows for a connection between people that is at once intimate and interactive. Especially within organizations that have reached a certain stage of growth and complexity, tools that make possible real-time video conversation are becoming indispensable. At Volcano Corporation, a medical-device vendor based in San Diego, leaders have installed videoconferencing units at each of the company's main locations. "We started out with one per site, and now we're adding more, because they're always booked," says Scott Huennekens, president and CEO. "We do most all of our meetings on video, instead of doing just a telephone conference call. Seeing people adds depth to relationships." Many of those video-enabled meetings are multiperson events that draw participants from the roughly twelve hundred people who work at Volcano. But over time, Huennekens says, he has also come to rely on the video channel to conduct one-on-one conversations with fellow executives and with customers: "It feels like we've really touched each other. Then, when we see each other in person, it doesn't feel like we've had six weeks of phone calls; it feels like, 'I just saw you last week!' It's an interesting human dynamic."

Facing Up to Culture

Interactive technology, a "hard" asset, requires the support of "soft" assets before it can yield value. Organizational conversation flourishes when leaders are open to leveraging such technology and yet refuse to lean on it—when they aim, first of all, to build a robustly interactive culture. *Culture,* in this context, refers to the array of values, norms, and behaviors that together come to define the spirit of a company. It's the sum total of assumptions and practices that set the default mode for how people treat each other. The success of any effort to enable interactivity within an organization thus hinges on the answers to a few culture-defining questions: Are higher-level employees collegial or condescending in their relations with people at lower levels of the organization? Do employees at every level experience the flow of ideas and information as a dynamic, two-way process, or do they tend to view each corporate message as "the last word" on a given subject? Does the organization exhibit a dense pattern of sociability, or do its people interact with each other mainly in formal settings and on an as-needed basis? Is there a widespread understanding that knowledge exists to be shared, or is there a tendency to guard it jealously, as though it were the prize in a zero-sum game?

One organization where leaders have sought to make their culture safe for information sharing is ManpowerGroup. Beginning roughly in 2009, that company undertook an initiative to change how it operates globally. ManpowerGroup has long had offices in many countries all around the world, but until somewhat recently each regional office had functioned more or less as an independent entity. Over the past decade, however, many of the clients to which ManpowerGroup provides staffing services have integrated their own worldwide operations, and ManpowerGroup leaders have seen fit to follow suit. "Our strategy has been to move toward more global solutions," says Mara Swan, executive vice president of global strategy and talent. (ManpowerGroup, based in Milwaukee, directly employs 33,000 people and handles job placement for about 4.5 million people each year.) "As a result, we need different behaviors from our employees. It's really a culture change. We've had to align the organization around not just our values, but also common goals—which we never did before."

Communication practices have proven to be a key factor in the work of aligning ManpowerGroup's internal culture with its new strategy. To encourage thousands of employees in multiple regions to see themselves as developing a cohesive set of global solutions, Swan and her fellow executives have revamped the way that they interact with their workforce. "Before, it would have been just communicating one-way out to people," whereas today company leaders emphasize "two-way conversation," Swan explains. "One-way communication is not very effective. It's really about creating a culture that's focused on passion for the brand, the client, our candidates, and our values." Within ManpowerGroup, Swan adds, she and her colleagues refer to that process as "changing the conversation and deepening the dialogue."

A sure sign that the culture within ManpowerGroup has changed, according to Swan, is that employees now participate actively and without hesitation in an organization-wide dialogue. "They're asking better, deeper questions," she notes. More to the point, they're posing questions that openly challenge senior managers. "I'll give you a good example," she says. "There's a guy who works out of Sweden. I've never talked to this guy in my life; I don't even know how he knows who I am. He sent me an e-mail that said, 'Mara, I'd like to give you feedback on this process that you did last year. Here is what needs to change and why.' So I wrote back to him and said, 'That's really cool. I appreciate your sending that to me. I'm going to look at it, I'll see what I can address, and I'll let you know what I can change.' People just feel free to do that." No intranet platform, no blogging application, no videoconferencing capability can give employees the cultural permission that they need to take such liberties. "Before you put in any tools or technology, you have to work on making your culture open and safe," Swan argues. "If you don't have a culture that's free of fear, then you're not going to have open communication, no matter how many great tools you have."

In a fully interactive organizational culture, not only does communication remain as *open* as possible, but it also tends to be as *direct* as possible. Even in companies that necessarily and effectively adopt the newest of new media to enable organizational conversation, unmediated communication—face-to-face communication, in other words—continues to be an essential channel through which leaders and employees gain critical information. "There are so many mechanisms of communication now that they become substitutes for real human interaction," says Ken Bagan, a veteran oil-company executive. "We forget that people like to see your face and watch your eyes. Telecommunication and videoconferencing notwithstanding, there's really no substitute for just talking to people. And the more that you can do that in a live conversation, standing right in front of them, watching them as well as listening to them, the better the level of understanding will be."

Opportunities for that sort of interaction are increasingly rare at many companies, and the value of newer communication technology often lies precisely in its potential to serve as a "substitute" for in-person conversation. Real-time video tools, in particular, offer a semblance (and, perhaps, more than a semblance) of the traditional face-to-face experience. Nonetheless, conversationally adept leaders appreciate the power of engaging in direct, you-are-there interaction with people in their organization, and they tap into that power whenever possible.

Face-to-face conversation is the mainstay of internal communication at Metabolix, a bioscience company based in Cambridge, Massachusetts. "You want to get people talking. You want to create a culture where they're willing to debate and challenge each other," says Rick Eno, CEO of Metabolix, which employs about 110 people at multiple sites in the United States and Europe. Eno and his colleagues are hardly averse to exploring up-to-the-minute technology. Their business, in fact, involves commercializing new discoveries in the field of biodegradable plastics. Inside the company, however, they rely far less on late-model communication tools than they do on methods that one might call "pretechnological." Metabolix produces no print or electronic newsletter for employees, and its leaders deploy the company intranet almost exclusively as a tool for keeping human resource records and for tracking intellectual-property assets. "My sense here is that communication is good," Eno says. "I'm not sensing that we're out of alignment because we don't use our intranet as a primary path for cross-functional communication."

How, then, do Metabolix leaders ensure that critical information circulates within the company? "The common theme is personal interaction," Eno says, and the principal channel on which he and his team rely is "management by wandering around." (The term *management by wandering around,* along with the practice that it describes, has been around for a while. Tom Peters and Bob Waterman picked it up from Hewlett-Packard back in the 1970s, and they popularized it in their book *In Search of Excellence*.) Eno travels frequently to wander among staff members at each company site, and the focus on direct communication extends to the organization's front lines. "We've got group leaders who are interacting with their teams, answering questions, making decisions on the spot," he says.

The case of Metabolix suggests a corollary to the notion that digital technology helps a large organization to feel (or at least to function) as though it were a small organization: Relatively compact organizations, in many cases, simply don't benefit much from the implementation of sophisticated intranet sites, elaborate video systems, and the like. They have other ways to foster interactivity among employees. "We're too small a company to get any real value from internal social media," says Scott Paul, CEO of Hoku Corporation, a Honolulu-based company that develops and sells clean-energy technology. "I'm definitely watching these technologies, and I can see how they will be of value when we are a bigger organization. But we're already flat, and there's already intimate conversation that goes on, live and in person." Hoku has grown to a point where it employs about two hundred people across four offices, and its leaders use videoconferencing tools to support communication between, say, its headquarters in Hawaii and a second major facility that it maintains in Idaho. In general, though, Hoku follows a low-tech course in its management of organizational conversation.

Any organization, whatever its scale, can be only as interactive as its culture. In a big company, the adoption of leading-edge digital technology can facilitate two-way communication in cases where it might not be feasible otherwise. Yet the leaders of a large organization will discover quickly enough that social media tools, for example, can't generate habits of interaction where those habits don't already exist. Small companies, meanwhile, frequently develop a culture that fosters back-and-forth communication—merely by virtue of the close proximity in which their employees work. Even in an organization of modest size, though, leaders will find that the level of interactivity will decline if they fail to cultivate values and behaviors that support open dialogue. "There should be a culture where people are comfortable asking questions and talking to anyone at any level in the organization, and where they feel that their opinion will be heard," Eno argues. "If you don't have that culture, the structures that you put in place won't be as effective as they should be." Or, to say it another way: The soft side and the hard side of organizational conversation must evolve together. They must, indeed, interact.

IN MANY CASES, not surprisingly, the leaders who have moved fastest to power their organizations with the aid of social technology are those who oversee high-tech companies. An organization that helps to create the hardware or the software of modern digital life has a strong incentive to test out the latest digital thing; it also has, among its employees, an ample supply of savvy testers. Certainly, that's true of Cisco Systems, a company whose products enable a broad range of social media capabilities. (Indeed, it's hard to talk about Cisco and its use of communication channels without sounding as if you're producing an advertisement for its products.) Yet the example of Cisco—as we will observe in the next chapter—shows that the smart use of interactive technology begins with a low-tech aptitude for back-and-forth communication.

CHAPTER FIVE

Walking the Talk

Cisco Systems

AT THE HEADQUARTERS OF Cisco Systems, in San Jose, a visitor sits at a semicircular table in a conference room. Across from him is an employee of Cisco. The meeting unfolds in much the same way as millions of other meetings that take place in corporate conference rooms all around the world every day. In this case, the visitor and the Cisco employee are discussing TelePresence, a Cisco product. They're also *using* TelePresence. The employee, as it happens, is sitting in an entirely different room from the one where the visitor sits. Indeed, from the visitor's perspective, the Cisco employee might as well be sitting in a room halfway around the world.

TelePresence simulates an in-person meeting by beaming life-scale video feeds between two distant locations. Using IPTV (Internet-protocol television) technology, it sends high-definition video images back and forth across a broadband network. As configured in rooms on the Cisco campus, the TelePresence package includes state-of-the-art video-recording equipment, along with a triptych of large screens that together create a wraparound effect for the user who sits in front of them. Also included is a specially designed meeting table that—at least in an ideal configuration— matches and mirrors the table on the other end of a TelePresence link. As a result, users on both ends of that connection feel as if they're occupying seats at the same piece of office furniture. "It's really the next best thing to being there," says Jackie Landsman, senior manager of corporate communications at Cisco.

The visitor can attest to the lifelike, "being there" quality of Tele-Presence. After sitting at that half-circle meeting table for a few minutes, he forgets that he's speaking to a screen and not to a physical human being. "This is much more engaging than any other type of video application that's out there," says Mike Mitchell, senior director of corporate communications. Mitchell is the Cisco employee whom the visitor has met across the membrane of a TelePresence screen. Although Mitchell and the visitor aren't able to shake hands in that context, they do make eye contact, and their meeting feels a lot like a routine face-to-face encounter. To the visitor, Mitchell is fully "present," just as he would be present in a standard in-person conversation—and just as he *is* present a short while later, when the visitor walks across the Cisco campus and finally shakes hands with Mitchell.

In one sense, a TelePresence meeting is simply a more robust version of a Web-based video chat, an experience that has become routine for most businesspeople. But in another sense, it provides a qualitatively different way for businesspeople to interact with each other. First, TelePresence delivers high-definition, real-time video; it has none of the delays or hiccups that typically mark online video performance. Second, and more important, it masters the critical matter of visual scale. "We studied meeting dynamics for a while before we developed TelePres-ence," says Bryan Hobbs, a demonstration engineer who works in Cisco's Executive Briefing Center. Among the factors of human behavior that Cisco engineers explored was this notable phenomenon: If the image of a person on-screen is less than 80 percent as large as his or her true size, then those who see that image will become "less engaged" in talking with that person, Hobbs explains. That's why someone who appears in a video chat window comes across as "just a person in a box," he says. Participants in a TelePresence meeting, by contrast, appear at life scale and thereby retain an aura of reality.

"Nothing is going to replace the initial handshake" that businesspeo-ple traditionally use to establish a direct connection with one another, Mitchell notes. Yet TelePresence goes far toward enabling many other essential facets of human conversation. "The technology is set up so that you look the other person in the eye," says Mike McFall, global sales director for business video, who uses TelePresence in his daily work life and who also sells the product to customers. Again and again, in watching potential customers as they give TelePresence a test drive, he has observed a pattern: "At first, people are looking around the room, looking at the cameras and the screens. Before you know it, though, they're completely engaged interpersonally. You see them playing off each other as they go back and forth."

"The Whole Conversation"

In the marketplace, TelePresence has become an increasingly common—and increasingly well-known—platform that organizations of all stripes use for high-end, long-distance videoconferencing. (Cisco has promoted the product in a series of widely aired TV commercials. In one of them, a TelePresence screen at the front of a school room serves as a magical window through which a group of kids in the United States wave to a group of kids in China.) Within Cisco, TelePresence forms the vanguard of a broad set of practices that leaders use to sustain richly textured organizational conversation among the company's roughly seventy thousand employees. In its approach to communicating with employees, Cisco exemplifies a trend toward leveraging the *interactive* functionality of advanced digital technology. "The mandate of communications has changed," says Abby Smith, director of global employee communications. "Technology has enabled communications to evolve, and there is a much larger need for interaction. It's no longer acceptable just to communicate one way. You can't just have talking heads that sit there and talk to you. Your employees want the opportunity to give feedback and to be collaborative."

Technical innovation in the kinds of channels that Cisco can deploy to reach its employees (or to let those employees reach their leaders) has certainly increased the potential for greater interactivity within the company. Yet, at Cisco and elsewhere, the interactive element of organizational conversation isn't a matter of technology per se. What emergent digital technologies make possible, rather, is the recovery of certain qualities that earlier communication technologies had necessarily undermined—qualities that allow conversation to be an immediate, spontaneous, back-and-forth affair. One Cisco leader, Randy Pond, explains this development by distinguishing between two modes of communication. "We've gone from a 'push' approach to what I would call an interaction on multiple fronts," he says. "We've always believed that the next big wave was going to be around interactions, both interaction inside the enterprise and interaction across enterprises. There is power in having the *whole* conversation." Examples of push media include traditional publishing and broadcast communication. Such channels convey information in one direction only, and either they allow for no feedback at all from those who receive that information, or they provide feedback that suffers badly from delay and distortion. "The problem with push [communication] is that push gets filtered and push gets interpreted," Pond adds.

As executive vice president of operations, processes, and systems, Pond bears top responsibility for managing how things get done inside Cisco. He knows well the cost to the company of communication that goes awry because of filtering or fragmentation. To illustrate what he means by "the whole conversation," he tells a story that makes its point by way of an amusing counterexample. One day, he took part in a videoconference with some colleagues. As he sat at his desk, he could see several of them on video-feed windows that appeared on his computer screen. At one point, Pond made a comment to the group. Then another participant, Pond recalls, "just put his head in his hands"— presumably in dismay at what Pond was saying, and presumably without pausing to think that Pond could see him. "I said, 'I can see you. If you disagree, *tell me*,'" Pond says. "And he said, 'Darn, I hate this video.'" In truth, everyone at Cisco seems to love what video communication, along with other uses of interactive technology, has done for the company. "The fact that you've got the visual really does make a big difference," Pond says. "You get the whole conversation done at once. I can't begin to tell you how powerful that is." In that example, Pond was able to engage with his head-shaking colleague *as a whole*, and he was thus able to grasp the *whole* story with respect to that colleague's views. A less interactive form of communication might have conveyed such information eventually, but it would have done so far less efficiently.

The ideal of wholly interactive conversation is clear enough. Even so, interactivity can occur in greater or lesser degree, and Cisco leaders are practical about interacting with employees in different ways and for different purposes. One common practice, for example, involves recording video sessions in which executives and others at Cisco discuss a given business topic—a product launch, say, or a new strategic initiative. Employees can then access this video-on-demand (VOD) content through the company's intranet. A VOD clip lacks the real-time immediacy of a live TelePresence session, but that's not to say that it lacks interactivity. Typically, executives conduct these videotaped sessions in a studio environment, complete with an audience. "We open it up to Q&A," Pond says. "That Q&A stimulates a follow-on conversation. Every question that we don't answer in the room, we answer afterward by posting an answer on the Web. Then we give employees the ability to interact." Once the VOD content appears on the Cisco intranet, any employee can post his or her own comments about it. In that way, even a form of communication that ostensibly follows a push model can incorporate and generate two-way conversation.

For Pond, who joined Cisco in 1993, the emergence of such capabilities marks a sea change in how the company operates. Whereas Cisco's top executives once communicated with employees primarily through messages that flowed in a single direction, down through layers of management, today those leaders use video tools, an advanced collaborative intranet platform, and other channels to build a direct, two-way connection with the company's workforce. "We've decided that some messaging shouldn't be filtered through the business," Pond says. "It's become a much more interactive environment than it was fifteen years ago."

They Get a Kick from Champagne

Cisco's exploration of interactive media was born both of necessity and of opportunity. "At Cisco, we are much more global than we've ever been—in more countries, doing more initiatives where decision making happens outside of headquarters. We've had to think differently about how we communicate, so we can reach everyone and have the same impact," says Blair Christie, senior vice president and chief marketing officer for worldwide government affairs. Given Cisco's complex, far-flung operations, moreover, merely having an "impact" on employees through one-way messaging is no longer sufficient. Cisco leaders, Christie emphasizes, need to ensure that "communication is definitely two-way." Similarly, rapid growth has put a premium on finding ways to preserve meaningful links between senior leaders and everyone else at Cisco. "Employees, despite our size, do feel a connection to the top," Pond says. But that connection, forged when the company was much smaller, is "hard to replicate without using some of the new tools and processes," he notes. "We try to drive that intimacy. It just doesn't scale easily across the globe, and that's where the new social networking capabilities, including video, really provide a lot of leverage."

Opportunity, meanwhile, comes to Cisco by way of the market for high-performance, interactive technologies. After all, Cisco *owns* many of those technologies, and it has a large stake not only in demonstrating the virtues of products such as TelePresence, but also in promoting usage of routers and other networking devices that form the core of its legacy product line. "Video as a market for Cisco is key," Christie says. "It has a huge impact on bandwidth and networking capabilities." (High levels of digital interactivity translate directly into high levels of band-width usage—and thus into higher demand for Cisco products.) Along-side that commercial incentive to encourage adoption of TelePresence and kindred products, of course, people at Cisco have an interest in making sure that those technologies work optimally. In Silicon Valley parlance, the company has naturally gravitated toward "eating its own dog food." Internally, Cisco leaders refer to the practice of developing and testing its products as "Cisco on Cisco." They also shy away from applying the term "dog food" to those products. As Hobbs notes, they prefer another saying: "We sip our own champagne."

Yet the affinity between Cisco and advanced forms of organizational conversation goes deeper than any single product. "We are a communi-cations company. That is what we do," says Kelly Lang, director of strate-gic communications. Every item in Cisco's product line, in other words, exists to support digitally networked communication. In that respect, the company doesn't sip champagne; it *guzzles* champagne. As a result, according to Landsman, Cisco has cultivated a "penchant for communi-cations" that "is driven through the entire organization." Consider, for example, the company's long-standing practice of providing communication support to a broad range of its leaders. Not only do its C-suite executives have communication managers who work directly for them, but so do many of its vice presidents and senior vice presidents. In all, about 650 professional communicators—or, roughly speaking, 1 communicator for every 100 Cisco employees—work at the company. And most of them work not at the corporate level, but at the group or team level. "Every functional leader at Cisco, from a supply-chain leader to our CIO, has their own communication platform. It's tightly linked to the corporate platform, but personalized for relevance to their team," Pond observes. Each such platform operates as a dedicated microsite, with a blog and a place to post video content. Leaders and their communication support professionals even measure traffic on their microsite in order to gauge its effectiveness. "We have a culture of communicating often," Christie says. "Everything here is about getting your messages across."

"Your CEO Unplugged"

At the crux of that culture is Cisco's chief executive, John Chambers. Known in business and technology circles for his charismatic approach to salesmanship, Chambers brings that same quality to bear on his leadership inside Cisco. "You do sell to your employees, and you've got to communicate, communicate, communicate," he says.[1] Lang, whose chief role at Cisco is to provide direct communication support to Chambers, explains her boss's contribution to the company's organizational conversation: "When you have a CEO in place who strongly drives business strategy using communication, you can't *not* have a culture of communications. John has a fundamental belief that everything that he does is driven by communication. We have all kinds of forums in place for him to be able to communicate, and also to keep a pulse on what's going on with employees." About every other month, for example, Chambers leads an event called a "birthday chat." It's a relatively informal Q&A session, and any Cisco employee whose birthday comes during the relevant two-month period can take part in it. Senior managers generally don't participate in this event, lest their presence keep attendees from speaking openly. "It's for rank-and-file employees," Smith explains. "It's intended to encourage really candid discussions, and to help management understand what's on employees' minds." Originally a small gathering with a few dozen people in attendance, the birthday chat now takes place on video and via satellite, and it includes as many as four hundred participants from around the world.

"We're very fortunate at Cisco to have a CEO who embraces and values communications and who is also such a natural communicator," Smith says. She and other Cisco leaders trace that quality in Chambers to another attribute of his: He's dyslexic. Marked with an apparent disadvantage, one that makes it hard for him to process written text, Chambers has developed a keen ability to express his thoughts through the spoken word. The spontaneity of direct conversation frees up his capacity to be powerfully expressive. "Being transparent about the challenges of dyslexia, that's very important for John as a leader," Lang says. "He doesn't type. He will admit that he can only type fifteen words a minute. But he can talk two hundred and fifty words per minute." Video-based communication, not surprisingly, suits the needs and strengths of a leader like Chambers exceedingly well. "There is very little room for misinterpretation through video," Lang observes. "Think about your tone, how you're telling your story, your body language. There is a quality when you communicate via video—when people can actually see the whites of your eyes—that sends a very particular message."

Among several channels that Chambers uses to communicate internally, one stands out: his blog, which he calls *On My Mind*. "If you'd have told [me] three or four years ago that I would eventually be blogging, I'd have said, 'That's not going to happen.' But blogging is now the way I communicate with our employees—almost all video," he said in 2009.[2] About once every month or so, he records a short video message, and out it goes to the entire Cisco workforce. His first video post, published in 2008, dealt with Cisco's latest appearance on *Fortune* magazine's annual list of the Best Employers to Work For. "We got such an incredible, overwhelming response," Smith says of that post. "Employees felt that it wasn't 'corporate' speaking; it was a genuine and authentic message from John to them. We very soon realized that it's the silver bullet of communications. To have your CEO 'unplugged' is very powerful." The practice of video blogging, Smith and her colleagues quickly learned, offers a big bang for a small buck. "Sending a message by video is very cost-effective," she notes.

A cardinal feature of *On My Mind* is its informality. It involves almost nothing that might come between Chambers's message and the employees who hit "Play" to watch his post. "He's not going to read a script," Lang says, noting that his dyslexia essentially rules out scripted communication. Staff members might prepare talking points for him, but he runs through them in a chatty, improvisational manner, Lang adds: "He'll see a keyword that's highlighted in yellow—'small-medium business'—and he takes off." To create a blog post, Chambers simply connects an Internet camera to his laptop, enters a few mouse-click commands on the device, looks into the camera, and starts talking. "You see a Diet Coke on his desk. You see pictures of his family, his coat hanging behind him," Smith says. Initially, Chambers needed to practice before recording a video post, but today he usually records each post in a single take. His video messages typically last two to five minutes apiece, and employees receive an e-mail link to them as soon as they appear online.

Despite the inherently push nature of a CEO video blog, Chambers and his team manage *On My Mind* in a way that incorporates interactivity. Smith explains: "He'll say, 'I've told you what's on my mind. Now you tell me what's on *your* mind.'" Like a standard blog, *On My Mind* includes a comments function that lets employees submit text responses that appear alongside the original blog post. More compellingly, Chambers encourages people to interact with his video blog by posting video messages of their own. "It started with text comments," Lang recalls. "But then he said to me, 'It really should be video—video all the time.' So employees will sit there with their CUVA camera, and say, 'Hey, John, just wanted to let you know, I've got something on my mind. I wanted to share this.'" (CUVA stands for Cisco Unified Video Advantage. Cisco, in another instance of sipping homegrown champagne, encourages use of its CUVA devices.) "John's video blog is a huge hit, with me and with everybody," McFall says. "I'm willing to bet that John gets more unfiltered feedback now, because he does the video blog. It helps people connect with him."

The success of *On My Mind* arguably derives as much from its medium as from any given message that Chambers puts out. "What video does is, it reduces the time to trust," Mitchell says. "When it's a video blog, you know that the message comes directly from John." By contrast, a text-only blog not only lacks the immediacy of video communication, but also carries the risk that employees will assume that someone has ghostwritten it. Meanwhile, even though video blogging is an intrinsically high-tech affair, Chambers's use of the medium has a low-tech, high-touch feel. "Because of the format that he uses, it's a casual interaction," Mitchell adds. "These are things coming from top-of-mind for John and going directly to the employee base."

See It, Believe It

Throughout Cisco, the fit between the company and the medium of video is remarkably tight. "We are a video culture," Lang says. Christie elaborates on that point: "Being very open and having direct communication has always been a part of Cisco culture. Video just extends that for us." Over the past half decade, in fact, the use of network-enabled video technology to foster organizational conversation has practically become a mandate within Cisco. "Every quarter, when we do a corporate-wide earnings announcement, we ask each leader in the organization to communicate about what this announcement means to their group—and we encourage them to do so using video," Smith says. At all levels of the company, employees have heeded that charge. By 2010, video usage accounted for two-thirds of all traffic on Cisco's internal network.

An array of video platforms is available to people at Cisco. There's WebEx, a widely marketed Cisco product that has become ubiquitous inside the company. It's a videoconferencing tool that lets users interact with each other from their laptop or desktop computer. Although WebEx delivers only a small-screen experience, it does allow employees to engage in face-to-face conversation with faraway colleagues. Then there's Cisco TV, an IPTV service that transmits a video feed to employees from within the company's intranet firewall. A common use of Cisco TV is to enable virtual attendance at quarterly earnings announcements and other company-wide meetings. Previously, employees who didn't work at or near Cisco's San Jose campus had no way to take part in those events. There's also C-Vision, which Mitchell likens to YouTube and which he describes as "an internal video wiki." Like Cisco TV, C-Vision is essentially a one-way medium, rather than an interactive one. Yet it serves to promote organizational communication at Cisco by inviting people throughout the company to create and share content with colleagues. "Any employee can upload a video," Mitchell says. Other employees can then access it on a VOD basis at the C-Vision Web site. Cisco professionals who work on geographically dispersed teams, for example, often rely on C-Vision to update each other on the status of their projects.

"There's interactive video, and then there's push video," Pond observes. But video of any kind, even in its push form, has qualities that set it apart as a medium of organizational conversation. "It isn't just a bland note," Pond says, referring to a one-way video message. "You get to see a speaker's inflection points. You get to see passion in the delivery of the message." The ability to *see,* of course, makes all the difference. It adds a human element to what would otherwise remain a detached and bureaucratic exchange of information. Although the video tools that Cisco people use are all very high-tech, the experience of communicating through them can seem to transcend technology. In effect, the technology becomes invisible: Users are able to see *through* it—and to focus instead on seeing, and speaking with, one another. "We can reach people very, very quickly with the technology; it's come so far. The quality is good, and you feel like you're actually meeting face-to-face," Christie says. Traditional text-based communication suffers by comparison. "The world is inundated by e-mail today," McFall notes. "If you have an emotional message that you want to convey, no one will pick it up in an e-mail. Recorded video lets you get the emotional content out to your people. If you're a sales manager and you want to rev up your team on a Monday morning, a video is going to work way better than an e-mail." Where communication involves words alone, Christie points out, the failure to use exactly the right term or to strike exactly the right tone can easily distort a message. "Video keeps it real," she says. "Video is absolutely key. It is the enabler. The power of visual communications to get a message across is just a stratosphere above anything we could do with text."

Along with the benefits that video technology confers on the practice of communication inside Cisco, it also makes interaction with people *outside* the company easier and more effective. Using video tools, Pond says, "you can introduce outsiders to the business in a way that you never could with the old, flat environment." Partners and customers now have a window into Cisco such as they never had before—and vice versa. Through state-of-the-art videoconferencing, for example, a value-added reseller can gain early, immediate insight into the strategic positioning and sales potential of a new Cisco product, and by the same token, professionals at Cisco can gain a very precise understanding of the needs and expectations of a key customer. "There has been a major breakdown in the wall between what stays inside the enterprise and what goes out to the ecosystem," Pond explains. "We'll actually put some of our development leaders on a videoconference with major customers to talk about the deployment of our technology in their businesses. The application of technology is becoming much more mission-critical. If I can make a better link between a development engineer and the guy who consumes our technology, it dramatically improves the performance of that technology inside the business. That's a big win for us. The customer loves it."

Present Company

With TelePresence, Cisco leaders render video-based organizational conversation as fully interactive as it can possibly be. Just as video communication marks a major qualitative improvement over text, so does TelePresence represent a notable leap in quality over standard video tools. "We're passionate about high-definition video. That's why Tele-Presence works so well," McFall says. Only a real-time, high-definition video feed, he explains, can provide full scope for the kinds of nonverbal cues that lend a sense of depth to in-person conversation: "It's not the big, obvious body language—it's not waving your arms—that helps people understand what your emotional state is. It's the microgestures. It's the way the muscles work around your eyes and around the edges of your mouth that really tells people how you're receiving a message." There are other attributes of TelePresence that make it an ideal medium for back-and-forth communication. Spatial-audio capability, for instance, eliminates the tinny, artificial sound of traditional electronic speakers and creates an effect whereby voices seem to fill a space naturally. "When I'm on the phone with people in Japan and we're talking about their requests for product features, their lips sync up. It's like I'm sitting in front of them," McFall says.

Chambers, quite naturally, has become a power user of this technology. "Past videoconferencing solutions didn't provide this level of in-person experience, so they were not heavily used," he says.[3] Today, Chambers organizes much of his schedule around TelePresence sessions. "I'll regularly meet with nine or ten people around the world at nine or ten different locations, and it's as though you're at the same table," he explains.[4] By conducting "TelePresence Theater days," Lang says, Chambers can span the globe without leaving the Cisco campus: "Instead of having John travel fourteen hours to Bangalore, we'll get him downstairs in a TelePresence room. He will go from eight a.m. their local time to five p.m. their local time, and he will have a full day of back-to-back meetings." A vital benefit of TelePresence, she notes, is that it "enables you to scale your executive." Not only does it multiply the number of chances for people to interact with Chambers in a face-to-face context, but it enhances efficiency as well. "We're giving time back to executives, keeping them off airplanes, saving travel dollars," Hobbs says. (As of 2008, the use of TelePresence within Cisco accounted for a 20 percent reduction in annual travel expenditures.)[5] For Chambers, benefits that aren't so easy to measure also come into play. "The so-called intangibles are just as important—the ability to read someone's expression and body language while you're trying to make tough decisions or make a tough sale. With TelePresence, you can literally see a customer's pupils dilate, or watch them cross their arms, and change your discussion based on these important nonverbal cues," he says.[6]

Thanks to TelePresence, Cisco has overhauled its approach to holding large organization-wide events. Like many companies, Cisco historically devoted considerable resources to bringing employees together to discuss new products, new sales goals, new strategic initiatives. Only meetings of that kind, according to long-held wisdom, allow for direct, back-and-forth interaction—for the sort of shared experience that produces organizational cohesion. Also like many companies, however, Cisco in recent years has sought to reduce the travel costs, the lost time, and the logistical headaches that come with putting on a big corporate gathering. While standard videoconferencing provides one alternative to such events, meeting via TelePresence goes much further toward replicating an in-person experience. A typical Cisco meeting held in 2009, for example, featured one group of presenters located at the Cisco Globalization Center in Bangalore and another group of presenters located in San Jose. In all, hundreds of people at six TelePresence sites worldwide took part in the event simultaneously. (Some fourteen thousand employees watched it live on an IPTV feed to their desktop computers.) "Because TelePresence is two-way, we're able to have questions answered from all over the world," Smith says. "We had somebody in Bangalore ask a question, and an executive in San Jose answered it live."

Today at Cisco, the application of TelePresence to organizational conversation goes well beyond its adoption by senior executives, or its use in large-scale events. By 2009, it had built more than 350 TelePresence meeting rooms at Cisco facilities throughout the world, and Cisco professionals had taken part in more than two hundred thousand TelePresence sessions. (Deployment of the technology inside Cisco began in 2007.) "It's just the way we communicate," Smith says. "It's now the standard way we conduct business internally." McFall routinely confers with people on his team via TelePresence. For one meeting that he recalls, members of his team dialed in from twenty-plus TelePresence rooms located around the world. People at one of those sites, moreover, took advantage of the immediacy afforded by TelePresence to bridge a large gap—geographic and experiential—that separated them from colleagues at another site. "The folks in Dubai said that they had never seen snow before," McFall says. "So the guys in Michigan went outside, scooped up some snow, and brought it back into the room." Apart from using TelePresence, he suggests, the only way to achieve "that kind of interpersonal connection" would have been to fly his entire team to a single site.

Along with building fully outfitted TelePresence rooms at Cisco facilities, the company has provided an increasing number of employees with in-home TelePresence units. These units don't offer a full-scale high-definition experience, delivering instead a smaller-scale video feed with DVD-quality resolution. Even so, they allow for a rich and highly convenient form of long-distance interaction. "We make video calls as often as possible," McFall says. "Often, we'll put up an instant message—'Are you there?'—and we'll do a TelePresence call. That's the beauty of TelePresence. It's just like making a phone call." He also uses his in-home unit to engage in a regular "virtual lunch" (as he calls it) with a fellow executive. "He's in San Jose. I'm in Pleasanton, California," McFall explains. "Sure, it's only a thirty-five-minute drive, but why do it when we can just connect live?"

The ultimate advantage of using TelePresence, McFall says, is that "it speeds decision making." For more and more businesspeople, in more and more situations, being physically present for an important conversation isn't an option. That's especially true in a company as large and as globally decentralized as Cisco. TelePresence, by providing what McFall calls a "high-def visual feedback loop" between participants in distant locations, helps Cisco leaders to address that challenge in a robust way. "Using TelePresence allows you to build trust faster, and having that trust between people allows you to make decisions faster and better. It makes for a more connected, easier-to-get-things-done environment," he says. Even a decision as weighty as the move to hire someone, McFall argues, can be made on the basis of a TelePresence connection. "Over TelePresence, I get a sense of the person, their skill set, and their emotional quotient," he explains. "We just hired an engineer from Washington, D.C., and I was able to interview him over TelePresence, as opposed to flying him out to California." The handshake moment, in other words, now often comes *after* the hiring moment.

It's Personal—and It's Business

At Cisco, the next frontier of organizational conversation involves integrating the numerous means and modes by which employees now interact with each other across digital networks. Step by step, division by division, the company has implemented a new system of internal communication that incorporates not only video media such as TelePresence and WebEx, but also e-mail, chat, and voice-based communication, as well as other applications and tools that people at Cisco use to create, store, share, and discuss the product of their work. This collaboration platform, as the new system is generically called, wraps all of those elements together in an environment that resembles a social media service. It looks more like Facebook, in other words, than it looks like a traditional corporate computing platform. "Think of it as a personalized portal," Pond says. "It's how you want to execute your work and how you want to interact inside Cisco." In effect, it serves—and greatly expands upon—the function of a standard intranet portal. Over time, according to Pond and other Cisco leaders, the new platform is likely to supplant the company's existing intranet site.

Today, Cisco sells its collaboration platform to outside users under the name Quad. Yet, in a twist on the company's usual modus operandi, Quad isn't a variety of "champagne" that Cisco set out to cultivate for external consumption. Indeed, the reverse is true. Before there was Quad, there was a platform called IWE, or Integrated Workforce Experience, which emerged as part of an effort to boost Cisco's own operational efficiency. "We were never going to 'productize' this thing. We were just going to deploy it internally," Pond says. "It was an IT project." Two goals lay behind that project: to "drive down the overhead" that comes with employee use of multiple applications, and to "drive up the key interactions" that make for productive employee collaboration. At a demonstration of IWE, however, John Chambers saw in this new platform an opportunity to extend Cisco's reach into a new arena. "When John saw it onstage, he said, 'We're going to sell this product.' I almost fell out of my chair," Pond recalls.

What initially sold leaders at Cisco on the need to invest in such an ambitious internal project was a worsening problem that leaders everywhere cite: information overload. "It's just increasing exponentially, in terms of content," Landsman says. "With all of this material, people are overwhelmed. What are they supposed to focus on? How do they get the materials that will help them do their job?" Just as the volume and variety of data have proliferated, so have the channels through which employees can retrieve and exchange such information, and so have the tools that they can use to process it. The task of bringing all of those inputs together is, arguably, the foremost challenge that most people at most companies face today. It's also, as the developers of IWE recognized, primarily a communication challenge. Cisco leaders decided, moreover, that the company couldn't resolve that challenge for its employees in a comprehensive, top-down fashion. Instead, they had to give employees a better, smarter way to interact with each other—and with the vast resources of the entire company—on their own terms. "The idea here was to take advantage of social networking capabilities and to create a seamless experience for people in which the materials that they need bubble up to the top," Landsman explains.

Three principles characterize the design of the IWE platform. First, there is *personalization*—a move to replace the one-size-fits-all model of traditional channels with a model that lets users tailor communication channels to their needs and habits. "From the employee's perspective, we're a very complex business, so it's difficult for us to create a single portal," Pond says. By allowing employees to "personalize how they interact with the business," he adds, "we mask the complexity of the business." With IWE, as with Facebook or any other social network service, each user has a personal home page that he or she can customize by adding or subtracting elements. That page, called MyView, includes a section that features top-level corporate news. But employees can also subscribe to news feeds related to their organizational function, for example, or to an area of professional interest. Each MyView page also incorporates information from its user's e-mail, calendar, and contact applications, and the user can customize those features as well. Another feature of IWE borrows from the personalized nature of many popular consumer Web sites. "It's similar to Facebook or Amazon," Landsman explains. "The power of the knowledge of your friends, or those who are like you, surfaces information for you in a very simple way. If you pull up a document that's relevant to you, it will say, 'People who looked at this document also looked at X, Y, and Z.' So, all of a sudden, you're not having to search for those other things."

A second principle that underlies the IWE platform is *resource integration*. In particular, the developers of IWE have sought to integrate the growing set of electronic channels that Cisco employees use to communicate with colleagues, customers, and partners. From within the platform, users can access and manage tools that let them reach people through e-mail, chat, videoconferencing, or voice calling. They can go to their contact list or to the company-wide directory, click on the entry for a colleague, and immediately initiate an e-mail, an instant message, or a phone call to that colleague. In many cases, they can even launch a TelePresence session with that person. IWE also integrates productivity tools and other digital resources that employees use to do their jobs. "Instead of logging in and out of twenty-five or thirty applications every day, you can create a work environment that makes those applications part of a single process," Pond says. (Within the collaboration platform, for example, salespeople at Cisco are able to deploy tools offered by the software provider salesforce.com.)

Finally, and certainly not least, the principle of *access to expertise* strongly informs the way that IWE works. The platform allows Cisco employees to tap into other employees' knowledge, first by locating relevant colleagues quickly and easily, and then by interacting with them directly and efficiently. "We talk about 'the wisdom of the crowd.' Well, we've got a huge crowd here," Landsman notes. The key to finding the right face in that crowd lies in the employee directory. "Most business directories have your name, title, office number, telephone number, department, and maybe employee number. At Cisco, we added depth," Pond says. A new version of the Cisco directory, introduced in early 2010, includes an expertise-tagging function that lets employees populate their directory entry with keywords that flag their areas of technical and professional knowledge. Through IWE, users can search the directory by reference to these expertise tags, as well as by criteria such as department and location. "That expertise function is definitely a kind of new medium in which to communicate," Christie says. Pond offers an example of how Cisco employees leverage that medium: "If you're sitting in a room with three or four people and given a specific question, you can query our directory and bring up a list of available employees with relevant expertise. It will show you who is available and how you can reach them. Then you can bring them into the meeting, get the answer you need, and send them back out again as the meeting continues."

Other components of the IWE platform amplify its power as a vehicle for sharing expertise, and those components incorporate common social media features. Each user of IWE, for instance, can create a personal profile page that resembles a public Facebook page. There, employees can maintain their own blog, offer links to recommended resources, and share information about their current projects. A company-wide knowledge base called Ciscopedia, meanwhile, follows the iterative, all-hands-on-deck model of *Wikipedia*. On Ciscopedia, employees throughout the company interact to generate, edit, and update articles on Cisco products, processes, and projects. Another highly participatory aspect of IWE is its community component—a network of specialized discussion groups that call to mind similar discussion boards and chat rooms on the public Internet. "This is where a lot of the conversation happens," Landsman says.

Rollout of the IWE platform within Cisco began in 2009 and has expanded through the organization in the years since then. The goal of IWE, Landsman explains, is to improve performance with respect to "how fast we can innovate, how fast we can bring products to market, and how fast we can respond to customers' requests." The purpose of the platform is to provide employees with (in Landsman's words) a personalized "one-stop shop" for interacting with others and with the company—yet in a larger sense, it's not really about employees. "We're not doing this just because it's fun," Landsman says. "The goal isn't to be like Facebook. It's to drive business value."

Three Pillars of Wisdom

Cisco, founded in 1984, passed its twentieth anniversary with a framework of organizational conversation that lacked an institutional center. Then, about half a decade ago, the company reconfigured the various departments that create and disseminate messages on its behalf. "Until then, there really wasn't a communications organization," Christie recalls. "There was corporate PR; that was in one organization. There was technology PR. There were two forms of internal communications—one at a corporate level, and one at an HR program level. There was investor relations, which sat in finance." Ad hoc rather than intentional, Cisco's approach to communication had developed pragmatically and organically. In that respect, the company had merely followed a pattern that's typical of fast-growing organizations, especially those based in Silicon Valley. In 2006, though, Cisco leaders decided that the time had come to unite the company's multiple communication functions into a single unit. "When you integrate communication disciplines together, you get a huge multiplier effect in terms of the resonance of your message and the impact that you have on different constituents," Christie says. "Whether you're communicating to employees or shareholders or the media or industry pundits or partners or customers, you can't be saying six different things. It all needs to start from a place of consistency."

By the time Cisco reached its quarter-century mark, it had successfully brought its disparate communication efforts under one institutional roof. A central corporate communications department, led by Christie, now took responsibility for coordinating the company's organizational conversation. That change in formal structure occurred alongside other changes in how Cisco leaders manage that conversation. Their shift away from a reliance on one-way message delivery, for example, accelerated during this period. "We also made it much more two-way," Christie says of Cisco's evolving practice of employee communication. "We started leveraging technology around discussion forums and wikis, and we're using that technology to get more input from employees." Pursuit of "the whole conversation," to use Pond's term, thus played out at multiple levels as Cisco revamped its overall communication framework.

Equally holistic in spirit, and no less significant, was the emphasis that Cisco leaders began to place on tying the various strands of its organizational conversation to a clear, shared *agenda*—an agenda based on broad strategic goals that the company intends to pursue. Today, the "place of consistency" from which Cisco and its people aim to start any conversation aligns closely with Cisco's position in the technology marketplace. The company's official tagline encapsulates that position in aspirational language: "Cisco is the worldwide leader in networking that transforms how people connect, communicate, and collaborate." Christie, in explaining the strategic model that her department now follows, makes a similar point: "The underlying foundation is that we believe the network is the platform. What we do at the company is drive networking and build networking."

Upon that foundation, there are "pillars," as Cisco leaders call them— key categories of organizational endeavor that correspond to market opportunities in the field of network-based computing. Not long after the 2006 reorganization, Christie and her colleagues undertook an analysis of the "big bets and must-wins" that drive Cisco's competitive strategy. "We came together and created an integrated planning process," she explains. "We decided that there were going to be three pillars of our communications strategy: video, virtualization, and collaboration. Every story that we tell needs to connect to one of those pillars, so that we can start connecting the dots between all of the activities at the company." Certainly, defining the main pillars of corporate strategy simplifies the work of planning and conducting Cisco's external communication efforts. Thus, under the rubric of each pillar, the company has developed white papers, messaging playbooks, and other apparatus that helps its people to talk up Cisco's position in the virtualization market, say, or in the market for collaboration software.

Within Cisco, meanwhile—in the interaction that takes place between leaders and employees, and among employees in general—the practice of building a conversational agenda around three strategic pillars has a powerful logic behind it. For one thing, it adds clarity to all such interaction. "We realized that the noisier you are, the less people hear," Christie says. "If you're pitching a new product and you're not connecting the dots for customers, they won't understand. Same thing with employees. If you're throwing all sorts of programs and strategic initiatives at them and you're not connecting the dots, they're going to walk away without an understanding of where they can take action." For another thing, as Christie explains, keeping the pillars of Cisco's external strategy in constant view brings a sense of purpose to the company's internal communication: "If you're going to build an employee communications plan, first you need to connect it to the key priorities of the company. Even if you're going to talk about a compensation change, or about an upcoming meeting, those key priorities have to be part of that conversation. You have to constantly tie it back, so that employees understand why you are doing something and how it affects their world."

The overall model that Christie and her colleagues use to manage organizational conversation matches a model that other Cisco leaders use to manage the development and marketing of Cisco products. "We call it *Vision, Strategy, and Execution.* It's the way that we look at any new market, any opportunity, any function," Christie says. Each part of the model aligns with a certain time frame. *Execution* involves actions to be taken over the next twelve to eighteen months. *Strategy* deals with goals to be achieved in a span that lasts from eighteen months to three years. *Vision,* finally, concerns an aspiration to be realized within three to five years. "One of our customer segments is the service-provider market.

That customer group has a vision, a strategy, and an execution plan for going into that market. We do the same thing for our function," Christie says. In her department, generally speaking, the aim of execution is to generate content (interactive and otherwise) for near-term use, while the purpose of strategy is to increase medium-term understanding (internally as well as externally) of the pillars that will support Cisco's growth. And atop those pillars is a vision—a "big, hairy, audacious goal" that Christie frames in these terms: "We believe that we are responsible for the reputation and the perception of Cisco, and we want Cisco to be recognized as the most important technology company in the world."

IN ORGANIZING BOTH ITS INTERNAL and its external communication work around the three pillars of its corporate strategy, Cisco displays a commitment to what we call conversational *intentionality*. (So, too, with its leaders' "audacious" goal to position the company at the center of what amounts to a worldwide technology conversation.) With the expertise-sharing components of the IWE collaboration platform, and with video-sharing tools such as C-Vision, Cisco fosters conversational *inclusion*. By investing in TelePresence and other videoconferencing capabilities, meanwhile, the company has achieved a robust mechanism for enhancing conversational *intimacy*. John Chambers, for his part, seeks to maximize that quality by way of his video-blogging efforts and his bimonthly birthday chat with employees. Underlying Cisco's entire approach to promoting and managing organizational conversation, however, is the high value that its people place on *interactivity*. Through its use of homegrown social technologies such as TelePresence and the IWE platform, Cisco illustrates the role that back-and-forth communication can play in powering its internal culture as well as its external performance.

CHAPTER SIX

Talk, Inc., Points (TIPs)

One-Way, Two-Way, *New* Way

WHEN IT COMES TO organizational communication, "one-way" is very often the easy way to go. Unfortunately, it's also very often the wrong way to go. Only by creating channels that operate in two directions— back and forth, *to* employees and *from* employees—can leaders harness the flow of energy that emerges when real, human interaction takes place. Yet there's more to enabling back-and-forth interaction than merely flipping a switch that toggles from one-way to two-way. Organizational conversation, in fact, amounts to a new way to think about both the media of communication and the people who use those media. The ins and outs of shifting from monologue to dialogue within a company are various and complex; finding the right way to deploy conversation-friendly technology, in particular, is no simple task. Here, though, are some pointers on how leaders can carve out an opening within their organization where interactivity can flourish.

Don't Be So Remote

Conversation thrives when participants are able to be *present* in each other's company—present, ideally, both in mind and in body. Two forces in organizational life today undermine people's capacity to bring that sense of presence to a meeting or a chat. First, the globalization of business has made long-distance collaboration a normal part of the working day for more and more employees. Second, the pace of business has taken a toll on the degree of focus that people bring to a conversation; their minds wander even as they remain bodily present. Among the tools that leaders can use to counter those forces, and thereby to make presence possible, is high-quality videoconferencing capability. A video link, everyone agrees, will never wholly replace the experience of an in-person meeting. But the use of video channels to minimize the feeling of distance, if not the reality of distance, has become a signal feature of organizational conversation at many companies.

At Cisco, the deployment of video technologies such as TelePresence helps CEO John Chambers and other top leaders to connect with employees, notwithstanding the company's vast size and scope. "It drives up the intimacy on a much broader scale," says Randy Pond, executive vice president of operations, processes, and systems. Mike McFall, meanwhile, prizes the way that TelePresence helps him to close deals with customers in physically remote locations. For one deal, he recalls, a TelePresence link allowed him—from the comfort of his office in Northern California—to form a key personal connection with a prospective customer in Melbourne, Australia. "It makes the globe smaller," says McFall, global sales director for business video.

McFall notes as well that a video connection, unlike a voice-only connection, gives participants in a conference call a clear incentive to be fully present for it. "There are so many modes of communication coming at employees these days," he says. "So it's very easy not to pay attention on conference calls—to be doing e-mail or something like that. When you're on TelePresence, it forces you to pay attention to *that* conversation. For me, the ability to be 'in the now' during a conversation is invaluable."

Strike a Balance

Smart handling of the tools of organizational conversation depends upon a careful analysis of what each tool can and cannot do. It also means weighing those capabilities against the particular needs and work habits that prevail in an organization. Do people prefer to compare notes in short, frequent bursts of informal communication, or does formal, in-depth conversation suit their work style best? Do they need to retain a record of messages that they send? How much of their interaction involves matters that are highly time-sensitive? Answers to such questions should guide the way that leaders select and manage communication channels.

At Hoku Corporation, CEO Scott Paul and other leaders have shied away from using many of the latest digital media practices, such as blogging and social networking, to facilitate internal communication. "We haven't reached a critical mass where we would see value in social media. At this point, it would just be a distraction for most people," Paul says. Yet he and other members of the Hoku team have embraced one medium that relies on digital technology. "We do use IM [instant messaging] quite a bit internally," he says.

An IM platform offers a fast, convenient, firewall-protected channel for swapping messages back and forth with colleagues. It also leaves behind a record of each message. For Paul, though, the primary advantages of this medium is that it resembles—and yet improves upon—the age-old practice of poking one's head inside a colleague's door to ask a question or to pass along a bit of news. "If I walk down the hall and knock on somebody's door, I'm interrupting them. If I send them an IM and they can respond immediately, they will. If they're in the middle of something, then they'll respond in a minute or two," he explains. E-mail, by contrast, lacks that sense of urgency. "There's an unwritten law that IM is meant for real-time conversation," Paul says. "It achieves that fine balance between immediacy and interruption."

Take the High Road

More and more of the day-to-day work of organizational conversation takes place on corporate intranet portals. Employees, meanwhile, are less and less willing to tolerate workaday, second-rate intranet content. Accustomed to the high production value and the attention-grabbing appeal of external Web content, people now expect to see those same qualities when they visit their employer's internal site. Conversationally savvy leaders, therefore, invest in creating an intranet platform that aims to reach people on a high plane.

The PNC Financial Services Group, for example, in 2009 invested about $1 million in upgrading its internal platform, adding video-on-demand capability and a Facebook-like directory to a site that was already publishing an average of four news stories every weekday. "We want our intranet to provide an experience that would be comparable to something that you might find on a media Web site," says Donna C. Peterman, executive vice president and chief communications officer.

"Every company today is a media company. I don't care what it's producing; it's a media company," PR consultant Gary F. Grates argues. "It has to get people's attention in an environment where nobody is listening and there's too much noise." Ronna Lichtenberg, a longtime communication professional, echoes that point: "As a communications consumer, I'm used to being catered to. As an employee, I'm no different from that consumer. One-size-fits-all, low-production-value communications aren't working." Equally "nonfunctional now," she adds, is the assumption that "emotional content is inappropriate for an internal communication." Leaders, on the contrary, should model their approach to interacting with employees on the heart-touching approach used in many TV commercials. "If you want people to innovate and to come up with creative solutions, you need to inspire them," Lichtenberg says.

Put Yourself Out There

It's not really possible to interact with people from behind a mask. So, when leaders decide to open a channel of organizational conversation between themselves and people in their company, they must bring to that venture the courage to show their true, unadorned face. Interactivity, no less than intimacy, calls for authenticity. One place where that dynamic very much comes into play is the executive blog site.

"Blogs are a double-edged sword," says communication consultant Jacqueline Taggart. "Sometimes, I think that it's better to do a blog than not to do a blog—but only if you have something to say and only if you're going to show your personality there. If it sounds like a press release, it immediately loses credibility." A leader who lacks the time to create blog posts, or who lacks a genuine aptitude for blogging, should feel no qualm about forgoing that option. Publishing a blog that's ghostwritten, or even just stiffly written, is generally worse than publishing no blog at all. "It has to really be a *blog*," Taggart says.

In the past, leaders could easily put up a false front whenever they communicated with employees. "When travel was limited and there wasn't video and you didn't really see the leader, you could craft an image that made him appear as something that he was not," says Nora Denzel, a senior vice president at Intuit. Those days are all but gone. Denzel notes, referring to her own communication efforts: "All of the employees interact with me—even if I haven't met them—through video, voice, et cetera. And they would totally know if my blog was not written by me. They would just stop reading it." Her advice to other leaders might fall into the category of "easier said than done," but it's nonetheless apt. "Just be who you say you are. Be yourself," she says.

Let Them Question Authority

At the most basic level, a commitment to interactivity entails an openness on the part of leaders to questioning from every quarter of an organization. Behind the mute faces that employees often present to their bosses, there lurk inquiring minds that want to know more about the latest company developments. By making it easy for employees to put questions to them, therefore, senior managers put in place a crucial building block of organizational conversation.

"You need to have a feedback channel that creates a two-way mechanism," says Chris Hayes, manager of internal communications at Cenovus Energy Corporation, an integrated oil company based in Calgary. "If you're telling everybody to pedal in one direction, you have to find out if they've got questions about that direction, or if they're not sure about it." In many organizations, people typically channel such questions through their supervisor. But that method, effective though it can be, isn't always sufficient. So leaders at Cenovus make sure to create specific opportunities—small-group Q&A forums and the like—for employees to interact with them. Hayes also cites a mechanism that he and his colleagues created at EnCana, an energy provider that in 2009 split into two separate companies (one of them being Cenovus): Using an intranet-based service, any EnCana employee could direct a query straight to the company's corporate office, and an EnCana leader would promptly respond with an answer.

A traditional venue for Q&A activity, of course, is the big town-hall meeting in which leaders allow audience members to raise questions from the floor. Yet in many cases—and for many employees—a crowded room isn't the best place to put forth a tough, probing question. Tony

Holcombe, former CEO of Syniverse Technologies, cites a practice that helps leaders at that company to get around this problem. (Today, Holcombe serves as vice chairman of Syniverse, a mobile-technology provider based in Tampa, Florida.) Using a tool on the Syniverse intranet, employees can anonymously enter questions that they want executives to address at the company's next town-hall gathering. "We found that if we ask people to submit them in advance, we get a much more diverse list of questions, and people are much more comfortable asking those questions," Holcombe says.

Power Down

Any tool that's powerful enough to be helpful also has the potential to be harmful. Thus, a tool designed to help people interact with one another can wind up hindering their efforts to communicate. Even as digital technology opens up new channels for organizational conversation, it generates new ways to obstruct those channels and new means by which to avoid interaction. When that problem arises, often the best solution is simply to put the tool down—in other words, to disconnect from the digital world long enough to connect with an actual person.

"There are so many different ways to communicate—phone, e-mail, instant message, Facebook, blogging," says Laura Cave, director of partner promotions at XO Group. (Previously, Cave served as corporate communications manager at the company.) "Sometimes you get to a point where the e-mail piles up so much that you can't get anybody to respond to you. Then you actually have to walk down to someone's office and just ask a question. That's the only way to get things done." A digital tool such as e-mail can create the illusion that highly efficient communication is taking place—when, in fact, communication has ground to a halt. In effect, a promising two-way technology can become a *no*-way technology.

The opposite situation, in which people respond quickly to an e-mail, carries another potential hazard. "You get sixteen e-mails, with people going back and forth, when really everyone should have just gone to a room and hashed it out," Cave says. True, an e-mail exchange *can* be the digital equivalent of a productive in-person conversation. But it can also be an exercise in which participants talk past one another. That's why, in many cases, it pays to take the low-tech road. "As great as technology is, nothing is as fast as speaking to one another," Cave suggests.

PART III

Inclusion

CHAPTER SEVEN

Give and Take

The Triumph of Employee-Generated Content

WHEN TWO PEOPLE COME together to talk, they bring not only an array of ideas and a set of facts, but also the full range of their own strengths and weaknesses, their own emotions and preoccupations. They bring *themselves,* that is—and the more of themselves that they bring, the deeper and livelier their conversation will be. Before a conversation can attain that high level of personal involvement, however, its two participants must achieve a measure of reciprocity between themselves. Both of them must be able to contribute actively to the ebb and flow of comments that drive the discussion forward. If one of them does all or most of the talking, their conversation will fall short of what interpersonal conversation ideally can be. Person-to-person conversation, in its optimal form, enables both participants to take a share of ownership in the substance of their discussion. Neither participant, therefore, claims exclusive authority over what they will talk about or how they will talk about it.

This element of *inclusion,* as we call it, applies to organizational conversation as well. Leaders who treat employees as full-fledged partners in that conversation, who count them among a company's official or quasi-official communicators, take what has traditionally been a *corporate* endeavor (in every sense of that word) and turn it into something that's considerably more personal. By inviting employees to contribute some of the content that sustains organizational communication, those in charge of a company not only expand the variety and increase quantity of such content; they also raise the level of emotional investment that employees are apt to bring to all aspects of company life. An inclusive approach to communication transforms employees from receivers of corporate messaging into messengers in their own right. It's a twist on Marshall McLuhan's dictum that "the medium is the message": Here, a new kind of *messenger* becomes a new kind of medium—a new channel for communicating the ideas, images, and information that serve to define an organization.

Conversational inclusion builds upon the elements of intimacy and interactivity that we addressed earlier. If the essence of conversational intimacy is the close, trusting relationship that exists between parties to a successful conversation, then the essence of inclusion is a commitment to full *participation* by all parties. At an organizational level, inclusion is the obverse of intimacy. Its point of focus is the role and conduct not of company leaders, but of their employees. For leaders to vow that they will listen to employees is one thing; for employees to gain the ability to speak up, often on official company channels, is something else.

Like interactivity, meanwhile, inclusion draws upon the two-way nature of real human conversation. Yet inclusive communication goes a crucial step further: It extends the practice of back-and-forth interaction in a way that entitles people to give as well as take—to provide their own ideas, and not simply to parry the ideas offered by others. Within an organization, the practice of inclusion enables employees not just to interact with managers and colleagues, but also to serve as frontline *content providers*. In recent years, as that practice has taken hold at many companies, the overall structure of how organizations develop content has undergone a noticeable shift.

Corporate communication professionals, working with other leaders, used to create all or most of the content through which an organization told its story—to internal and external audiences alike. Those professionals developed static messages and built carefully structured campaigns around those messages. By and large, they viewed communication as a control function, and they kept a tight rein over what people wrote or said on any of a company's official channels. When employees read a company newsletter, or when they listened to speakers at a company event, they became members of an essentially passive audience. They were mere spectators of the organizational story, in much the same way that people who watch a Hollywood movie or a network TV show have always been mere consumers of those media. What's more, because employees were consumers rather than producers of organizational content, the scope of employee communication remained fairly narrow, and so did the purpose of such communication. That purpose, for the most part, was to deliver information and instruction that would help employees to thrive in their functional role.

More recently, a different approach to content development has come to the fore. The old emphasis on producing carefully framed messages has given way to a more fluid and variegated style of communication, and the campaign mentality has yielded to a preference for collaboration. Most important, employees are becoming an integral player in that collaborative enterprise. "Communication today is really about establishing and maintaining a relationship with employees, rather than top-down command and control," says Nora Denzel, of Intuit Software. "It's about participation and contribution as much as it is about information sharing." Leaders, in other words, have come to take the process of communication as seriously as they do its product. More and more of them recognize that including employees in that process sends its own kind of message, not least to employees themselves. The term *employee communication* has thus acquired a provocative new meaning. Where it once referred primarily to communication aimed *at* employees, it now encompasses communication performed *by* employees.

A give-and-take model of communicating with employees, as we'll see, can follow a variety of patterns. It can focus on internal matters, or it can involve aspects of a company's external communication. It can result in the creation of a standard media product (an article, a photograph, a video clip), or it can exhibit the dynamic and spontaneous character of spoken conversation. The common denominator in all such practices is that employees don't rely on authorized communicators to say what needs to be said, or to tell them what they need to know. At his public-relations firm, for example, Richard Edelman and his colleagues have allowed employees to migrate a share of the company's intrafirm communication to a Facebook page. "They write to each other on 'the wall', and it's all good," he says, referring to the virtual bulletin board that is a distinguishing feature of the Facebook platform. New media, he notes, reconfigure the relationship between those who create messages and those who receive them: "It's a big mind-set change. It used to be that you'd send out an employee newsletter. But we've got to go where our people are, whether it's on their cell phone, whether it's on Facebook. We're saying, 'Let's inform the conversation.' It's consumer-generated content—meaning, in our case, employee-generated content. And we're saying, 'Hey, put it anywhere you want.'"

Employee-generated content is a common term of art for this kind of bottom-up messaging. It's a variation on the idea of *user*-generated content—a principal facet of the Web 2.0 paradigm of online communication that has emerged over the past decade. According to Web 2.0 theory, the Internet in its early days largely resembled traditional mass media. In that so-called Web 1.0 phase, the operators of Web sites produced content and distributed it to visitors, much as the operators of a TV network create programming and then broadcast that programming to viewers. In the Web 2.0 phase, by contrast, "users" replace "visitors," and these users leverage social media tools to help generate the content that appears on their favored sites. Examples of user-generated content range from the book reviews that readers post on Amazon.com to the images that amateur shutterbugs upload to photo-sharing sites such as Flickr. With a social networking platform like Facebook, moreover, the line between the producers and the users of content blurs to the point of disappearing altogether.

"Web 1.0 is the democratization of access to information, and Web 2.0 is the democratization of creation of information," says Mike Wing, vice president of strategic and executive communications at IBM. "It's literally the case today that any individual in the world can become a global publisher for free in five minutes. Any individual has access to capabilities that were beyond the fondest imagination of William Randolph Hearst, William S. Paley, or Rupert Murdoch. And that's a big deal." It's a big deal, not least, for those at the commanding heights of companies large and small: Just as media titans in the tradition of Hearst, Paley, and Murdoch no longer monopolize the means of gathering and distributing news to consumers, so executives and their communication staff no longer hold complete sway over the process of shaping and sharing information within their organization.

Among businesspeople, the Web 2.0 trend finds expression under the label Enterprise 2.0, and manifestations of that trend have become increasingly evident at a growing number of companies. The reason why isn't hard to discern: Conversational inclusion fosters employee passion. Encouraging people at all levels of an organization to write blog posts about their work or to share snapshots of life at their company, for example, spurs them to care about both their work and their company with a renewed sense of intensity. Passion of that kind, in turn, helps fuel greater innovation, faster execution, and other ingredients of improved organizational performance. "The goal is to have engaged employees," says Larry Solomon, of AT&T. "If you're an engaged employee, you're going to score high on your commitment to customers, your loyalty to the company, your overall happiness as an employee. You're going to stick around, and you're going to act as an ambassador for the company when you're talking to your friends and family. And one of the key factors in having an engaged workforce is creating an environment where people feel like they're being listened to." Leaders at AT&T and elsewhere now listen to employees in part because those employees now have something to say—not just on their own behalf, but also on behalf of their organization.

Developing Content

The job of finding, organizing, and packaging company information has long been precisely that—a job, a specialized endeavor undertaken by professionals. Typically working out of a corporate communication department, those professionals often boast degrees in journalism or communication studies; many of them have experience as reporters, editors, and producers at mainstream media outlets. Hiring them to create the content that other employees consume is, from a traditional standpoint, a perfectly sensible division of labor. Yet more and more leaders are calling upon the amateurs in their midst to help generate the material that sustains organizational communication. "I just don't have enough staff within the PR department to cover everything that I need to have covered," Larry Solomon says. "And I have a lot of great employees who want to help who are good writers. They're right there on the front lines. Why not tap into these employee citizen-journalists to provide content for our intranet portal?" Solomon and his colleagues at AT&T, as we pointed out earlier, have sought to model the company's intranet site on the consumer-facing sites of major media brands. "The only way to do that," he says, "is to have relevant, fresh content all day long." Today, big-time news organizations often feed their content stream by inviting audience members to send in story ideas and even full-fledged stories. (CNN, for example, does so through its iReport feature.) And there's no reason, Solomon argues, why AT&T and other companies shouldn't follow suit.

By encouraging ordinary employees to become producers as well as consumers of information about an organization and its activities—to become, as Solomon suggests, internal amateur journalists—leaders broaden the range of content available for use within that organization. They also, at a more profound level, transform the process of creating and delivering such information. Even in cases where employee-generated content assumes a fairly standard form, the fact that employees are providing it makes that effort inherently conversational. Here, then, is a sampling of how employees are providing content in areas of organizational communication that were once the sole bailiwick either of top executives or of designated professional communicators.

PRODUCT INFORMATION. The task of making sure that employees are knowledgeable about a company's product line is a staple of internal communication. If the company's own people don't have a clear understanding of its product offerings, they won't be able to sell, service, and otherwise support those offerings. The default way to handle that task is to give employees the same kind of slickly produced marketing material that goes out to media figures and to prospective customers. But an alternative method is to let employees take part in spreading the word about a new product to their colleagues. Often enough, those employees use the product, and they're in a good position to sing its praises— perhaps literally. "We have employees who are musically inclined," Solomon says. "We'll launch a new product, and they'll go down to their basement and record a song about it. They'll send us the song, and we'll post it on the intranet."

On a more serious note (or, at any rate, on a more systematic note), AT&T has sponsored a group of "mommy bloggers"—women who work for the company, who happen to be mothers as well, and who welcome the chance to discuss the highs and the lows of being a working mom. In 2008, Solomon and his team recruited about a half dozen employees who fit that description and gave them an internal online forum where they could publish text and video posts. "We push those blogs by our in-house mommy bloggers out to all employees," he says. Working mothers have a lot to talk about, of course. Both the "working" part and the "mother" part of their status bring a wide range of challenges, and they face the additional challenge of balancing those two parts of themselves. Moreover, because many of these challenges involve staying in touch with people (colleagues and customers on the one hand, kids and caretakers on the other), working moms are a natural market for the kinds of products and services that AT&T sells. Which means that the AT&T mommy bloggers aren't just internal corporate journalists; they also serve as consumers by proxy, or as quasi-official product testers. "They write about how they use our technology to manage their busy home and work lives," Solomon says.

Take the FamilyMap service, which AT&T launched in 2009. For a monthly fee added to their regular phone bill, the service enables AT&T customers to track the GPS locations of other members of their family. "Our mommy bloggers are writing about how awesome it is. It allows them to keep up with their teenage kids," Solomon explains. "So, instead of just posting a bulletin to our intranet site—'We launched a new service called FamilyMap'—we have our mommy bloggers, who are helping bring it to life for employees." Along with conveying news-you-can-use information to other AT&T working mothers, therefore, the mommy-blogger crew provides everyone else in the company with a real-world, user's-eye view of the value that AT&T products offer to customers. "I'm a fifty-five-year-old male," Solomon notes. "I'm not on Facebook. I'm not using Twitter. But now I'm watching a video of how a thirty-five-year-old mom is using every technology that we have to help run her household."

EVENT REPORTING. People put a lot of effort into business meetings, but often it's hard to tell exactly what they get out of such gatherings. The problem, in many cases, is that there's no easy way to capture and convey what people say over the course of a meeting. One time-cherished solution to that problem is to charge an attendee with writing up a report that meeting organizers then distribute to other attendees—usually days or even weeks after the event. Another common approach is to send attendees away with a stack of presentation slides, together with other documents that people have developed for the meeting. In the digital-age version of that practice, meeting organizers give each attendee a flash drive that contains a slew of PowerPoint files. "I mean, who is going to go back and look at those? Nobody," says Jason Greenspan, director of global strategic communications at McDonald's. Greenspan calls this solution that doesn't solve much of anything "the memory-stick syndrome."

In mid-2009, Greenspan and his colleagues conducted an experiment of sorts to see whether blogging might offer a better solution to the problem of generating event-based content. For each of two major organizational meetings, they recruited someone to serve as a dedicated event blogger. Their hope was that McDonald's—the company that pioneered fast-food delivery—could excel internally at the fast delivery of information. The first event was a Big 10 meeting, so called because it featured marketing executives from ten key regions where McDonald's does business; the second was a People Summit, which brought together leaders from the company's HR, IT, and operations divisions. "Each meeting had a hundred twenty-five people or so," Greenspan explains. "We had a blogger literally in the back of the room, capturing what they were hearing and getting it up live." The benefits of blogging these proceedings included "real-time sharing of information and not having to wait for a meeting recap," he notes. Plus, even those who couldn't attend the events in person were able to benefit from timely access to meeting-related content. The blog that accompanied the People Summit, for example, attracted nearly one thousand unique visitors, or roughly eight times as many people as attended the live event. Overall, the use of blogging proved to be a success at both meetings. "It brings a real voice to the content," Greenspan says. "It's just more authentic, and it makes you feel like you're there." (The "special sauce" in blogging, one might say, is the sense of personality that it adds to otherwise dry forms of communication.)

Yet not all blogs are created equal. The blog written for the Big 10 marketing event scored notably higher on the authenticity meter than the one written for the People Summit, according to Greenspan. The reason for that discrepancy is simple: At the Big 10 meeting, it was an employee from the company's marketing division who took charge of posting news and observations about the gathering. As it happens, that employee was a woman who had already set up a personal blog of her own. "So it was cool. It had a little bit of flair to it," Greenspan says of her event blog. For the People Summit, by contrast, it was a corporate communication specialist who took up the blogging reins. One finding of this experiment in event blogging, therefore, concerns the value of including frontline employees—along with, or instead of, professional communicators—in ventures of this kind. Greenspan suggests that it might have been wiser to tag an employee from the company's HR department to act as a blogger of record for the People Summit. "I don't know if next time I would have someone from corporate communications doing it," he says.

CORPORATE IMAGE-MAKING. For decades, companies have relied on photographers for hire to capture images that will cast their brand, their people, and their products in the most favorable light. Proper-looking corporate communication material, according to long-prevailing wisdom, must feature glossy photos of the kind that only highly paid professionals can produce. But the advent of digital photography, and the corresponding ease with which amateurs can take and share pictures of reasonably high quality, have thrown that assumption into question. Today, any employee with a camera (or perhaps just a smartphone) can produce eye-catching photos that illuminate varieties of organizational activity and accomplishment that official company photographers are unlikely to glimpse. As a consequence, leaders now have access to a rich new source of images through which to tell their company story. Furthermore, by drawing upon that source, they give employees a new way to participate in a conversation about what that story is—or what it might be.

At General Electric, a bid to encourage people to share photographic content succeeded on both of those fronts. It helped to "bring good things to light" about the company (to quote a classic GE slogan), and it did so in a way that truly engaged employees. "We did an employee photo contest," says Susan Bishop, director of communications at GE Capital. "The idea was, 'Let's tap into the pride that our employees have in the company.'" The contest, which took place in December 2008, called for employees to submit photographs of their own that illustrated some aspect of their experience at GE. During the contest period, they uploaded some eight hundred photographs to InsideGE, the corporate intranet site. People throughout GE then viewed those photos online and voted on which ones they liked best. The posted photographs, grouped into categories such as *Innovation* and *Globalization,* formed a de facto album of corporate life. One shot featured a gathering hosted by GE at a company site in India. Taken on the occasion of Holi, an annual Hindu festival, it showed employees and their families taking part in the Holi ritual of covering themselves with brightly colored powders. Other photos celebrated the work that GE employees do and the products that they create. "We make wind turbines, and these things sit one hundred meters up in the sky. So we got a lot of pictures taken from the top of these wind turbines by our engineers, who were up there either fixing them or installing them," says Bishop. "Those were crowd favorites, because they were just beautiful photos."

The photo contest, for GE leaders, was the opening phase of a longer-term investment in using employee-supplied imagery. Having brought forth a wealth of inspiring photographs, Bishop and her colleagues have seen fit to include many of them in official organs of GE corporate messaging. "Some of them are just amazing," she says. "We've used them in our annual report. We use them on our intranet. We use them on GE.com. We sometimes use them as attachments to press releases." (GE.com is the company's main consumer-facing Web site.) In 2009, Bishop and her team followed up the photo contest with a video contest that invited employees to submit dynamic footage of GE people in action. Later that year, the company began posting some of those "homegrown videos," as Bishop calls them, to an external Web site called Meet GE. There, journalists and consumers could view slices of GE life as seen through the eyes of GE's own people.

The still photos and the video clips created by GE employees do more than help the company to tell its story. Such content, GE leaders have discovered, also helps them to find new stories to tell. A photograph of a seemingly mundane medical device, for instance, led Bishop and her colleagues to gain a novel perspective on that facet of the company's product line. "Someone sent a picture of one of our MRI machines at a hospital in Mexico," Bishop explains. "It was a very funny picture of this giant MRI dressed up to look like an elephant. It was in a children's ward, and the children were intimidated by getting rolled into the MRI machine. Our on-site sales staff, plus the hospital staff, built this huge decoration that attached to the machine and made it look like an elephant. We ended up doing a whole story on the intranet about how our team worked with the local team to make children more comfortable with the machine, and how this is the extra value and service that a GE team provides to a customer. But we wouldn't have known about that story if it weren't for the photo contest."

THOUGHT LEADERSHIP. It's a truism (but nonetheless true for being so): To achieve market leadership in a knowledge-based economy, an organization must first pursue *thought* leadership. Frequently, that means asking a consultant or an in-house professional to draft speeches, op-ed articles, white papers, and the like—vehicles that demonstrate to the public or to the marketplace that a company is operating at the leading edge of its industry. Top executives usually put their stamp, and their name, on such content; they are the public face of the best thinking that occurs in their company. But what if the most forward-looking "thought" within an organization occurs not at the senior "leadership" level, but at the levels where people develop, test, and create new products and services? In that case, empowering some of those people to create and promote thought-leadership material might be the smartest, quickest way to bolster the organization's reputation among key industry players.

In the view of top executives at Juniper Networks, the path toward thought leadership in the networking-technology industry passes through the ranks of the company's working engineers and technicians. In recent years, therefore, Juniper has sponsored an initiative to bring many of those employees out of their labs and offices—and into public venues where industry experts and customers can see them strut their intellectual stuff. "We're engaging our great technical talent across different forums, either with customers or in other, larger settings," says Steven

Rice, executive vice president of human resources. Part of what Rice and his colleagues straightforwardly call their "thought leadership agenda," the initiative aims to convey to the world "our differentiated point of view," he explains. "We have a deep bench of distinguished engineers and Juniper Fellows who are working on the next wave of silicon, systems, and hardware, and we want to connect them with customers who are asking, 'What do you think is going to happen in the next five years? What do you think these trends in the marketplace represent for us? What do you think will happen as the macroeconomics of the Internet start to shift?' We have a unique perspective and an innovation agenda in each of those areas." To communicate that range of perspectives to relevant audiences, Juniper dispatches some of its most accomplished engineers (among other employees) to national and international technology conferences. With support from company leaders, Juniper technologists also prepare and distribute white papers, and they meet with customers at company-run briefing centers.

"Our thought leadership agenda shows that we think about solving customer problems differently," Rice contends. By including some of its down-in-the-trenches employees in efforts to convey that agenda, Juniper overcomes the often cumbersome division between value-adding innovation, on the one hand, and the work of developing content that explains and promotes such innovation, on the other hand. Conversational inclusion also gives critically important employees a higher profile—not just in the eyes of people outside the company, but also in the eyes of other employees. Engineers at Juniper, for example, conduct regular whiteboard sessions that allow them to debrief colleagues on what they have learned at conferences or in meetings with customers. The company also holds an annual engineering forum at which technologists present to one another the white papers that they have created over the previous year. Such practices, by bringing the thought-leadership conversation full circle, boost employee engagement throughout the Juniper organization. "Encouraging our employees to serve as external ambassadors enables them to engage directly with customers and to gain much-deserved recognition for their work," Rice says. "The input that we receive during these customer experiences helps our folks to say, 'Gosh, I'm working on something that's going to be relevant, something that our customers really want.' We're driving all of that customer feedback into the organization, so that people can see how they're making a difference."

Sending Out a Message

As the example of Juniper shows, leaders today aren't limiting their practice of conversational inclusion to the realm of internal communication. More and more of them, in fact, have begun to engage employees in the wider conversation about their company that takes place outside its organizational walls. Out in the marketplace and in the public square, an array of third parties—mainstream journalists and online gadflies, satisfied customers and disgruntled citizens, eager investors and eagle-eyed analysts—are constantly feeding and shaping that conversation. Whether they're talking up the company's stock, bad-mouthing its products, or musing on the quirks of its latest advertising campaign, those external players can have a cumulatively large impact on its brand, its reputation, and its overall public image. Organizational leaders, of course, have long sought to conduct this external conversation on their own terms. Deploying specialists in public relations and investor relations, in branding and marketing, they have worked to craft and control any information about their company that might enter the public domain. But in this realm, too, the limits of relying on professionals alone to handle organizational conversation have come sharply into focus over the past decade. Amateurs, as it turns out, have a lot to contribute with regard to helping a company spread its message. "Corporate America is really starting to realize that using employees as advocates for a company or a product can be a hugely powerful tool," says Kim Carpenter, of General Motors.

Part of that realization stems from a growing awareness that (as we noted previously) employees have become a highly trusted source of company information—a more trusted source than a company's top executives, or than its official spokespeople. Inadvertently or implicitly, employees already convey messages about their company that resonate with outsiders. For leaders, a logical response to that development is to authorize and equip employees to speak on behalf of their organization in ways that are active and explicit. Viewing employees as trusted (and trustworthy) communicators has a further implication for leaders, according to Bob Pickard, president and CEO for the Asia-Pacific region at public-relations firm Burston-Marsteller. Instead of treating influential outsiders as the primary target of any messaging initiative, he argues, company leaders "should communicate first with those who are part of their most intimate core audience" and then proceed outward in concentric circles to address other audiences. Senior executives occupy the innermost circle, but employees as a whole should come next, followed by customers, investors, opinion leaders, media representatives, and the general public.

Another factor behind the move to include employees in outside messaging efforts is the steady waning of the once-bright line between internal and external communication. Under pressure from new technologies and new work practices, that barrier has nearly disappeared. No longer can leaders separate what employees say from what outside parties hear. Or vice versa. An employee at her desk can easily and immediately glean the latest news about her company, or the latest rumor of a company scandal, from any number of online sources. Her colleague in the next cubicle, meanwhile, can polish or tarnish the company brand merely by e-mailing an internal document to a reporter or a blogger, or even to a group of friends. "When I came into this role, in 2003, the traditional model of internal communication was breaking down very rapidly," says Mike Clement, reflecting on his experience as the top communication executive at Bank of America. "Today, audiences really are indivisible. So you need to prepare any internal communication with an eye to having it go external, and any external communication with an eye to your internal audience." Organizational conversation is, at bottom, a unitary affair—a single give-and-take process that involves many participants, including employees. "The word *internal* is a misnomer," Pickard says. "Employees, as a constituency, have become so interconnected with a whole system of stakeholders that the distinction between what's inside and what's outside [an organization] is becoming irrelevant."

Amid these shifting circumstances, inclusive leaders make a virtue out of necessity. Casting those inside their organization as potential evangelists or ambassadors to the outside world, such leaders seek to integrate ordinary employees into the public-messaging work that has traditionally been the responsibility of brand marketers, PR agents, and senior executives. Kris Gopalkrishnan, of Infosys, notes that he and his colleagues have little choice but to treat staff members as corporate envoys without portfolio. "Our employees are, on a daily basis, in interaction with clients. There's no way that we can control that," he says. "We have to let them represent the company—and, by and large, they do. In today's world, and in the services business, it's extremely important that you have empowered employees, so that they can be ambassadors for your company."

Even in organizations where most employees don't routinely face customers, leaders put an increasingly high premium on enabling their people to act as company advocates. At Cenovus Energy Corporation, according to communications manager Chris Hayes, he and his colleagues are striving to build "an ambassador base" that consists of "people who understand not only how we operate internally, but how the industry works." The involvement of Cenovus in the business of resource extraction and energy development naturally raises hot-button issues among the public, and its employees must be ready to respond appropriately when such buttons get hit, Hayes says: "They should know our stance on things, so that they can reiterate that stance if they're at a family barbecue, say, or if they're talking to someone in line at a grocery store."

Other leaders engage employees in outward-facing communication projects in order to boost the level of company pride within their workforce. In 2008, for example, GE was a top sponsor of the Summer Olympic Games in Beijing, and encouraging its people to share in that commitment was a high priority for the company. "We had an internal portal dedicated to our involvement in the Olympics," Susan Bishop says. "Employees could go there, and they'd read stories about the technology that we were developing that went into the games. So they learned about the company strategy, and about how much revenue our sponsorship brought to the company." At the portal, employees could design an Olympic-themed kite and enter their design in a contest; GE then distributed kites based on the winning design, and the winning contestant was able to attend the event in Beijing. "She [the winner] was one of the people who blogged from the Olympics. She talked about the experience of going there and seeing her kite printed," Bishop explains.

(As we've seen, GE employees also play an active part in outside messaging by creating photographic and video content that the company then repurposes for external audiences.)

At Sealed Air Corporation, similarly, top executives emphasize the internal benefits—the positive impact on employees themselves—that come with including employees in external communication. Each year, in an effort to promote its Bubble Wrap brand, the company hosts a contest for students in grades 5 through 8. (Typically, the contestants are between ten and thirteen years old.) For the event, students offer innovative ideas on how to use Bubble Wrap, and the winner overall receives a $10,000 prize. (One year, the top prize went to a student who had devised a plan to save energy by using the product to insulate home refrigerators.) To handle outreach for this project, Sealed Air doesn't rely on professionals from its PR or corporate-relations department. Instead, its leaders invite employees from various parts of the company to venture out into schools and to act as contest judges. "We've got plants in twenty-three states, and we generally have a ready supply of employees who volunteer" to participate in the Bubble Wrap contest, says CEO William Hickey. "I've always looked at it as a way to get employees involved in the brand."

In Depth: A Case of Coke

Nowhere is the inclusion of employees in the conversation that occurs outside their company more pertinent, or more evident, than at Coca-Cola. Leaders at Coke, an organization celebrated worldwide for the power of its brand, focus with predictable intensity on promoting and maintaining the company's illustrious image in every possible way and among every imaginable audience. And the audience inside the company attracts at least as much of those leaders' attention as any other audience. "There are many stakeholder groups that you can name, whether it's the media or the government or others. But you have to start with your associates," says Diana Maria Martin, former director of internal communications. Kari Bjorhus, former vice president of enterprise communications, echoes Martin's emphasis on the role of employees: "What any communication function wants to do, ultimately, is to drive strategic alignment throughout the organization—so that everyone is talking off the same page, so that employees have an understanding of the company's goals and strategies, so that they sense a connection to those goals in their everyday work life." (Today, Bjorhus serves as vice president of global communications at Ecolab, a cleaning-supply provider, and Martin is a senior vice president at Citizens Financial Group, a subsidiary of Royal Bank of Scotland.)

In recent times, Coke leaders have grown more acutely aware of the need to reinforce that connection—the need not only to keep employees "talking off the same page," but also to involve them in talking about the external fortunes of their company. "As I see it, everything we do has to drive the bottom line," Martin says. "Ultimately, what's Kari's job or my job? It's to sell more beverages. It's about making sure that we're constantly reinforcing our brand benefit, and making sure that we maintain a competitive advantage in the marketplace." That job, for leaders at Coke, has become harder over the past decade. Health concerns on the part of consumers (regarding the risks associated with artificial sweeteners, or the link between obesity and consumption of high-fructose corn syrup) have caused difficulty for the entire soft-drink industry, and international controversies (allegations of water contamination in products bottled in India, entanglement in labor troubles in Colombia) have beset Coca-Cola in particular. As a consequence, this most fabled of brands has come under regular assault in the public sphere. At the same time, the mass-media tools that Coke has long deployed to extend and defend its brand message have begun to lose much of their efficacy, while newer social media tools have started to undermine its leaders' ability to control that message.

Those challenges from without have spurred the leaders of Coke to look within. To help keep the company's external image in good shape, executives now make a big push internally to engage employees in the greater life of Coca-Cola. That push combines outside-in and inside-out approaches to organizational conversation. In the first instance, company leaders bring into that conversation a wide range of information about developments out in the world and in the marketplace that relate to the Coke organization. In the second instance, they provide employees with tools to support the Coke brand and to spread the Coke message beyond the confines of the company proper.

One outside-in practice is the Café Conversation, a regularly held small-group gathering. "It's an informal discussion between a subject-matter expert inside the company and associates who sign up for it," Martin explains. Topics of conversation range from intriguing sidelights on Coke and its brand (such as the history of Coke's iconic skirt-shaped bottle) to "hot-button issues," Martin says. "We want to make sure that associates can speak to accusations that Coca-Cola makes you fat, for example." (Most Café Conversation sessions take place at the company's world headquarters in Atlanta, but there are variations on this practice at Coke facilities everywhere.) Another recurring practice exemplifies the outside-in approach yet also points toward the inside-out approach. Called a Red Alert—and named after the universally familiar color used in the Coke logo—it's an e-mail message that goes out to all employees. "Red Alerts are news-driven, and they focus on our flagship Coca-Cola brand," Martin says. Early in 2009, for instance, the company issued a Red Alert about a report that members of the incoming Obama administration tended to prefer Coke over competing cola brands. Unlike garden-variety forms of internal communication, Red Alerts don't cover executive promotions or other staples of intracompany news. "They address external-facing things that associates would find interesting enough to distribute virally to friends and family," Martin notes.

When an employee does forward a message about Coca-Cola to someone outside the company, a shift occurs, practically small but large in its implications: By helping to convey the company's message in an inside-out fashion, that employee joins the great open conversation about the Coke brand that unfolds in homes and offices, in retail stores and restaurants, and in the court of public opinion. "From our perspective, having ninety thousand informed associates adds a sales force of ninety thousand people to the company," Martin says. "It's a powerful force for getting the facts out." (Coca-Cola employs that number of people directly, in its corporate functions and in its wholly owned bottlers. The entire Coke system, which includes franchised bottling companies, encompasses about one million employees.) In effect, those employees are a vast cadre of corporate ambassadors.

In fact, Coca-Cola has created a formal Ambassadorship program, aimed at encouraging employees to promote the Coke image and the Coke product line—to advance the company cause in speech and in practice. The program even has a slogan: "Drink It. Live It. Love It."

At a dedicated Ambassadorship area on the Coke intranet site, the company presents an array of resources. There's a page called Know the Business, which offers links to information both on Coke's storied past and on its current operations. There's a tool called Get Involved, which connects employees to company-sponsored volunteer activities. There's an icon labeled What's Your Story?, which invites employees to "inspire others by sharing how you are being an ambassador." The centerpiece of the program, though, is a list of nine ambassadorial behaviors. That list starts on a simple note ("Make it a point to enjoy Coca-Cola, the epicenter of our business!") and ends on a rather ambitious note ("Model what it means to live an active, healthy life"). In between are suggestions on how to support company goals in a more direct way. One suggestion reads, "Help us win at the point of sale" (by cleaning up merchandise displays in retail outlets, for example). Another item asks employees to relay sales leads back to the company and to report instances in which a retailer has run out of a Coke product.

One of the nine ambassador-worthy behaviors calls on employees to become, in effect, adjunct members of Coke's public-relations team: "Learn the facts in order to confidently promote our products." The online Ambassadorship material includes a page called Get the Facts, which outlines Coke's position on some of the contentious issues that surround the company and its products. That page features data on beverage ingredients and their effects on consumers' health, for example. "There is so much inaccurate information out there, whether it be related to aspartame, high-fructose corn syrup, caffeine, or obesity," Martin says. Coke leaders hope that employees, in their daily lives, will step up to counter charges that stem from those issues. "Our research indicates that when people hear something from an employee of the company, they tend to find that information to be highly credible," Bjorhus says. By providing tools and talking points to use in defending the Coke brand against outside critics, she and her colleagues enable the people who work for Coke to *speak* for Coke.

Telling employees how to play an ambassadorial role goes only so far, however. In the spirit of also showing them how to carry forth the Coke message, company leaders have produced a series of short video segments that illustrate some of the nine desired behaviors. "They're designed to have low production quality," Bjorhus explains. "We don't spend a lot of money on them. We have employee actors. They're kind of goofy." In one video, titled "Lesson 1: Merchandise Our Products," an off-duty Coke employee strolls through the beverage aisle in a grocery store and notices a couple of merchandising horrors: a poorly stacked twelve-pack of Minute Maid Lemonade cans and an upended two-liter Coke Classic bottle. After acting out scenarios that show what not to do in response to this calamity—don't ignore it, but don't be silly about it, either—the employee demonstrates the correct approach. He pauses, quickly straightens up the wayward items, and proceeds with his shopping. The staging of this action, together with the background music that accompanies it, recalls the hokey style of a 1950s-era corporate training film. Bjorhus describes another entry in the series: "We have some folks in a restaurant where Coke is not being served: What do you do when someone offers you a competitor's product? We have somebody at a neighborhood barbecue where the host isn't offering our brand." A Coke ambassador, in short, is *always* on duty. These brief videos convey that idea with a light touch. "They're fun, but they also help you think, 'Yeah, I could do that.' The response has been very positive," Bjorhus says.

Of course, when it comes to recruiting employees to become ambassadors, Coke has an advantage that few other organizations can match. "People who work at Coca-Cola really love the brand," Bjorhus notes. "There's a magic about Coca-Cola; it's not just a regular company. So people here are more inclined to want to do this." Yet the benefits of deploying employees as public advocates are vividly clear—and they're at least potentially applicable to any company. At Coke, those benefits reveal themselves both externally and internally. "If we have more ambassadors out there, that becomes a competitive advantage in the marketplace. It's good for business," Martin says. Meanwhile, employees who uphold the Coke brand outside the workplace tend to bring that attitude back inside the Coke organization. "If we can encourage employees to support the company and to represent the company after their working hours, that has the effect of increasing engagement, commitment, and loyalty," Bjorhus says. "People live up to your expectations, and I don't think that we've expected as much of our associates in the past as we should have."

Relinquishing Control

The flip side of allowing employees to generate organizational content is accepting a certain loss of control over the messages that go out under corporate auspices or through corporate channels. In an Enterprise 2.0 world, managers relinquish much of their capacity to manage what their people say, or where and how their people say it. That's a scary prospect for many business leaders, and it's a potentially unsettling development for anyone who occupies a position of organizational responsibility: How much unfiltered communication can a company actually bear? If a leader invites employees to post content to a corporate Web site, for example, who knows what they might put up there? The pursuit of conversational inclusion casts the entire function of corporate communication in a new and uncertain light. "It moves the role from being the vehicle of a control culture and saying, 'Here is the message, so please understand it,' to being the stimulators of a conversation and trying to guide that conversation. That's completely different from sending out corporate announcements," says communication consultant Michael Croton. "Companies will be wrestling over the next few years with what the democratization of communication actually means in practice."

What many leaders have done, in practice, is to embrace the new logic of conversational democracy—a logic that calls on them to loosen their grip on organizational communication. "The old 'We can control the message' world is disappearing very quickly," says Peter McKillop, of UBS AG. "We know that to gain control, we have to give up a certain amount of control." Lurking within that Zen-like paradox is a signal piece of wisdom: Only by allowing employees to take part in telling the story of their organization can leaders ensure that the story will remain compelling and viable. "There's a dialectic between control and credibility," Richard Edelman says. "The more control, the less believable. Joe Stalin communicated a lot. I don't know if people believed it."

For communication leaders especially, the shift toward greater inclusiveness presents a new opportunity. "You can no longer control messages. You can no longer control channels," Mike Wing observes. "Some people look at that situation and think, 'What are we going to do?' I look at it and think, '*Now* we can actually do some real work.'" Even during the heyday of top-down corporate communication, there was an element of pretense in the notion that certain designated professionals could tightly manage the way that information circulated to employees. "We fantasized that we were in control: We were the 'communicators,' and they were the 'audience.' Now we understand that *they* are the communicators and we are their assistants," Wing says. Frontline employees should take precedence over back-office functionaries, he argues, because "the source of information has to be authentic." In his view, serving as "a catalyst or a facilitator" of organizational conversation—helping employees to make the most of that process—is more satisfying and more viable than trying to mastermind it.

At the CEO level, leaders are coming to view this new, less control-oriented model with enthusiasm—or at least with equanimity. Scott Huennekens, CEO of Volcano Corporation, suggests that a looser approach to communication has enabled organizational life to become less stifling and more productive than it used to be. He recalls the experience of working at another company in an earlier era: "It was fifteen or twenty years ago. You had to get people to sign off on something if you were going to send it to the whole company. It was all about risk aversion." A notably different spirit prevails at his current organization. "There's more of a free flow of information today than we could have had in the past. And we don't try to control it," he says.

At Infosys, Kris Gopalkrishnan and his colleagues allow open and uncensored discussion to unfold on the company's intranet site, in part because they know that their people always have the option of posting online content elsewhere. "Whether we like it or not," Gopalkrishnan notes, "our employees are part of social networks outside the company." So letting them comment freely on the Infosys intranet (even when their comments reflect negatively on the company) is a way to reckon with one of the unavoidable facts of life in a Web 2.0 world. "You can't control it. You can only try to manage it," Gopalkrishnan argues. Infosys leaders manage the company's internal conversation, he says, by insisting that employees follow a tried-and-true rule: "You can disagree, but you can't be disagreeable."

Quite often, leaders have discovered, an ad hoc system of self-regulation by employees fills the void that's left when top-down control ebbs away. "What happens over time is that the community self-polices,"

Larry Solomon says, referring to his experience with allowing AT&T employees to comment on articles posted to the company intranet. "You'll see somebody come out with some outrageous comment. But then you'll see the sentiment swing back to the middle." While AT&T does have a policy that bars (for example) the release of proprietary information and the posting of what Solomon calls "incendiary comments," he reports that the company has largely avoided the need to enforce those rules formally. Jacqueline Taggart, a communication consultant, notes that basic self-interest provides the foundation for self-policing behavior. "What do you think employees are going to do?" she asks rhetorically. "Are they really going to put up a career-limiting comment? I find it strange that people think that employees would really do that." Of course, to make a regime of self-regulation work, leaders must be rigidly controlling in one key respect: They must require every employee to attach a name to any message that he or she transmits through company channels.

The move toward conversational inclusion entails considerable trade-offs—big potential rewards, as well as big risks. Yet the matter is by no means clear-cut. It requires, according to communication professional Ronna Lichtenberg, "a new way of thinking about risk management." Any lawyer or PR manager can point out the downside risks that come with yielding control over organizational content. But company leaders should "really explore the upside" of promoting "a more full-bodied communication among all employees," Lichtenberg says. Arguably, moreover, any effort to impose discipline over what people say carries its own kind of risk. The flow of information between top leaders and their employees runs (or should run) in two directions, and leaders must keep in mind the cost of constricting that flow. "There are issues that sometimes do not make it to the top, because there's been too *much* control of the communication channels," says Laura Cave, of XO Group. "So I spend more time trying to encourage people to give their input, or to disagree, or to propose a different direction, than trying to control what they say or think."

THERE'S A TENSION BETWEEN running a tight ship and inviting members of the ship's crew to talk about what happens onboard. Those who stand at the helm of a company can't wish that tension away. Nor can they forfeit the benefits of conversational inclusion—the benefits of engaging with their crew in a give-and-take manner. Consider EMC Corporation, the subject of our next chapter. When EMC engineers design a data-storage system, they bring to that work a control-based mind-set: The task of making sure that EMC hardware and software products will remain stable and secure requires a precisely calibrated approach to execution. In the realm of organizational conversation, however, company leaders have come to emphasize inclusion more than they do control.

CHAPTER EIGHT

Walking the Talk

EMC Corporation

VIEWED FROM THE OUTSIDE, the main offices of EMC Corporation, in Hopkinton, Massachusetts, have a lot in common with the computer-storage devices that the company sells (along with a vast array of related software and solutions): Box-shaped and nondescript, made from materials that gleam with the look of pure efficiency, they reveal almost nothing about what exists inside. But inside EMC are a culture and a set of practices that place its 40,000-plus employees—and the passions that drive them both personally and professionally—very near the center of its internal and external communication efforts. *Passion*, of course, isn't a word that quickly comes to mind when one thinks of EMC. As the world's largest computer-storage provider, the company projects a public image that focuses on business-to-business reliability, not on consumer-oriented appeals to emotion. Nonetheless, over the past several years, EMC has sought and found multiple ways to tap into the wellspring of what motivates its people. It has done so, in large part, by moving toward a policy of greater conversational inclusion. Polly Pearson, a longtime EMC executive who helped initiate that shift, describes the attitude that underlies the company's emerging framework of communication. "You let the people do it. And you provide an environment where they can thrive doing it, where they feel safe, where they can share knowledge with one another." Today, in one area after another, leaders at EMC enable and encourage employees to generate much of the content that makes up its organizational conversation.

Item: When CEO Joe Tucci announced in the fall of 2008 that EMC needed to undertake serious cost retrenchment, one employee took matters into her own hands. On EMC|One, the company's internal social networking site, she started a discussion thread in which she asked fellow EMCers to offer ideas from the corporate grass roots on how to reduce expenses. (The term *EMCer* applies to any member of the EMC community; people inside the organization use it widely.) Pearson explains the spirit behind that initiative as follows: "Here are these smart types at EMC, right? 'Don't give me a platitude. Engage me. I want to help.' So this woman starts a thread and says, 'Let's share some constructive ideas on cost savings. Don't just bring your complaints. Let's join in.'" Within a few months, employees had posted several hundred responses to that thread, and the discussion had received more than thirty thousand page-views. More important, analysts from the office of EMC's CFO reviewed the ideas put forth there, and in 2009 the company had begun to implement many of them.

Item: When EMC leaders need material to support the company's submission to *Fortune* magazine's annual Best Companies to Work For survey, they don't go the usual route of preparing that material in a centralized, top-down fashion. Instead, using the capabilities built into EMC|One, they let employees do much of the work. "The normal model," Pearson explains, "is that a few people in corporate communications get together and write all this documentation—'How we listen,' 'How we inspire,' 'How we celebrate.' Our model here is: Let's put this in the network and let our people tell us how they are inspired or how they experience celebrations. And they can post photos and videos and whatever else to support that. It's community-sourced, if you will."

Item: When the head of EMC's competitive group needed to add a member to his team, he used EMC|One to enable an internal recruiting effort. According to Pearson, he was looking for "somebody who really understood the CLARiiON product and who could write." He ran a search on EMC|One for content about CLARiiON, a line of midrange storage systems, and read what various EMCers had written about that line of products. The posted writings of one employee caught his eye. After using EMC|One to solicit comments about this EMCer from other people, the executive interviewed and eventually recruited that employee. "Here's a guy who got a promotion as a result of his work and his insights," Pearson notes. "He was an engineer in North Carolina. In the old world"—the world before EMC began its highly inclusive use of social media—"he could have lived and worked under the corporate radar forever."

Item: When Chuck Hollis, vice president and chief technology officer for global marketing, needed to assess the functional possibilities and the strategic necessities of emerging Web 2.0 technology, he didn't authorize a study, and he didn't turn the matter over to social media professionals. "Everyone agreed that Web 2.0 is big, but there wasn't much information out there. It was just a bunch of consultants," Hollis says. "So I started writing a corporate blog." Among his fellow executives, he recalls, "there were a lot of white knuckles" when he told them that he would be publishing his unfiltered thoughts on potentially sensitive topics. (His site, which he simply calls *Chuck's Blog,* bears the tagline "An EMC insider's perspective on information, technology and customer challenges.") But over time, the blog attracted a loyal following both outside and inside the company, with employees accounting for about one-third of his audience. A sure sign that the practice of employee blogging had fully arrived at EMC came just a few months after Hollis launched his blog, in 2006. At an EMC board meeting, one of the company's more prominent directors—John R. Egan, an IT leader with a long and storied career at EMC—approached Hollis and said, "Chuck, I read your blog." Receiving that seal of approval led Hollis to conclude that he was on the right track. "We're using social media to solve social media problems," he explains.

These items, taken together, illustrate both the breadth and the depth of EMC leaders' commitment to conversational inclusion. "It's a two-way, equality-based dialogue," Pearson says, referring to the process by which internal communication (at its ideal best) now unfolds within EMC. "It is asking and listening, and then it's allowing them to own it in the process. It's not about controlling anymore. It's not a central organization telling people things." In each of those episodes, social media channels such as EMC|One played a critical role. Yet, as with Cisco, the adoption of interactive technology at EMC revolves less around fancy digital tools than it does around the employees who wield them. "Technology is not the issue. Blogging is a simple technology," Hollis says. "Blogs are about people." In fact, Pearson argues, the genius of social technology is that it gives employees a new way to invest emotionally in their company and in their work. "It's not money that motivates people. It's not money that's the satisfier," she says. "It's the softer things that social media is practically designed for: being recognized, feeling as though you make a difference, feeling respected, advancing your skills. Those are the things that make people want to sing and dance and run into work every day."

Through the inherently inclusive medium of social networking, and by other means as well, executives at EMC have supported initiatives that allow employees to start a conversation on their own and to find their own voice along the way. Internally and externally, online and in print, rank-and-file EMCers are developing and distributing content about their industry, about their company, and about themselves. EMC leaders, for their part, have learned to relinquish some degree of control over organizational content, and in return they have gained stalwart allies in the cause of promoting EMC—not only in the marketplace among customers, but also in the pool from which the company draws its employee talent. "It's a whole different interaction mechanism. Polly and I came up with the term *passion-led engagement,* or *passion-based communication,* to describe it," Hollis says. "This is transformational stuff."

Leading Indicators

For high-level EMC executives, the inclusion of employees in the work of sustaining organizational conversation has become nothing less than a strategic imperative. Behind the move to foster "passion-led engagement" within EMC's workforce lies a relatively dispassionate appreciation of certain deep changes that are affecting how EMC competes and how its people work. "I've been around for twenty years, and we've evolved as an organization," says William J. Teuber Jr., vice chairman of EMC's board of directors. "EMC was founded around a single product. In today's world, we have many products, we're worldwide, we have forty-seven thousand people, and the ability to keep those forty-seven thousand people in the know is absolutely critical. That's why we need many ways of communicating with them—because no one way is going to work for everyone." Jack Mollen, executive vice president of human resources, offers a similar perspective on how the company's vertiginous growth has sharpened the challenge of maintaining an optimal flow of information: "When I joined EMC, we were predominantly U.S.-based, and the majority of our workforce was here in Massachusetts. And the way that we'd communicate with that group was with an all-hands meeting. But when you truly have a global workforce, you have to bring in new ways of communicating. We're now in eighty-plus countries, and the vast majority of our revenue is from products and solutions that we've developed in the last fourteen months. So how do we get people in this global organization, with its fast product cycles, to innovate together? Because it's all about innovation."

The phrase *data storage* conjures up the image of a stable and static world, but there's nothing stable or static about the data-storage business today. "The industry is changing rapidly, and the ability to get your message out quickly and succinctly, and to reinforce it in various ways, is essential," Teuber says. "To create momentum in the marketplace, you need to get everybody moving in the same direction." EMC, Teuber and his fellow executives believe, has become ever more reliant on having a base of employees who can respond to diverse customer needs and to a fast-changing competitive environment—who understand not only the products that EMC develops but also the stakes involved in bringing those products to market. "Success, for companies in high technology, is built around speed and agility," Mollen argues. "So people have to understand: What is our strategy? What are the spaces in which we're playing? What is the potential of those markets? And they have to have that information at their fingertips, so that they can move fast in their job." The complexity inherent in EMC's line of products, moreover, makes back-and-forth communication a vital necessity for its employees. "People want to have conversations; they don't want just to be talked down to," Mollen says. "They want to feel that they can ask questions. We try to create an environment where people have the ability to do that, so that they truly understand the opportunities that these new technologies bring."

By virtue of its place in the data-storage industry, EMC finds itself at the eye of the mighty information storm that has been sweeping across the entire economy with increasing ferocity. Mollen points to a series of "Digital Universe" studies that the research firm IDC has conducted on behalf of EMC. According to one recent study, for instance, people worldwide are now doubling the amount of data in existence every two years.[1] "With that much information being created, we have to make sure that we give our employees tools so that they can quickly get to the information that's meaningful to them," he says. Tools such as EMC|One have arrived just in time to help EMC address that need. "Now, with social networking, it's changed the game. This is how we integrate," Mollen says. Again, though, what matters most is the *social* aspect—the conversational aspect—of social networking. Very often, the best way for an employee to gather crucial information is by communicating with another employee. Thus, to ride out the storm of knowledge accumulation, people must be able to talk about what they know (or about what they don't know).

Building a conversation-friendly environment, therefore, has become a keenly felt priority among top company leaders. "EMC is probably one of the flattest organizations that you'll see, for a company of our size," Teuber says. "Joe Tucci, myself, all of the senior executives—we're out in the field a lot, so that we hear the concerns and opinions of people at the lowest levels of the organization." Being accessible to people at every level of the company is a key part of the EMC leadership model, he notes: "We value the kind of conversations that can make us better. There's no e-mail that Joe Tucci gets from an employee that goes unanswered. Same with me." Yet direct, face-to-face interaction with employees remains paramount. "I'm a huge believer in being in front of people," Teuber says. "I travel the globe to make sure that people understand that there's real humanity to EMC, and to the executive team. You've got to be seen, you've got to be heard, and you've got to listen. And you have to do it in person." In his travels from one EMC outpost to another, Teuber often delivers a standard presentation that outlines company strategy. "But that's just an enabler for conversation," he says. "Unless you enable two-way conversation, you're not going to be successful." The attitude that EMC leaders strike when they talk with employees is also critical to organizational success. "Style trumps everything," Teuber contends. "As long as you're real, as long as people don't think that you're just giving out corporate-speak, they get really engaged by it."

"Something Special"

Engaging current and prospective employees in the life of EMC has become a prime objective within the company. That's why, in 2006, EMC leaders tapped Polly Pearson to serve in a newly created role: vice president of employment brand and strategy engagement. It was a role that bridged the company's human resource function with its marketing function. On the employment-brand side, Pearson's mandate was to court talented would-be employees; on the engagement side, her goal was to promote a deep sense of organizational commitment among existing EMCers. Those ostensibly separate efforts are actually "two sides of the same coin," Pearson argues. "One is connecting with the talent market outside our doors, and the other is connecting with the talent market inside our doors—connecting *with* them, not just communicating *to* them." In 2010, EMC executives dissolved the position that Pearson had taken up. In no small measure, they did so because she had succeeded in meeting the goals that they had set for her. "There is no longer a need for someone to spark the fire. The fire is now burning," says Pearson, who continues to consult for EMC on issues related to recruiting, engagement, and communication. That *fire* (to translate Pearson's term into the language of our model) is a highly inclusive conversation that extends across the EMC organization, and beyond.

In every phase of this conversation, company leaders work to signal that EMC is an organization toward which people can and do develop a passionate attachment. With respect to employee engagement, those leaders seek ways to inspire their people on an individual level. "Did you ever have an experience, when you were a kid, when somebody told you that you could be something special? Well, that's what engagement does inside a company. It's the same experience," Pearson explains. "They're all smart people here. We just need to figure out how to connect with them, how to unearth and unleash all that's in their minds." When it comes to building an employment brand, meanwhile, EMC leaders aim to heighten the sense that EMC is "something special" *as a company*. "My favorite definition of a brand is that it's a relationship like the kind that you would have with a friend," Pearson says. "That's what I would love to have with the talent market—a relationship with people who feel that they know us."

The notion that EMC should even *have* an employment brand didn't come easily to company leaders. "We put so much effort into our B-to-B marketing to customers," Pearson says. "But we'd never really thought about who we are as a company, as a culture, as a place to work, or about how we should market all of that." She paraphrases an outlook that was once prevalent among EMC executives: "We're B-to-B. We're not going to fund branding. That's ego stuff. What we do is build a great product and sell it to our customers." Over time, though, gruff skepticism has given way to a ready awareness of the need to "sell" EMC to current and future employees—the need to attract, motivate, and retain the kind of talent that enables the company to create value. "We have a largely professional workforce," notes Mark Fredrickson, former vice president of marketing strategy and communications. "They're knowledge workers. They're professionally portable. They can and do move from one company to another. They are the biggest asset that we have, and that asset walks in and out of the building every day. That's not just a cliché." Pearson, for her part, emphasizes the ultimate value that the people of EMC provide to the company. "I believe in my soul that this is the most valuable audience that I could be trying to reach," she says. "It's more important than investors. It's more important than the media. It's not necessarily more important than customers, but I'd argue that it's your *people* who do the best job of communicating with your customers."

The practice of employee engagement and employment branding at EMC has a self-reinforcing, do-it-yourself quality. Support for employee-generated content begets employee passion, and that passion begets an eagerness among employees to keep the organizational conversation going, not only inside EMC but also in places where potential recruits look for information about the company. Internally, engaged corporate veterans become carriers of the EMC culture through their participation in channels such as EMC|One. "The original founders of EMC inspired and motivated us," Pearson explains. "You take that model, and you sprinkle Miracle-Gro on it. We have employees at every level and at every location who are doing the role-modeling here." Externally, EMCers carry the company's brand message as they venture into online forums, or into real-world professional settings. "Engagement is up, employees are doing the work for us, and we've got a reputation that is cool," Pearson says. (By showing employees how to do this work on their own,

Pearson essentially rendered her old position obsolete—a point that she acknowledges. "It's now integrated into the organization," she notes, referring to the engagement mandate that she pursued for four years. "It was always set up to be that way.")

The main effect of what Pearson and others have achieved on the employee-engagement front has been "to humanize EMC, to personalize EMC," she says. And executives at the company have come to appreciate the human, or personal, side of that achievement. In 2009, Pearson created a presentation that featured photographs of employees, alongside responses by those employees to the question "What inspires you about EMC?" When she delivered the presentation to her fellow company leaders, it "hit people's heart-strings," she recalls. Clicking through one slide after another, Pearson demonstrated just how special many EMC employees believe their organization to be. "These employees were saying everything that you'd want your kids to say about you as a parent: 'I feel so motivated to get up every single day. I feel like part of a team. I've got the best product to sell. I can make anything happen at this place. The executives are approachable. And I wouldn't want to be anyplace else.' That's passion. That's how you win," Pearson says. "You know what the bottom-line impact of those quotes is? These people are just *pushing* it. They're working here because they love it, and their customers see it on their faces, and it pays all sorts of dividends."

Mothers of Inclusion

The real work of engaging employees "has nothing to do with technology," Pearson says. "It's all behavior." As if to prove that conversational inclusion at EMC isn't dependent on using the latest digital gadgetry, the company in 2009 published a traditional printed book—a softcover tome of coffee-table-book size, just shy of 250 pages, written by and for EMCers. It's an old-media monument to the idea of letting employees tell the EMC story, and to the related idea of letting them tell their *own* story. Called *The Working Mother Experience,* the book gathers personal essays by ninety-seven EMC women from fifteen countries (along with one essay by an EMC man). The essays deal with the highs and lows of being both a successful EMCer and a mother (or, in that one case, a single father), and they cover personal and professional matters alike. "They're about raising kids, and the things that give these women joy and pride, and working at EMC, and being able to balance everything," says Fredrickson, whose department took charge of designing the book and coordinating its production. (His colleagues also made the book available in an electronic format on its public site, EMC.com.) In one contribution, an EMC program manager discusses her telecommuting regimen, her use of the company's backup child-care service, and other factors that make her "daily balancing act" possible. In another essay, a member of EMC's legal team writes: "It is remarkable how much like my two-year-old many of our sales reps can be—they need it now, they need it right, and they often don't understand how they reached their current predicament!" The book also features a chapter titled "Tips and Best Practices," in which EMC working mothers distill the wisdom that they have accumulated over many years of negotiating the ever-shifting line between work life and home life.

Producing a book of this kind isn't out of the ordinary for a big company like EMC. In a standard corporate communication model, however, such a book would emerge as part of a top-down, professional-driven campaign to promote a specific organizational objective. Not so in this case. "It was a peer-level idea, and the people ran it," Pearson explains. "It wasn't the corporate inclusion office, it wasn't the corporate communications office, it wasn't HR. It was born from the passion of people, from friends talking to other friends at work and saying, 'Hey, let's give this a try.'" (Here, Pearson uses the term *inclusion* to mean something different from what we mean by that term. She's referring, of course, to the function that's called corporate diversity in many organizations.)

The prime mover behind the book project was Natalie Corridan-Gregg, who at the time was a principal product manager at EMC. Frank Hauck, executive vice president of global marketing and customer quality, had expressed an interest in efforts to "make women feel connected to each other and to EMC," Corridan-Gregg recalls. So she took her idea for a book to him. "This was not going to be a rah-rah book," she says. Instead of offering a PR-spun feel-good message, it would present (in her words) "a snapshot in time" of the way that working mothers at EMC live now. Hauck immediately signed on to the idea. "It was a request and a yes. Within twenty minutes, he was saying, 'I'm going to fund it. Go do it,'" says Corridan-Gregg, who is now a director of technology analysis.

EMC has distributed copies of *The Working Mother Experience* both internally and externally, and on each front the book has attracted enthusiastic attention. "People want to embrace a positive project," Corridan-Gregg says. Inside the company, the book has helped EMC women to send a message to their leaders—and especially to the men in that group. "It's a decoder ring for male managers," she suggests. By reading the stories that women tell in the book, men come to a better understanding of what makes working moms at EMC tick (or, in some cases, what ticks them off). The book also lets men send a message of their own to colleagues. "Male managers can project concern by putting the book on their desk," Corridan-Gregg notes. The physicality of the book, in fact, makes it an ideal tool for starting a conversation. William Teuber describes one such encounter: "I had that book in my house. A woman I know was there, and she picked it up, and she immediately bonded with it. She said, 'You know, this personalizes EMC in a way that I had never understood.' I said, 'If you like the book, you can have it,' and she took it home with her. She doesn't work for EMC, but she's a working mother, and she identified with a lot of stories in the book."

In casual interactions like that one and in other settings as well, *The Working Mother Experience* has had a wide-ranging impact on people outside EMC. Out in the talent market, candidates have seen the book and have responded well to it; according to Corridan-Gregg, some female recruits have chosen to work at EMC partly on the basis of what they have read in its pages. Pearson argues that precisely because the book was a bottom-up operation—because "it reads so genuine and true"—it makes a powerful case for EMC as a women-friendly workplace. "This is doing more to serve that purpose than any artificial, consultant-oriented powwow that tells people, 'Inclusion is important. Hire women, and treat them with respect,'" she says. Customers have received a similar message from the company. "Our people are using the book to reach out to customers," Corridan-Gregg says. "Connections are happening that wouldn't have happened otherwise." More generally, people with an interest in "the working-mother experience" have taken note of *The Working Mother Experience*. In 2010, for example, Simmons College in Boston hosted a panel discussion that focused on issues raised in the book. Professionals from other companies, meanwhile, have contacted people at EMC to gain insight on how the book project has helped to further a conversation about women in the workplace. In response to those queries, Corridan-Gregg offers up a simple lesson. "It couldn't be a corporate mandate," she says. "It couldn't be a top-down thing."

Community Service

With its foray into social media, as with its support for the *Working Mother Experience* project, the leadership team at EMC has exhibited a hands-off approach that lets rank-and-file employees take the initiative in starting a conversation. The place where that approach is most evident is on EMC|One, the social networking platform that the company launched in 2006. There, EMCers of every stripe can join an online community, or create a new one; contribute to an ongoing discussion, or start a fresh discussion thread; comment on a colleague's blog post, or launch a blog page of their own. EMC continues to maintain a standard intranet site, called Channel EMC, which offers benefits information, policy documents, company news, and the like. That site, Fredrickson explains, presents "the company's voice to employees." EMC|One, by contrast, plays host to the many voices of individual employees, and not only does it amplify those voices, but it allows people to attach a face and a personality to their voice as well. On the platform, any EMCer can create a profile page that highlights his or her professional and personal interests, and colleagues all across the world can then find and interact with that person. "It's your Facebook inside, behind the firewall," Pearson says of EMC|One. It's also, in effect, a cornucopia of employee-generated content.

A feature on the main page of EMC|One exemplifies the inclusive sensibility of the site. Called Meet the Community, it's a short piece in which one employee profiles another. Site managers publish new profiles regularly, and in some cases the subject of a profile gets to choose the colleague who will be profiled next. "It was an employee's idea, to 'meet' a fellow employee," Pearson says. "I just love it because, again, it's owned by the community. It's much more powerful, coming from a peer, than it would be coming from somebody in an ivory tower somewhere." The heart of the site's main-page content, meanwhile, is a continuously updated discussion area that draws in threads from various parts of EMC|One. Posted topics (to cite examples offered by Fredrickson) range from "How do we celebrate EMC?" to "Defect tracking metrics during the development phase." EMC leaders also post major company announcements on the network, and that news then becomes a topic of discussion. Responding to a cost-cutting announcement, for example, employees might debate the relative merits of a plan that relies on layoffs and a plan that relies on reduced travel expenditures. "Sometimes, they're more comfortable talking about it online than they would be in the hallway," Fredrickson says. Otherwise, he adds, a typical conversation on EMC|One isn't much different from an ordinary in-person chat: "It's just a good, normal back-and-forth."

Within the general community that is EMC|One, there are numerous smaller online communities, each with its own microsite and its own discussion area, and employees can join those that meet their needs. Scores of specialized communities thrive on the platform, and they cover a wide array of topics—from particular EMC business segments to issues of broad organizational interest. "We have communities that are based on certain products, on certain solutions, and they're communicating globally on a regular basis," Mollen says. "The more that we see this process as part of our normal way of life, the more powerful it becomes." As Mollen points out, this aspect of the EMC|One architecture provides an invaluable boon to employees who struggle to manage the profusion of data that is now intrinsic to business life: "It allows you to say, 'I'm going to be involved with these three or four communities, and I'm not going to worry about the other ones.'"

The community-based structure of EMC|One also opens an opportunity for employees to explore personal interests that they have in common with fellow EMCers. "We have an artists' community," Pearson notes. "Every month, they have discussions about their art project for that month, and then they post photos of what they created. So they get to do the things they really love—which brings that flush and that smile to their face." Similarly, there's a community area where EMC employees who love photography can post a link to a slide show of their work on Flickr, an external photo-sharing site. "They get their gallery debut, if you will, and that connects them to other people who are photographers. They're exemplifying their passion by sharing it," Pearson says.

Granting employees license to generate personal content reflects one of the guiding principles behind the formation of EMC|One. "Even if it's not directly related to business, even if it's photos of your kids, that's okay," Hollis says. For EMC leaders, the thinking goes like this: When employees are able to relax and to interact with colleagues on a personal level, they forge bonds within the company that can give them a professional edge. "EMC|One is a friend machine. It enables like minds to find one another," Pearson says. The use of social media "enables safe conversations and safe ways for people to connect," she argues. "You start with the personal. Then it's, 'What do you do at EMC?' And then it's, 'Oh, I was just thinking of an idea on that subject,' or 'I've got a customer in that space. Could you help me?' And then all of these other types of connections happen."

Connection, community, conversation. Behind those soft-sounding concepts is a hard truth about the value that EMC|One and other social technologies deliver for EMC. "It's about accelerating your learning and improving your ability to move faster," Mollen says. He recalls an incident from the early days of EMC|One in which a customer in China asked an EMC sales representative for information on a newly released product. "In the old days, that salesman would have to go up the chain of command to the country manager, and then to the regional manager. The regional manager would have to get somebody down in the product-line division, here at the home office. And then the information would have to go all the way back up," Mollen explains. "Who knows how long it would have taken us to prepare that sales rep for a talk with his customer?" In this case, though, the salesman was able to log into an online chat room, where he interacted with people who had direct knowledge of the new product, and they helped him develop a customer-ready presentation in the space of a single day. "It hit home that we'd reduced the cycle time" on that process, Mollen says. Today, meanwhile, others at EMC rely on social media tools to shorten cycle times at the front end of the business. "We innovate products using EMC|One," Hollis says. To solve a product-design problem, for example, engineers who work out of different offices might form an ad hoc online community in which they can trade and track relevant ideas and documents.

"Technology allows a big company to get small," Hollis says, referring in particular to the technology that drives EMC|One. "It lets us have a small-scale conversation." Other EMC leaders frame the benefits of EMC|One in similar terms. Fredrickson, for example, notes that top executives at the company watch the flow of discussion on the platform in order to gain a more intimate sense of what employees are thinking and feeling: "Being able to see people's opinions and reactions in writing really seems to have grabbed hold of senior managers. They really care about what employees think." For that reason, he suggests, EMC|One has become "a great management tool." Mollen, going a step further, argues that the adoption of this technology has ramifications that are external as well as internal. "It's a tremendous competitive advantage for EMC to have this capability to communicate so fast and so effectively, on so many issues, with our global workforce," he says. "If you're a competitor of EMC, and if EMC has this capability and you don't, that should make you nervous—because we can reach our employees so much quicker, and in such a rich way."

Voice Recognition

Among the richest lodes of employee-generated content at EMC is a large and growing collection of employee blogs. Under the umbrella of official or quasi-official company sponsorship, EMC employees today maintain several dozen blog sites in all. Keeping a blog has become a way for EMCers at all levels of the organization to showcase their knowledge and talent, as well as their engagement with EMC-related issues. Corridan-Gregg operates a blog, *Natalie's Corner*, whose tagline says it all: "This blog is about the intersection of wife, mother, and employee." Hollis, as noted previously, uses his blog to write mainly about broad trends in technology and business. EMC employees account for about one-third of his readership, he says; customers and other external readers make up the remainder. Some EMC employee blogs reside exclusively on EMC|One and enjoy a largely internal following, but many of them are accessible on the public Internet as well. In either case, this practice has proven to be an outstanding way for employees both to find a voice and to gain recognition for it.

Consider Steve Todd. An engineer with more than 170 patents or patents pending, Todd helped invent the RAID storage technology, which remains a core element of many EMC products today. "Before he started blogging on EMC|One, he was fairly anonymous at EMC. He was just keeping his head down, writing code," Pearson notes. "He found his voice through our social media network." In 2007, with encouragement from colleagues such as Hollis and Pearson, Todd launched a blog. At first, the blog was available to internal readers only, but within a year he moved it to an external site. It's called *Information Playground*, and it carries the tagline "Building Software for the Information Storage Industry." The title and the tagline are somewhat misleading, however, since Todd's blog features not just technical content, but also commentary on the dynamics of innovation, career-management advice for his fellow engineers, and insights into what it's like to work at EMC. "I really wanted it to reflect well on my company," Todd says of his initial vision for the blog. According to Pearson, he has done extremely well in that regard, especially when it comes to reaching young engineers who might apply to work at EMC. "I shared with him our message architecture," she says. "He internalized it, and he's out blogging externally, using our messages in everything that he does. He's probably one of the best spokesmen for the company now."

For Todd, becoming a content provider has brought significant rewards. Before, he was primarily a technician, and that's how he saw himself. Today, he says, "I see myself as a writer." Indeed, along with generating posts for his own blog, he has written for such Web sites as Vault.com and CNBC.com, and he has written two books. Meanwhile, his star has also risen within the company. In 2008, EMC named him a distinguished engineer—a title held by only a few dozen of his colleagues. "We get leverage from him, and we give to him as well," Pearson says. "It's a mutually beneficial two-way street."

Enabling rank-and-file employees to raise their profile inside EMC has become an important undertaking for Pearson and other company leaders. Over a period that began in 2009, for instance, Pearson hosted an online interview program called Visual Talk Radio, which people throughout the company could access via EMC|One. For each episode of the show, she and an employee cohost would chat with a couple of EMCers both about their work and about themselves. Guests and cohosts alike were thus able to bask in the glow of the social media spotlight. "You're feeling honored, you're talking about what you love, and people are asking you questions as if you're a VIP celebrity," Pearson says of the effect that the show could have on participants. "It's a free form of recognition that just spreads the happy vibe." Through blogging, moreover, employees have an even greater chance to increase their visibility and their sense of belonging within EMC. "For people who have blogs, being a recognized subject-matter expert does a lot for their motivation and their feeling of personal value," Mollen says. It does a lot for their professional stature, too. "The blog is the new résumé," Hollis argues. At EMC, in short, such tools have the capacity to transform employees from cogs in a corporate machine into stars that shine across a galaxy.

Blogging, in addition, has the capacity to extend an employee's voice into regions that lie beyond EMC. "Once you start blogging externally, you get more recognition than you know what to do with," Pearson says. The EMC Community Network, a section on the EMC.com site, offers links to more than two dozen public-facing employee blogs. "We have this whole community of people who got their water wings inside EMC|One and are now blogging outside," Pearson explains. To any employee who might want to make that move, she and her colleagues deliver an encouraging message: "We're going to teach you how to swim. We're going to catch you. You're not going to fail. When you're ready to go outside, you can do that." It's an arrangement that enables EMC to communicate with industry movers and shakers, and with other key audiences, in a new and compelling way. "We know that the more that customers look at our blogs, the better they feel about EMC as a supplier," Mollen says. Of course, helping employees to amplify their voice in the technology marketplace also allows them to boost their visibility in the market for talent—and greater visibility often means greater mobility. "The downside is that their brand follows them," Hollis notes. Even so, he says, "the benefits are priceless."

Rules of Engagement

Reckoning with an inability to control the brand identities that employees develop externally is merely one example of a larger challenge that EMC leaders now confront. The more extensively those leaders include EMCers of every rank and role in the work of creating organizational content, the less able they are to control such content. On the whole, company executives have decided that the best way to engage employees in organizational conversation is to dispense with the pretense that they can apply elaborate rules to that effort. "A lot of people look at EMC|One, and they're amazed at how deep it is. They say, 'Could we get a copy of your policies?' But we don't have policies on it," Mollen says. "It's self-governing." He notes, further, that self-governance will succeed only if there are people who are equipped to undertake it: "A fundamental guiding principle at EMC is that we only hire adults, and we treat people as adults." On the basis of that principle, Mollen and his colleagues have built a system in which employees effectively police each other in venues such as EMC|One.

During the development stage for EMC|One, a few executives suggested that the company should establish an array of online communities that employees would be able to join. But Pearson, as she recalls, argued successfully in favor of allowing that process to occur "organically": "I said, 'No, we're not going to start any communities. We're going to let the people determine what communities they want, what they want to talk about, what they're interested in.' We had to learn to stop being command-and-control." By the same token, she and other leaders have learned to take a live-and-let-live approach to the blog posts, discussion comments, and other content that employees publish on EMC|One. Ultimately, Pearson contends, there's no reason to treat communication on a social network any differently from other forms of intracompany communication. "In a physical meeting, you might have a guy who says something stupid, or you might have somebody who sends a stupid e-mail every now and then," she says. "You might pull them aside and say, 'That didn't make you look very good. That wasn't cool.' And if it were really uncool, you'd have HR come in and do what HR does best. Same thing here. There are norms." In any case, she points out, no organization would try to control every meeting or every e-mail exchange in a top-down fashion.

"Old-fashioned executives who are less-information-is-more types are becoming a rare breed," Fredrickson says. Indeed, Pearson argues, "if you grew up in a turbo command-and-control company, you could be at a disadvantage" when it comes to leading the organizational conversation at a company that allows employee-generated content to flourish. In

a typical corporate communication department, people take on a polic-
ing role in order to protect "the best interest of the brand," she notes.
"They set the message, and each message is used by official people, and
no one else is allowed to speak." The emergence of social media renders
that model increasingly untenable. Moreover, that model has always had
serious limitations. "The conversation happens with or without you,"
Pearson says. In a traditional organizational setting, much of the
inevitable chatter among employees takes place not only outside of leaders' control, but also outside of their awareness. By empowering people
through bottom-up communication, leaders empower themselves as
well. "Participating in the conversation is a way for them to have control—to help steer the conversation," Pearson suggests.

As it happens, one control-oriented corporate practice nearly thwarted
a highly promising employee-initiated project—that is, before EMC lead-
ers used EMC|One to rectify the situation. In 2008, an EMC employee got
the idea for a company-wide event in which EMCers would snap photographs that captured the experience of working at EMC. The woman, a
program manager in EMC's engineering group, had no official connection to the company's marketing and communication apparatus. But
that incidental fact didn't keep her from approaching Pearson with her
idea, as Pearson recalls: "She says, 'Gee, wouldn't it be fun if we had a
day-in-the-life photo contest?' And I said, 'That would be great. Run it.
You're anointed.'" Soon enough, the woman ran into a roadblock.
Company policy, as it turned out, barred employees from bringing cameras into an EMC facility. Although the policy was "laughable" in its
existing form, Pearson notes ("Every cell phone has a camera on it now,
right?"), changing it would entail reckoning with legitimate security and
privacy concerns.

The usual approach to revising such a policy, at EMC and elsewhere,
would be to set up a lengthy committee process. Pearson helped initiate
an alternative approach that she summarizes as follows: "Just take the
policy as it stands, post it on the social network, and let the community
propose a new one." The result was a case of employee-generated corporate governance. EMC executives had final authority over any changes
to the policy, of course. But they found that by using the EMC|One plat-
form, they could easily leverage the distributed intelligence of people
throughout the company. (Thus, even as social media tools lessen a

leader's ability to control organizational communication, they compensate for that loss by enabling greater efficiency.) "The community, within the course of about forty-eight hours, had a more bullet-proof, more modern photo policy," Pearson says. "These guys were tougher on security concerns than the old guards in PR or legal would have been. They thought like human resources people. 'What if somebody didn't want their photo taken? Should we ask permission beforehand?'—they considered all of these things. And they created a new policy. It sailed through PR, it sailed through legal, and off we go."

The event took place on October 9, 2008. That day, more than four hundred EMCers at sites all around the world brought cameras to work and took photographs with the aim of turning slices of EMC life into digital imagery. They then uploaded their snapshots to EMC|One, where these photos became part of a feature called A Day in the Life of EMC. Within less than a week, the feature had logged twenty-nine thousand page-views, as employees checked in to see images of themselves and their colleagues at work—and, in at least a few shots, at play. "As you saw your peers from around the world, it hit something very magical," Pearson says. "Do you know how awesome it was to see that our peers in Utah see mountains and ski slopes out of their windows, and our peers in Bangalore have a permanent rock-band set in their cafeteria, and in Japan they're in this gorgeous skyscraper overlooking a waterway? Suddenly, you felt a part of a community."

LEADERS AT EMC CONSCIOUSLY treat communication to, from, and among employees as a vital factor in the company's ability to adapt to lightning-fast changes in its technology environment and in its competitive landscape. In fact, they view their communication even with potential employees from a strategic perspective. Thus, EMC displays its capacity for conversational *intentionality*. Through their deep investment in EMC|One, a platform that enables robust discussion among employees, EMC executives have increased the company's level of conversational *interactivity*. By striving to build a flat organization in which employees have regular access to senior managers, those leaders have demonstrated a willingness to pursue conversational *intimacy*. (Likewise, their decision to encourage employee blogging and other forms of employee-generated content signals a high degree of trust in their workforce.) Finally, EMC's support for a broad range of employee-driven communication efforts—from the *Working Mother Experience* project to the proliferation of employee blogs—indicates an unusually strong penchant for conversational *inclusion*. For EMC leaders, engaging their people and including them in organizational conversation go hand in hand.

CHAPTER NINE

Talk, Inc., Points (TIPs)

Amateur Hour

FOR MOST PEOPLE MOST of the time, conversation is a habit or a pastime or, perhaps, an art form. But it's not a profession. So one upshot of recasting organizational communication in a more conversational mode is that it opens up a chance for amateurs—employees, in other words—to go where only professionals were formerly able to tread. Engaging a wide range of employees in the give-and-take of organizational communication, both internally and externally, entails an upfront commitment to letting all kinds of people contribute all kinds of messages. It also involves a commitment to letting go of the need to control every last message. But once the spirit of conversational inclusion has taken hold, leaders face the practical need to translate that spirit into action. Here, then, are a few ideas on how to enable and to leverage employee-generated content.

Let Them Build It

Conversational inclusion starts, quite simply, with a resolve to include employees in the real, nitty-gritty work of gathering and sharing company information. It means drawing them over to the active, constructive side of the communication process. To invert a popular movie phrase: If you let them build it, they will come. And they will come with a higher level of engagement than they're likely to have if top leaders and professional communicators insist on doing all of the work for them.

Or, to shift from one metaphor to another: Sometimes people should be able to bake their cake and eat it, too. Leaders at King Arthur Flour, a baking-goods company located in Norwich, Vermont, follow that principle in their approach to producing *The Tablespoon,* the company's internal newsletter. "It's user-generated," says Sarah McGinley-Smith, director of corporate communications. "Anyone from throughout the company can contribute an article or a picture and talk about what's going on in their area—issues that they have there, help that they may need." The newsletter, which appears weekly on the King Arthur Flour intranet site, covers both work and personal matters that are of interest to employees. There's even a recurring feature, called The Scoop, a free digital marketplace where employees can put items of their own up for sale. "It's not intended to be a flashy, fancy marketing piece," McGinley-Smith says of the newsletter. "It's meant to have a lot of different voices in it."

Inclusion of this kind comes rather naturally to King Arthur Flour, since the boundary that separates the organization from its employees is already somewhat permeable. The company operates under an ESOP (employee stock ownership plan)—which means that the vested members of its 160-person workforce are also its shareholders. "We are one hundred percent employee-owned," McGinley-Smith notes. Yet the ESOP structure doesn't obviate the need for leaders who bring an inclusive attitude to employee communication. Steve Voigt, the chief executive of King Arthur Flour, makes a point of demonstrating that support for *The Tablespoon* comes straight from the top. "Every week, our CEO sends an e-mail to every person who contributed, thanking them for their contribution and talking about the highlights of that week's issue," McGinley-Smith explains. "That's one of the ways that we remind people that it's important to contribute."

Open Up the Floor

Seen from one angle, conversational inclusion is a matter of conversational expansion—expansion of the range and number of people who contribute to organizational messaging, and expansion of the range and number of ideas that are available to drive that messaging. Smart leaders, accordingly, open up institutional space where people from all parts of a company can participate in creating and telling the company story. In that space, employees should be able to contribute to both message development and message delivery.

Bob Pickard, drawing on his expertise as a PR executive, offers a term to describe this model: "The whole phenomenon of *cocreation* is the most important change in what's going on right now. You get the best, most authentic communication if you cocreate your messaging by consulting with employees and by engaging them in a dialogue." By fostering what amounts to an open-source approach to content generation, leaders can inspire "employees to proselytize, to 'own' what they talk about, to advocate enthusiastically for their company," Pickard argues.

One way to instill a spirit of cocreation among employees is to make a game of it. In 2008, leaders at the restaurant chain Ruby Tuesday held a Brand Champion contest in which any of the company's 46,000-plus employees (or their family members) could submit material that celebrated what the company offers and what it stands for. The aim of the contest was to spur "all of our team members throughout the country to share a story about what makes them proud of the brand, or proud of where they work," says Kimberly Grant, executive vice president and chief operations officer. Employees didn't limit themselves to entering standard written submissions, however. "We received a couple hundred entries," Grant says. "We had three-year-olds who sent in colored pictures. We had people who put together slide shows—really high-tech, high-touch slide shows. We had people who made YouTube videos. So there were a lot of great stories." Along with awarding prizes for the most compelling entries, the company posted much of the material created by its in-house Brand Champions on its intranet site.

"It was about strengthening our internal culture more than anything else," Grant says of the Brand Champion contest. All the same, some of the messages developed by employees have found their way into the stream of Ruby Tuesday's external messaging. "We created a series of Brand Champion statements, based on items that our team members were particularly proud of," Grant explains. Using those statements ("We have a farm-fresh garden bar," for example), her colleagues compiled a series of Brand Champion banners that appear as images on the screen saver for the company's point-of-sale system. "Because those computers, in a lot of our restaurants, are visible to our guests, they noticed the artwork," Grant says. "We were communicating with our teams, but it spilled over to our customer base, and we realized that it was a powerful communication tool."

Throw an Inside Pitch

Companies deploy armies of salespeople and spend millions of precious marketing dollars to get the word out about their products. No doubt, most of that effort and expense is unavoidable. But inclusive leaders know that bringing non-sales employees into the sales process can offer a low-cost, high-impact way to generate interest in their company's latest offering. Word of mouth, ideally, starts at home.

"The number one audience that most companies miss in introducing a product is their own people," says PR consultant Gary F. Grates. He advises clients to set up intranet-based tools, podcasts, or other vehicles through which engineers, designers, and managers can talk to employees about new (or existing) products: "You start off with the premise that you want to make your employee population smarter about your products, so that they will become stronger advocates or ambassadors for the company. Then you create destinations inside the organization where you give them information on those products." If employees can get the inside scoop on a new offering, he adds, "they'll be more apt to talk about it" outside the company.

The key to turning employees into eager and effective pitchmen (and pitchwomen) is to assure them that they don't need to act like stereotypical salespeople when they chat with friends and family members about what their company offers. On the contrary, they should come to understand that a little plain talk usually beats a hard sell. Take the model used by leaders at General Motors. Not only do those leaders actively encourage ordinary employees to help sell GM cars and trucks, but they also look for ways to include employees in the sales-training process. One year, the company produced a video in which several employees discuss how they practice the art of the pitch. "It was interesting just to hear the different approaches," says Kim Carpenter, who was then manager of global internal communications at GM. "One guy always makes his pitches at gas stations. When he's filling up at the pump, he says, 'Do you like that car?' That starts a conversation. We have another person who arms himself with research." What these pitch styles have in common is that they avoid both marketing-speak and traditional car-sales lingo. "Rather than talking about the 'sleek, athletic stance' of a car, we'll say that it hauls your groceries and it's a nice car for commuting to work," Carpenter says. "We take the tools that our external communicators develop for automotive media, and we try to make them personal."

Shine a Light

Allowing employees to step up and speak is a natural corollary of encouraging leaders to step back and listen. Where a spirit of conversational inclusion prevails, moreover, employees are frequently able to speak out in situations that give them high visibility: They occupy center stage, as it were, while the top executives who usually perform in that spot retreat to the wings. By conferring attention on people who typically work in the organizational shadows, leaders enable employees to gain a higher profile inside (and, in some cases, outside) their company.

David Liu, in his role as CEO of XO Group, initiated a practice in 2010 that lets people throughout his company have an occasional turn in the limelight. About once a month, he conducts an interview with an employee, and afterward he posts a transcript of that conversation on his blog. "Because we have such a disparate and complicated company, I thought it would be fun for people to get an idea of what various groups are working on, and to have a window on a 'day in the life' of some of our staff members," Liu explains. "The goal was to create a talk-show-like interview with a colleague." Rather than making himself the focus of organizational attention, as CEOs often do when they open up a standard Q&A session with employees, Liu places the focus of each interview on an individual who works at the departmental front lines. "David will sit down with a designer and just shoot the breeze: 'Where did you grow up? Where did you go to school? What's been your favorite part of your job here? What's been the worst part of your job?'" says Laura Cave, who formerly helped manage communication at the company. Other interview subjects have included a customer-service representative, a project manager, and a systems engineer.

The practice of chatting with employees in this fashion provides them with a valuable sense of recognition. But it can also have a notable impact on how a leader sees his or her company. In one instance, Liu says, an employee interview helped shine a light on an area about which he had previously been in the dark. "I asked one of the customer-service folks, 'What thing that has happened in the last year did you take the most pride in?' She talked about dealing with a very challenging client call, and how she was able to rectify a very complex situation and to make the client happy," he recalls. "And I was happy to hear that. But I began to question how that situation had ever come about. When we started pulling the thread, we were able to track down an enormous issue that was creating problems for our clients. The genesis of the hunt for that issue came from that one interview."

Give It Up

For company executives, letting employees join the fray of organizational conversation means letting go—letting go of the eminently understandable impulse to monitor and restrict what people say on company-sponsored communication channels. The advent of social media raises a particular challenge for leaders: Should they seek to impose rules on a medium that appears to be as unruly as it is powerful? But there, too, inclusive leadership requires a willingness to give up the need for control, together with a faith in employees' ability to control themselves.

When EMC Corporation launched its EMC|One internal social network, its top leaders had to decide whether to edit or censor the content that employees generated on the new platform. "There were concerns: 'What, are you nuts? People can express opinions without any filtering?' It took about a year to get to a certain level of confidence and trust," says Chuck Hollis, vice president and chief technology officer for global marketing. At that point, "the willies went away," he adds. "We started seeing that we could find value and that the world wouldn't end." He and his colleagues created a governance committee to oversee EMC|One and to consider adopting specific rules for its use. The mere existence of that committee allayed many people's worries, Hollis says, but ultimately "it wasn't really needed." In fact, the committee ended up meeting just twice.

"Policing this stuff cannot be done with old tools," argues Jack Mollen, executive vice president of human resources at EMC. In managing how employees contribute to EMC|One, company leaders emphasize "guiding principles and not policy," he says. "It comes back to the environment that a company creates." And the main guiding principle of EMC's online environment is that participants will police one another's conversational conduct. "The culture enforces rigor. Inappropriate behavior lasts about thirty seconds," Hollis says, referring to the set of norms that governs use of EMC|One. "It's a complete alternative to a command-and-control culture." Early on, it became apparent that users of the internal network who behaved unprofessionally would encounter a different kind of control. "Their fellow employees would tell them to tone it down or to be more objective. It wasn't management doing this. It was their peers," Mollen explains. (Significantly, employees can't participate in the network anonymously; their name automatically appears with any content they post.) About the launch of EMC|One, Mollen says: "People took it seriously. They acted like adults. It's adding great value for us and to them personally, and it's been a home run. We could never go backward."

PART IV

Intentionality

CHAPTER TEN

Open and Close

The Quest for Strategic Alignment

A RICH CONVERSATION BETWEEN two people is open, but it's not aimless. Although each person might appear to be "going with the flow," neither of them will remain engaged in the conversation for very long if they lack a coherent sense of where they hope it will lead, or of what they hope to get out of it. They do well, in other words, to have an agenda. This agenda doesn't need to be one that they have consciously formulated, and it doesn't need to be elaborate or extensive. What matters, however, is that people come to a conversation with some kind of goal in mind. Our preferred term for that state of mind is *intentionality*. The goals that motivate participants in a two-person conversation can be as various as the goals that people bring to any sort of endeavor. One participant might seek to instruct or to learn from the other, to understand or to entertain the other, to persuade or to humor the other.

In the absence of conversational intent, talk tends either to wander or to run into a blind alley. Where conversational intent does exist, it confers order and meaning on even the loosest and most digressive forms of interpersonal chatter. The quality of intentionality enriches conversation in one other way: It makes the effort of bringing a discussion to a close considerably easier. A good conversation, like any other good thing, eventually must come to an end. And having an end goal in mind, vague though it may be, enables people to find the right point at which to wrap up their conversation.

In an organizational context, intentionality is the element that gives shape, focus, and direction to what otherwise might be a scattered set of communication activities. It allows talk to segue into action, and it ensures that any such action will conform to a clear set of company objectives. Broadly speaking, conversational intentionality unfolds along two distinct but intersecting planes. First, there is *conversational strategy*, which pertains to the way that leaders envision and plan for the conduct of organizational communication over a given period. Second, there is *strategic conversation*—the process by which leaders develop communication practices that help to align their company and their people to the contours of a specific business strategy. We cite conversational strategy first because we'll be discussing that topic first in the sections below. Even so, the first step to take in pursuing conversational intentionality is to clarify a company's external strategy.

Organizational conversation doesn't exist for its own sake, after all. The main point of fostering dialogue within a company is to improve its internal and external performance. Leaders, therefore, must take steps to orient that flow of conversation to an agenda that supports the operational and competitive goals of their organization. The items on this agenda should address big questions that strike at the core of what drives a company: What business are we in? What challenges and opportunities do we confront in the marketplace? Where will our company be one year from now, five years from now, and ten years from now? Exploring such an agenda with internal stakeholders is no less critical than exploring it with any other stakeholder group. "These days, if you're running a large company, your messages have to be very consistent across different constituencies," says Anne Mulcahy, former CEO and chairwoman of Xerox. "It's really important that people understand where the company is headed and why they should believe in it—whether they're a customer, whether they're a shareholder, or whether they're an employee."

Along a couple of key dimensions, this final element in our model of conversation-based leadership differs from the three elements that we set forth earlier. Intimacy, interactivity, and inclusion all help to infuse an organization with energy. They are, in effect, sources of fuel that leaders can use to motivate employees and to unleash a spirit of innovation. But intentionality is what gives an organization the vital sensation of movement toward a specific destination. It's also what gives people in an organization the ability to translate conversational activity into operational activity: Beyond the up-and-down, back-and-forth, give-and-take work of opening up a conversation, there is the indispensable task of *closing the loop*—of making sure that strategically relevant action ensues from the push and pull of discussion and debate. By providing employees with a focused view of where their company is going, intentionality enables them to achieve closure amid an ongoing stream of utterances and interactions.

As we noted previously, senior leaders can't exert nearly as much control over employee communication as they did in an earlier era. Yet a loss of control doesn't entail a loss of responsibility: Managers still need to guide organizational conversation toward results that align with organizational goals. In fact, the need for guidance of this kind has only intensified in recent years. As employees have gained more and more autonomy as content providers, leaders have come to put a higher premium on increasing the level of business acumen throughout their organization. If employees don't have a reasonably nuanced understanding of the strategic dynamics that affect their company, then the content that they create and the messages that they send will be out of alignment with the company's overall purpose and direction. To prevent misalignment, smart leaders today speak with employees—regularly, extensively, *intentionally*—about the strategic vision that lies behind executive decision-making. This trend reflects a long-term shift in the relationship between organizational communication and organizational strategy.

In an earlier era, a closed system of strategy formulation and strategic execution kept most employees "out of the loop" when it came to understanding the broad organizational aims that their work was meant to further. The managers of corporate communication either ignored the topic of strategy or dealt with it by means of assertion—by simply telling people that one strategy or another was in effect. The idea of informing employees about a change of strategic direction was, at best, an afterthought. Leaders sought to align employees to their strategic plans through practices that were mandate-driven and rule-based; their goal was to command assent. As a consequence, employees tended to think exclusively in terms of their own functional area, and they waited for information about their company as a whole to cascade toward them through layers of management.

These days, by contrast, a high degree of strategic intent colors both the form and the content of organizational communication. Smart leaders expect all or most employees to develop a measure of strategic awareness, and they design their interaction with employees accordingly. They convey strategic principles not by assertion, but through explanation—not just by telling people what the current strategy happens to be, but also by showing employees the logic that underlies it. To align employees to a strategic vision, leaders adopt practices that are directive but also flexible. Their goal is not to command assent, but to generate consent, and cultivating employee buy-in is their default mode of meeting that objective. (That buy-in approach replaces the lock-in approach that leaders used to follow.) In this model, the communication function provides crucial support to the strategy function; far from being an afterthought, communication becomes an element of strategic execution that requires careful forethought. As a result, employees of every rank gain a big-picture view of where their company stands and where it's going. In short, they become *conversant* in matters of organizational strategy.

"The focus of corporate communication has changed," says Diane Williams, vice president of human resources at Silicon Laboratories, a semiconductor company based in Austin, Texas. "Years ago, the focus really was on the employee newsletter. Now it's become very well thought-out, very structured, very strategic—a long way from the employee newsletter!" Silicon Laboratories employees about eight hundred people at several locations, and Williams and her colleagues aim to instill in them a detailed sense of the company's key priorities. "My job is to make sure that if I stop any employee in the hall, they can tell me the top three or four things that we as a company are trying to get done this year," she explains. "They need to understand why we do the things that we do, instead of saying, 'What a bunch of idiots! Why did they do that?' Or, 'I don't understand why we're spending money on this.' Or, 'Why am I working on this project?' They need to be able to map what they're doing to those overall goals."

Employees, indeed, now expect that kind of engagement with respect to top-level strategy. "There is a real, fundamental difference in society today," says communication consultant Jacqueline Taggart. "People are saying, 'We won't work with you for life just because you gave us our first job. We have to feel valued. We have to understand that what we do has a purpose.' It's all interrelated: It's about 'what we're trying to accomplish,' and 'what we expect of you,' and 'how what you do contributes to it,' and 'how you'll be rewarded for that.' Sure, a CFO gets a lot more business information than an entry-level person, but it's just a matter of degree." As a recruiter who specializes in working with communication professionals, Taggart has an obvious incentive to trumpet the contribution that those professionals make to a company. Yet she argues compellingly that communicating with employees has become a "strategic necessity" that senior executives, too, must take responsibility for: "If you want people to follow you into whatever market battle you're entering—and to be there through thick and thin—they have to believe in you, and they have to know why they're doing it, and they have to understand what their role is. And that only happens with communication."

Top leaders have come to recognize that it's their job not just to make strategy, but also to talk about strategy. "The primary purpose of internal communication is to make sure that everybody is on the same page—that everybody understands where we're going, why we're going there, and how we're going to get there," says Bruce Crair, former CEO of Local.com. In that regard, he adds, "there's no such thing as over-communication." Of particular concern to Crair is the need to place the efforts of individual employees into a broad organizational context. "I'm a big believer in goals," he explains. "In our company, everybody has goals, right down to our receptionist. We set those goals quarterly, we measure them quarterly, and we pay bonuses based on achievement of those goals. And in order for everybody to set goals properly, they have to understand what our strategy is." Although "not everybody will have the same goals," Crair says, company leaders must aim to "ensure that people are all heading in directions that are congruent and complementary." Framing organizational conversation in strategic terms carries an additional benefit, according to Crair: When employees hear a leader talk about what their company's strategy involves, they gain clarity about what it does *not* involve. "There are a lot of cool things that we could be doing, and some of them may even be profitable," he notes.

"But we're a small company; we can't afford to do everything. We need to make sure that people focus on the things that are most important, and that's what goals help us do."

For Scott Paul, CEO of Hoku Corporation, discussing matters of strategic importance is one facet of organizational conversation that he prefers not to delegate. "I consider it my job to maintain communication within the company so that everybody knows what our biggest challenges are, what our biggest opportunities are, and why we think our stock is moving up or why it's getting beaten up," he explains. More generally, Paul views employee communication as an endeavor that promotes closure as well as openness. "It's how we close the loop and how we get things done," he says. "It's making sure that people understand what the task is, what the strategy is, and how we define success with respect to that task or that strategy." Only by talking about how they "define success" can leaders keep their company—and the conversation within their company—on track and on target. "By and large, CEOs get it," says communication consultant Michael Croton. "They know that they need to be out and about in their organizations, enrolling people into a big picture." Thinking big and painting a picture are, as we'll see, key aspects of what it means to be intentional. What matters most, though, is being clear about where one wants a conversation to go.

Following a Plan

At first glance, the idea of having a strategic plan for organizational conversation might seem like a contradiction in terms. Isn't conversation, almost by definition, fluid and unpremeditated? Isn't spontaneity one of its principal charms, and isn't improvisation one of its most attractive features? The ever-changing, topsy-turvy nature of present-day business life, moreover, raises the suspicion that planning conversational activity very far ahead of time will leave you far behind the strategic curve. "There's no such thing as a communications plan today," says PR consultant Gary F. Grates. "By the time you write a plan for a communications opportunity—by the time you finish it and vet it—the opportunity has passed, because things are happening too fast. So it's not about the communications plan per se. It's about planning for communication constantly and consistently."

Yet just because it's foolhardy to create a set-in-stone plan doesn't mean that leaders can or should neglect the need to forge a conversational strategy. Grates himself, for example, lauds an initiative undertaken several years ago at General Motors. In that instance, company leaders plotted out a carefully structured course of action for interacting with employees. "They instituted standards for communications," he explains. "They created a *habit* of communications, an *expectation* for communications." Departing from what had been a more ad hoc style of organizational conversation, GM leaders adopted a regimen that included "four or five key common processes." Among those processes were a regular state-of-the-business meeting led by managers at each GM facility and a quarterly videoconference in which top executives and regional managers discuss the company's performance with employees. "Creating that line of sight between the marketplace, the business, and an individual's contribution—that's phenomenal. That's seeing the organization holistically," says Grates, who worked with GM leaders around the time of this initiative. Developing and maintaining a standard tempo for employee communication is one way to capture the benefits of planning, even in an environment where planning has become problematic.

To say it another way: Planning for organizational conversation is different from trying (usually in vain) to control it. Conversationally adept leaders allow for the unpredictable quality of open, two-way communication, but they also put in place structures and processes that help to channel the flow of organizational content so that it coheres with an intentionally devised pattern. For most such leaders, the task of thinking through the inputs of employee communication warrants just as much attention as the task of thinking through the business outcomes that they aim to achieve. "In my mind, you can't decouple your strategy from the where and when and how of your communications," says Nora Denzel, of Intuit. "The difference between a hallucination and a strategy is how many people can see it. So we try to reinforce our strategy early and often." With any new strategic initiative, she adds, "we have a really deliberate communications plan" that applies to the period "leading up to, during, and after" the initiative in question. An effective conversational strategy does more than simply convey information to employees, Denzel suggests. It becomes, in effect, a vehicle for executing corporate strategy. "The role of communication is to ensure that the business strategy is understood and supported," she says.

Formulating a cohesive communication plan for an organization is, inherently, an effort that entails some degree of centralization. But that effort can be more centralized or less so, depending on the strategic positioning of the organization. The PNC Financial Services Group, for instance, operates at one end of that spectrum. "We're highly integrated and highly centralized. Our messaging and all of our programs are driven from the core of the organization and then executed out into the regions," says Donna C. Peterman, executive vice president and chief communications officer. PNC, based in Pittsburgh, is the sixth-largest bank in the United States, yet it attained that status somewhat recently, following a series of acquisitions that took place over the past decade. As PNC has grown, its leaders have made a strategic push to unify the company internally. Peterman describes the challenge of bringing one especially big cohort of new employees up to organizational speed: "My focus, obviously, is on making sure that we integrate those folks as fast as possible into the PNC culture, the PNC values, the PNC way of doing business—and, at the same time, making sure that our legacy folks are marching in step with our corporate vision. So we're trying to create one company very quickly, and communication is one of the drivers of our integration success." Another of those drivers was One PNC, a $400 million initiative that the bank launched in 2005. "The basic purpose was to identify ways to become a much more efficient and effective organization," Peterman explains. "It was employee-led. There were a number of employee teams, and everybody could contribute ideas." Over the course of the initiative, PNC logged more than sixty-five hundred employee-generated ideas and implemented a great many of them. "We got rid of all these little business silos, and we moved to a more central type of organization," Peterman says.

To sustain their tightly integrated organization, PNC leaders have cultivated an acutely intentional model of organizational conversation. When Peterman arrived at the company, in 2004, she met with CEO Jim Rohr, who told her to develop a list of priorities for PNC's communication function. "I came back with about five items," Peterman recalls.

"One of them was an observation. I said, 'The department does not have an agenda. It's very good at responding to what people think they need, but it has no point of view on how it contributes to the company's success. And because it doesn't have a point of view, it doesn't have a game plan.' That's changed here, I think." Today, Peterman and her team generate an annual communication plan that summarizes achievements from the previous year, lays out objectives for the current year, and outlines messaging tactics for reaching various constituencies. In conjunction with that process, she works with Rohr and other executives to maintain a "corporate message platform" that serves as the basis for every phase of PNC's organizational conversation. Each year, PNC leaders also choose a broad theme and several key messages to help structure that platform. In 2009, for example, "Together Building a Great Company" was the annual theme, and "Challenging Environment, Significant Opportunity" was the first of several key messages. Everyone who creates organizational content at PNC takes his or her cue from this messaging platform. "In essence, we're saying, 'This is the way that we want you to convey who PNC is and how it does business,'" Peterman says.

Toward the opposite end of the planning spectrum is Manpower-Group, the international staffing-services company. Like PNC, ManpowerGroup has made internal alignment a major priority in recent years. Traditionally, the company had allowed managers a high level of autonomy—a policy that corresponded to the high variability of national and regional labor markets. "We didn't really need to operate with a global footprint, even though we were a global company, because we were serving very local communities," says Mara Swan, executive vice president of global strategy and talent. But many client companies have become less exclusively local in their operational scope, and ManpowerGroup has retooled its strategy to meet their needs. To support a strategy based on offering truly global solutions to customers, Swan and her colleagues have revamped the way that they talk with employees. "Communication has changed dramatically," she says. Broad-brush statements from the CEO about, say, financial results or corporate values are no longer sufficient; these days, ManpowerGroup must chart a conversational strategy aimed at "aligning people around a common purpose," Swan explains. All the same, shifting to a fully centralized structure hardly makes sense for an organization with operations in more than eighty countries. Therefore, instead of constructing an all-embracing *platform* of the kind used at PNC, leaders at ManpowerGroup have devised a relatively open *framework* that leaves ample discretion over messaging to people who work in its field offices.

"What we've done is focus our communications around what we call our strategic execution framework," Swan says. "It takes into account our long-term goals, our vision, our brand, and what we're trying to deliver to clients, and it really articulates what needs to be done, and why." A new framework emerges each year from a round of consultation that involves a broad swath of ManpowerGroup executives. Those leaders "cocreate" the framework, according to Swan—"It's a very interactive process," she says—and Swan then distills the results of their cocreation into a one-page memo that goes out to all ManpowerGroup employees. "Everybody in the company, all the way down to our staffing consultants, will see it," Swan notes. "I was just in Dubai and Shanghai and New Delhi, and everybody has it on their desk." That document sets forth organizational objectives at a global level, but regional leaders have the authority to adapt it into a framework that more specifically fits their market. "They're not being told what to do," Swan explains. "They're saying, 'Here's what we want to get done'" in the context of a global framework.

While the strategic execution framework used at ManpowerGroup is (obviously) a vehicle for planning corporate strategy, it effectively serves as a vehicle for planning organizational communication as well. It sets the terms of discussion for people throughout the company, providing them with common points of reference as they talk about ways to serve clients and to build business in a complex global environment. Swan and her colleagues use a framework-based approach not only to help employees get things done, but also to make sure that people say things right—right, that is, from the standpoint of the company's brand and messaging model. "Our communications has really been about establishing a common language, a common tone," Swan says. "No one has to approve people's communications. Instead, we provide frameworks for people so that they can operate independently." According to one "tone framework" statement that ManpowerGroup leaders have developed, for instance, employees should aim to be "human, contemporary, and purposeful" in any messaging work that they do for the company. At ManpowerGroup, a framework is what connects many diverse parts to an organizational whole, and it's what aligns the way that people communicate with the way that they pursue organizational goals. "We really think about the communication lever, and we apply it to strategic change and strategic execution," Swan says. "Communication, frankly, is just noise if it isn't done for a purpose."

Before leaders can follow a plan for organizational conversation, they need to create it. And before they create it, they do well to sound out the resources and the constraints, the opportunities and the challenges, that mark their organization's current array of communication practices. By conducting a communication audit, as that sounding-out process is typically called, leaders are able to develop a conversational strategy that matches the way that people in their organization think and act, the way that they work and create, the way that they talk and listen. "It's important to do an assessment up front, to understand what you're trying to achieve," says Peter Broderick, former vice president of corporate communications at Abt Associates, a research and technical-assistance firm based in Cambridge, Massachusetts. When Broderick joined Abt, in 2002, his first step upon arriving there was to undertake a wide-ranging audit of the activities, needs, and resources of the firm as they pertain to organizational communication. "I talked to about fifty people inside the company and asked them similar questions," he recalls. "I asked them what they thought of the company's communications vehicles, internal and external, what they thought were the obstacles to communication, and what they thought were the key issues to address. A lot of learning came out of that, and it formed the basis for developing a communications strategy."

Central to Broderick's audit was an analysis of the factors that distinguish Abt Associates as a company. Abt provides domain expertise and project management in fields such as economic development, public health, and social policy; although it's a for-profit enterprise, its clients consist mainly of governmental and nonprofit entities, including chiefly the U.S. Agency for International Development. It relies on a "highly credentialed workforce" with "a mix of multidisciplinary capabilities," Broderick explains, and among its 1,300-plus employees are large numbers of economists, health professionals, and other people with advanced degrees. "We're a professional-services firm," Broderick notes. "We are not unlike a law firm or a management-consulting firm."

Abt, in short, is an organization dedicated to knowledge work. For its leaders, therefore, a pivotal insight that emerged from the audit was that they must talk about matters of genuine interest to the knowledge workers whom they employ. Like other well-trained professionals, employees at Abt retain a much stronger affinity for their work and for their clients than they do for their firm, and they have scant patience for the sort of content that corporate communication has traditionally delivered. "It doesn't matter what else you do," Broderick argues. "If they don't think of you as sharing their commitment to projects—if they think of you as being all about business performance—then you'll never be on the same page as them, and they'll never really internalize anything that you communicate to them."

At the end of the audit process, Broderick devised a highly intentional plan for how Abt leaders would now interact with employees. They would, for example, break their habit of speaking primarily about financial metrics, regulatory compliance, and other matters unrelated to the real, client-facing work of the company. While they couldn't avoid those issues altogether, they could and did shift the firm's internal communication away from administrative topics and toward topics that engage its internal stakeholders. "We made a very specific strategic decision to focus much more of the company conversation on our project work, as opposed to talking to employees just about our business performance," Broderick says. As we'll see later in this chapter, he and his colleagues recalibrated "the company conversation" at Abt in ways that encompass external as well as internal aspects of organizational communication. Yet they couldn't move in that direction—they couldn't decide which kind of conversation to have with people both inside and outside their organization—until they had first plotted out a conversational agenda that took into account the kind of company that they lead.

Drawing a Picture

At King Arthur Flour, CEO Steve Voigt holds a town-hall meeting with employees every month, and he typically starts the event with a presentation on the company's recent financial performance. To that standard-issue CEO practice, he has added a couple of small yet notable twists.

To convey one key data point—cash from operations, as that figure relates to King Arthur Flour's all-important profit-sharing pool—he uses an image that plays upon an eminently appropriate baking metaphor. It shows an ordinary kitchen one-cup container, with hash marks at various levels and with filled-in colors that indicate how actual performance compares with the company's goal for a given period. In effect, the image functions like a classic United Way fund-raising thermometer. "You know: Is it half-full? Is it quarter-full? Is it getting close to the top? Is it overflowing?" says Sarah McGinley-Smith, director of corporate communications. "That's a lot more tangible than just looking at a cash-flow number."

When it comes to talking about King Arthur Flour's performance at a big-picture level, Voigt deploys another kind of picture. "It used to be that at town-hall meetings we'd put up the financials," McGinley-Smith recalls, "and if you were in the front of the room, you could wave your hand and people's eyeballs wouldn't move." Today, using iconic round yellow face images ("with either really happy faces, happy faces, sad faces, or really sad faces," McGinley-Smith explains), Voigt highlights critical financial metrics in an eyeball-grabbing way. These "smile charts," as Voigt and his team call them, signal where the company stands with respect to meeting its principal strategic objectives.

The leaders at King Arthur Flour have an especially strong incentive to sharpen employees' understanding of marketplace realities: It's an employee-owned company. Yet many other organizational leaders have come to value practices that give their people an evocative, wide-angle view of their company's competitive prospects. Consider the case of Jim Rogers. In 2002, when he was CEO and chairman of Cinergy, Rogers grew concerned that employees had lost sight of the company's overall strategic position amid a major restructuring effort that was then under way. Speeches and talking points, he knew, wouldn't be enough to bring Cinergy's forward path into proper focus. Nor would they be enough to clarify the obstacles that lay along that path. So he charged a team of Cinergy professionals with developing an alternative approach to internal strategic education. The result was a series of "image maps" (as people at Cinergy called them)—graphic renderings of the complex competitive environment that existed outside the company's own sphere of operations.

The first image map that Rogers and his team devised, for example, bore the legend "Cinergy and the Changing Energy Landscape." It depicted the company as a Jules Verne–style airship held aloft by a pair of hot-air balloons; each balloon represented one of Cinergy's two main business units. Dark clouds labeled "External Market Forces" loomed overhead, and gust-like forces called "Winds of Uncertainty" blew in the distance. Even as competing energy companies flew (or crashed!) all around, the good ship Cinergy was navigating toward a sun marked "Bright Future." That image, along with others in the series, produced a shared visual vocabulary that employees could use to discuss the link between their work and the competitive challenges that the company faced. About one such image, a Cinergy employee later said: "You know what? That map created meaning for my job. It's no longer a chart. I actually have a lot more meaning in what I do."[1]

Whether they do it through imagery, through charts and graphs, or through words, leaders who practice conversational intentionality strive to *draw a picture* for employees—to provide employees with an enlarged sense of what their organization aims to achieve, and of where they fit on the broad canvas of the organization's strategic environment. Such leaders strive, that is, to turn organizational conversation into strategic conversation. By making sure that people throughout a company are able to grasp its strengths and weaknesses, the risks that it confronts as well as the rewards that it seeks, these leaders also ensure that communication inside the company remains aligned with the objectives that it's pursuing externally. "You can't execute if people don't know where you're headed and don't know their role and don't have some kind of emotional connection to it," Nora Denzel argues. "That's the role of communication: How do you parse out your strategy?"

The picture that leaders draw for their workforce needn't take the form of an actual visual image. What matters is that they evoke and sustain a strategic vision. In that way, they help to keep employees' eyes on the prize, as the saying goes. At the same time, they keep organizational conversation from veering off-track. "We begin with the end in mind: What does it look like when we've won?" Denzel explains. "We paint a picture of what it will be like when we get to our goal. The more that people can see it, the sooner they will internalize it."

From 2008 to 2011, Denzel was in charge of a division at Intuit called Employee Management Solutions; it's a $400 million unit that provides online payroll services to employers. In that role, she spent a lot of time talking with her people about the strategic position of that division, both with respect to the corporation as a whole and with respect to the larger business ecosystem. Her intent in doing so was to instill a sense of context and a sense of mission in members of her team. "We always share our financial goals, and then connect the dots as to how we plan to achieve those results. That's the business lens," she says. "The other thing that we communicate is *why we exist*. We exist to make employers more efficient in the way that they hire, pay, and retain employees. There's a lot of communication around all of that: What does *efficient* mean? Who are these employers?"

The habit of putting big-picture issues at the top of the conversational agenda makes Intuit employees more efficient as well, according to Denzel. "It really enables people to make better decisions in their jobs," she says. "We just eliminate a lot of churn in the group. We don't have a lot of meetings where we say, 'Are we going left or are we going right? Are we going fast or are we going slow?' People in the group have a common language. They have common stories. And they get to work quickly." That high level of strategic alignment, moreover, depends crucially on leaders' willingness to explain—and employees' ability to understand—the motivation and the reasoning that underlie a given strategy. "Say that I'm the captain of a ship, and I say, 'Wipe off this table.' If you're just taking orders, then you're won't be able to exercise any judgment. But if you know that someone is going to perform an operation on the table, or that someone is going to eat on it, or that someone is going to finger-paint on it, you might approach your job differently," Denzel says. As she points out, the same principle applies to the vessel that she helps to command: "If every single person in our organization intimately understands the strategy and how they can contribute to it, then we can have a much more effective organization."

Intentionality, at its core, involves having clear reasons for doing what you do—clear reasons for deciding what you decide. Conversational intentionality, meanwhile, entails a commitment to explaining what those reasons are. Several years ago, leaders at the restaurant chain Ruby Tuesday instituted a policy that puts explanation at the forefront of organizational communication. "I spend about seventy percent of my time in our restaurants," says Kimberly Grant, executive vice president and chief operations officer. "I would be out in a restaurant, and we would have changed a recipe or changed a uniform standard, or whatever it might be, and people would bombard me with questions: 'Why did we do that? Who came up with that crazy idea?' And it occurred to me that we weren't sharing the business reasons for what we were doing." To correct that problem, she and her colleagues added a feature to a template that the company had previously developed for all of its messages to employees. Now, immediately after presenting the issue at hand ("the what," as Ruby Tuesday leaders call it), each message includes an item ("the why," in Ruby Tuesday parlance) that provides key background information. Company leaders have even created a special rubric for this feature; they call it simply "the Y?"

"Change is hard for everyone, but it's harder if people don't understand *why* you're changing," Grant says. "So we decided, as a leadership team, that we weren't going to do anything without explaining the why. Now, people may not agree with the why of a certain decision, but at least they understand our reasons for making it." Conversational intentionality, therefore, can reinforce conversational intimacy: It can help to close the knowledge gap that otherwise separates those who initiate a change initiative, for example, from those who implement change on the organizational front lines. "As a leader, you sometimes forget that when you make a decision, you're privy to a lot more information than your team is," Grant notes. "You're privy to research. You're privy to results. You're privy to lessons learned in the past." The use of a feature like "the Y?" makes employees privy to the same kind of information. It peels back the executive curtain, so to speak, thereby allowing top leaders not just to inform employees, but also to engage them.

At some companies, the push to engage employees in strategic conversation is largely external in focus. "We don't want employees just to be 'generally informed' about happenings across the company," says Andy Burtis, vice president of corporate marketing and communications at McKesson Corporation. "Ultimately, we would like to create a thirty-five-thousand-employee virtual sales force. We're trying to help employees become brand champions, or brand evangelists, for the company as a whole." The idea of recruiting employees to serve as brand champions outside their company is one that we discussed earlier; it is, we argued, a prime example of conversational inclusion. Yet the viability of that idea depends crucially on whether leaders approach it with intentionality—on whether they actively cultivate a high degree of strategic awareness among their people. At McKesson, Burtis and his colleagues aim to boost "the level of business literacy" throughout their organization. "How do we make sure that someone in accounts payable knows enough to be 'dangerous'?" Burtis says. "How do we make sure that someone in HR, someone in sales, someone in product management, or someone in the legal department has at least a baseline understanding of what we do, and why it matters, and what their role is in advancing that agenda?"

The agenda that McKesson leaders seek to advance involves expanding their company's reach within the health-care services market. McKesson handles the distribution of medical and pharmaceutical supplies to hospital and pharmacy customers, for instance, and its core strategy is to broaden the range of solutions that it provides both to those customers and to new customer groups. "If that person in accounts payable happens to be at a backyard barbecue with a neighbor who happens to be a physician, we want that person to know enough about what we offer to physician practices that he or she can engage in a meaningful conversation about it," Burtis explains. To prepare employees for encounters of that kind, he and his team look for ways to provide "McKesson 101" training (as he calls it) in how the company serves various market segments.

In their conduct of organizational conversation, Burtis and his fellow executives also work to ensure that employees never lose sight of a "golden thread" (to use his term) that ideally runs through all forms of communication at McKesson. People throughout the organization, he argues, should be able to "see that everything that they read, whether it's from the community-affairs group or from the sales group, is tied to our broader mission as a company." Leaders such as Burtis might use different metaphors to describe their efforts—teaching a course, pulling a thread, drawing a picture—but in each case, their focus on organizational alignment remains vividly apparent.

One way to help employees see the big picture that captures their company's governing strategy is to let them take part in drawing it. In that spirit, the leadership team at Infosys has taken to including a broad range of employees in the company's annual strategy-development process. "Ideas can come from anywhere," says Kris Gopalkrishnan, cofounder and executive co-chairman. "It's not only top leaders who have ideas, right? We try to get as many ideas as possible before we narrow them down." Thus, in late 2009, as Infosys leaders began to build an organizational strategy for the 2011 fiscal year, they invited people at every rank and from every division of the company to join that undertaking. In particular, they asked employees to submit ideas on "the significant transformational trends that we see affecting our customers," Gopalkrishnan explains. Using the ideas that employees put forth, strategic planners at Infosys came up with a list of seventeen trends, ranging from the growth of emerging markets to the increasing emphasis on environmental sustainability. The planners then created a series of online forums where employees could contribute further ideas on how to match each trend with various solutions that the company could offer to customers. "We used technology and social networks to increase participation," Gopalkrishnan says. "That's how we got bottom-up feedback from the company."

Here again, the practice of inclusion amplifies the practice of intentionality. When employees help to design the strategic framework of their organization, they become more comfortable with that framework and more adept at operating within it. "If they're part of the discussion—part of the strategy-setting process—there's a lot more ownership, and there's a lot more awareness. It creates excitement within the company," Gopalkrishnan says. By and large, strategic planning at Infosys remains an inherently leader-driven process. Nonetheless, it has become a *conversational* process, and employees play an integral role in it. "They might not fully appreciate everything about our strategy, or they understand it only in the context in which they work," Gopalkrishnan notes. "But we do communicate it across the company, and they can leverage what is relevant to them."

Telling One Story

Organizational conversation, to the extent that it's truly strategic, guides its participants toward a shared, unified view of the organization that is the subject of conversational activity. On one level, to be sure, it will always be multifaceted and multidirectional, multifocal and multivocal—a buzzing cacophony of complaints and conjectures, of ideas and insights. It will be loose, freewheeling, open-ended. Yet, on another level, it will recognize and promote a singleness of purpose. It will reflect a fundamental, defining feature of all organizations, which is that they must be *organized:* They must display a strong sense of organic integrity, and their constituent parts must move into alignment with their whole. Consequently, the force of conversational intentionality must complement the forces that make organizational conversation spirited and spontaneous. Out of the many voices that make up that conversation, one vision must emerge. Or, to put it differently, one *story* must emerge. Toward that end, effective leaders create an environment in which employees come to see themselves as figures within a common narrative, and thus as members of a common enterprise.

The story of Abt Associates, which we introduced earlier, illustrates one way that leaders can build their communication efforts around a central organizing principle. Peter Broderick, who oversaw communication at Abt from 2002 to 2010, uses a term that neatly captures the notion of telling a single organizational story. Beyond the many phases and facets of organizational conversation—beyond the ebb and flow of internal and external discussion—there is *"the* company conversation," as he calls it. There is, in other words, an overall pattern of communication that both reveals and influences how people perceive that organization. Broderick connects this idea of a unitary company conversation to the idea of a company brand. "A good way to think about branding," he says, "is that it's the ongoing conversation that we have with our stakeholders." The people inside Abt, he adds, rank high among its stakeholder groups: "Employees are critical. If you lose them, it will cost money to replace them. And if they're not motivated, we can't be successful." It is employees, moreover, who create and sustain the culture of a company. "We can't have a successful branding effort that's at odds with the dominant culture," Broderick argues. "The culture has to be able to deliver the brand promise."

Broderick, upon completing his in-depth communication audit of Abt, concluded that the firm needed to build its company conversation around two themes: first, the research and technical-assistance projects that it undertakes on behalf of clients; and second, the professionals who take responsibility for those projects. "The dominant logic of our culture is that mission-driven project work is the essence of the company," he says. And it's Abt employees who make that work both viable and marketable. "People are our product," Broderick notes. "In my interviews, I asked staff members, 'Why do people choose to do business with us, as opposed to someone else?' And it's always about people and relationships. It's the people we put in proposals that win or lose business." The implications of that insight are simple, yet also profound and wide-ranging. "That cascades down to other kinds of messages: Our people make a difference. Their work makes a difference. They bring multidisciplinary expertise to a problem. They manage complex problems worldwide," Broderick says.

Guided by these findings, Broderick and his colleagues revamped their company's Web presence. Both on Abt's external site and on its intranet, they moved to showcase the company's project work and its professional talent. On the public site, for instance, a visitor today can scan story headlines under labels such as Recent Results and New Projects. They will also see, at the top of the page, a series of rotating portrait photos of Abt professionals. "We tried to make heroes of the people on our staff," Broderick says of the way that he and his team designed the new client-facing site. The updated intranet site, similarly, features photos of Abt employees. Making people and their projects "the driving force" of the company's online branding "really resonated with staff," Broderick says. "People love this. They love to have their work profiled and highlighted. One of the things that I noticed when I got here is how much they love to talk about their work." Externally, too, there were reverberations from the new approach to organizational conversation. "This whole idea of *making a difference*—we boil that down into a recruitment communications program," Broderick explains. "So it all starts to hang together."

Ultimately, for any organization, there is only one strategic conversation. As Broderick and other company leaders discovered, the conversation that sustains the Abt Associates brand and the conversation that takes place within Abt are fundamentally inseparable. What animates both sides of that conversation, furthermore, are the passions that animate Abt employees. "People don't come to Abt Associates to make a million dollars, or because we are a hot growth company like Google," Broderick says. "People come here because they want to pursue work in their field, and that's what they care about. That drove the whole communications strategy. It was so overpowering for me. Until we moved the company conversation around that principle, it didn't matter what else we did."

Recalibrating a company's entire communication strategy isn't always necessary. Some leaders, in order to align employees to a unified organizational vision, focus on developing carefully structured conversational practices. In 2010, for example, executives at Juniper Networks undertook an elaborate initiative—called the Next Generation Leadership Agenda—to talk with employees about the past, present, and future trajectory of their company. Thirty senior leaders, working in teams of three, traveled to Juniper sites all around the world and conducted a total of seventy-two hour-long sessions; through those sessions, they were able to speak with most of the company's seventy-five hundred people. "The agenda started with our legacy in terms of the problems that we were trying to solve when we first came together as a company," says Steven Rice, one of those thirty executives (he's in charge of human resources at Juniper). "From this foundation, we built and shared a storyline that focused on our current agenda in the marketplace, and on the connections between the voice of our customers and our brand identity." During each session, Juniper leaders collaborated with employees "to connect the dots between each of these components," Rice explains. "It was energizing to be in the room."

The mode in which Juniper leaders approached these agenda-setting discussions was rigorously intentional in its own right. "We wanted to have no more than a hundred employees in a session, if possible. We wanted to keep it as intimate as we could," Rice says. "We had scripts, and we had to lean into this body of work in a very thoughtful way. We couldn't wing it." To gauge the return on this investment in strategic alignment, Rice and his colleagues look to the results of Juniper's annual employee survey. "Scores have risen," he says, on questions that cover "the level of understanding of the vision and mission of the company." In one recent survey, he notes, the proportion of employees who indicate that they clearly see "the connection between the vision of the company and what they do" topped 87 percent.

For leaders at the oil company Enerchem International, strategic alignment in recent years has been partly a matter of linguistic alignment—or, to be precise, a matter of linguistic *re*alignment. A major business-model change, initiated in 2009, resulted in the need to find new language to tell a new organizational story. Previously, Enerchem was "what we would call a manufacturing company," says its president and CEO at the time, Ken Bagan. (He served in that role from 2008 to 2011.) Its primary aim was to sell the fixed throughput of Enerchem-owned petroleum refineries. Today, by contrast, Enerchem leaders position their organization as "a marketing company" that sells products from multiple sources. "The market creates our opportunity," Bagan explains. "When we reach refinery capacity, we'll look to other refiners and resell their goods into our market. We're much more about moving volumes now. As a result, our volumes are tremendously larger than they were two years ago." To orient employees to that shift in strategy, company leaders worked to shift the way that people talk about Enerchem and its business. "The first thing that we had to communicate was a different paradigm," Bagan says. "We had to use words that people weren't familiar with. There were probably a dozen new words in the lexicon that we started to use." Where employees used to say "sales," for instance, they now learned to say "marketing." Where they once spoke of providing "service," they now began to speak of generating "volume."

Words, of course, are the very stuff of conversation. Leaders who aspire to bring intentionality to their company conversation, therefore, will handle those essential building blocks with care. "The words that you use change the understanding. Then, once the understanding changes, the culture changes," Bagan argues. And yet, while making sure that people throughout an organization all "speak the same language" is necessary, it's hardly sufficient. Equally important is making sure that people embed that shared language within a fully developed structure of shared meaning. "What I seek is an understanding, from the top to the bottom of the organization, of what the company's objectives are," Bagan says. For Scott Huennekens, president and CEO of Volcano Corporation, sharing starts with owning. "You should be able to ask anyone here what our strategy is. You should be able to ask anyone what our key success factors are," he says. "Everybody here can rattle off what those things are. It's very important not only that everybody know them, but that they *own* them."

One crucial way that Huennekens and his team strive to generate a feeling of ownership is by telling stories. Volcano is a medical-device maker whose products help doctors to perform invasive heart surgery, and whenever one of those products reaches a key turning point in its development—a regulatory approval, a marketing launch—company leaders hurry to bring that event to life for employees. Of particular interest to everyone at Volcano are "first in man" studies in which surgeons use a Volcano device on a human subject for the first time. Such procedures "are the culmination of a lot of people's work," Huennekens notes. For that reason, he and his colleagues move swiftly to share news about them. "We send updates about those studies via e-mail, with pictures from the field. It's not a flat communication. We go deeper, explaining the case and the patient, how the device was used, and how it made a difference," he says. The value that employees gain from receiving those reports is considerable, he suggests: "It gives them incredible psychic returns. They all go home and tell their kids about it. They tell their family about the cool stuff that their company is doing." For the company, meanwhile, this practice has the benefit of bolstering "the whole culture in terms of getting things done and working together in teams," Huennekens says. "It's kind of 'back to the campfire': You reinforce your culture through the stories that you tell."

Over and above the tales of incremental triumph that Volcano leaders recount to their people, however, there is an extended storyline that they use to keep strategic conversation on track within their company— a broad narrative arc that establishes Volcano as an entity that operates intentionally across time. At a long-term level, Huennekens and his team construe that story as one that unfolds in a series of three-year-long phases. A start-up phase came first, followed by a pre-public phase, and then by a phase that centered on the process of becoming a public company. Next came the current phase, in which the company has focused on expanding into multiple divisions and across multiple global markets. "People understand that we're in this fourth phase," Huennekens observes. "They'll say, 'I joined the company in the second phase.' So they have a context for where we are and what we want to accomplish over the next three years." At a relatively short-term level, he and his colleagues articulate the Volcano story by reference to key success factors that they set forth on a quarter-by-quarter basis. And in between, over the intermediate time frame of one year, they build the company story around a single, overarching strategic theme.

In 2010, the theme at Volcano was *Build and Explore*. As Huennekens explains, the *build* part referred to the need to construct enough institutional infrastructure (in the form of "people, processes, control systems") to enable rapid growth, while the *explore* part indicated a need to preserve the qualities ("the innovation, the energy, and the creativity") that drove the company's initial success. "If we do those two things, then we have sustainability, profitability, scalability," he says. Leaders at Volcano treat their annual theme as a means of providing continuity—narrative continuity, and hence strategic continuity—across various forms of organizational conversation. "It's reinforced throughout the year at all of our company meetings and in other communications," Huennekens says. "I sign all of my e-mails 'Build and Explore.' It becomes part of the PowerPoint template that we use for all of our presentations." There's even a logo that's designed to capture key thematic messages for the year, he notes: "The *x* in *Explore* is basically an individual holding the globe. That's intended to be *you*, the employee: You have a responsibility. You're part of the global Volcano organization."

By developing an organizational story that proceeds on multiple levels and within multiple time frames, Volcano leaders run the risk that they'll promote confusion rather than alignment among their employees. But Huennekens and his team appreciate the need to follow a conversational strategy that clearly and deliberately supports the strategic conversation at their company, and they emphasize the way that each part of the Volcano story meshes with every other part. "It's all layered," Huennekens explains—from the latest "first in man" achievement to this quarter's key success factors, from this year's theme to the current longer-term phase. "You add up four quarters, you have a year. You add up three years, you have a phase. And everybody understands how that whole rhythm works," he says.

EACH ORGANIZATION DEVELOPS its own path toward strategic alignment and its own way to talk about staying on that path. People in a small, growing company can bind their culture and coordinate their operations in part by telling stories and practicing rituals that arise organically from within. A company of great size or one that is undergoing great change, however, must pursue intentionality by following a different kind of route. At Kingfisher PLC, a global retail holding company, leaders are trying to transform a group of historically discrete business units into "one team" (to use their term). As we will observe in the next chapter, those leaders present an ambitious model for how to open a conversation and then bring it to a productive close.

CHAPTER ELEVEN

Walking the Talk

Kingfisher PLC

PICTURE A MARKETPLACE, an actual physical space where vendors can set up shop and showcase their products, and where customers can stroll from storefront to storefront, hoping to spot a choice find. This market, located in a city on the Mediterranean Sea, has more than a little in common with the classic bazaar of Mediterranean and Middle Eastern legend. It's a noisy, compact area in which a scene of apparent chaos, marked by round after round of frenzied chatter, serves to conceal the orderly process by which eager sellers encounter willing buyers. Instead of wearing flowing robes of the kind that you might see in a traditional souk, however, the buyers and sellers who populate this bazaar wear sport coats and collared shirts, blouses and dresses, and other staples of the international business-casual style. And instead of haggling over the sale of carpets and cooking pots, they're keeping up a brisk trade in ideas—business ideas, to be precise, ideas that just might help them to run their company with improved efficiency or higher profitability. As it happens, the people who have come together to enact this ancient drama of buying and selling are in the *business* of buying and selling. They are retail executives, men and women who head up various operating units of Kingfisher PLC, the world's third-largest chain of home-improvement stores.

In the summer of 2010, more than two hundred senior leaders from Kingfisher came to a hotel conference center in Barcelona to attend the company's One Team Leaders Meeting. Midway through the three-day event, they gathered in an open area under the Mediterranean sun and took part in a session that conference organizers called Share at the Marketplace. Participants in the Marketplace (to borrow a shorthand term that organizers used for the session) fell into one of three categories. The top executives who form the group executive committee at Kingfisher acted as facilitators; they ambled through the market, providing words of encouragement and making friendly observations. A second set of participants, called "suppliers," were in effect purveyors of ideas. They each donned a bright-blue shopkeeper's apron, stood at one of twenty-two stalls in the Marketplace area, and presented a spiel about a business practice that people in their part of the Kingfisher organization had developed. The largest set of participants consisted of "buyers" who traveled from one stall to the next, examining the merchandise on offer and occasionally—yes—purchasing one of the ideas for sale. Using a special checkbook that conference organizers had issued to them, buyers could draft up to five checks in "payment" for suppliers' wares. Such transactions had no tangible meaning beyond the confines of the ninety-minute-long Marketplace session, but they conveyed a real message to suppliers. "It was recognition: 'What you're telling me is impressive, so I'm giving you a check,'" says Benedikt Benenati, director of group internal communication.

More to the point, this exercise in conceptual retailing gave suppliers and buyers alike a new way to talk shop with each other—a new way to trade the kind of business intelligence that enables people in organizations not only to get better at what they do, but also to align what they do with organizational objectives. Across much of the business world, the customary term for this process is *sharing best practices*. Yet Kingfisher leaders, starting with group CEO Ian Cheshire, shy away from that term. "In a lot of Latin countries, the idea of 'best' practice sounds very Anglo-Saxon: 'There is one way of doing it, and we will impose it.' Whereas the Latin approach is to say, 'Let's discover this. Let's make connections. Let's understand what people are doing.' And the human dynamic of that approach is much more positive, because you're doing something, as opposed to having something done unto you," Cheshire argues. While Kingfisher has a major presence in the United Kingdom and maintains its group headquarters in London, it also has operating units in Latin markets such as France and Spain (as it does in other parts of Europe, and beyond). Indeed, a principal goal of the Barcelona meeting was to strengthen the cultural and practical ties that connect one unit to another. "A guy running a store in France, say, might not know what people in the U.K. have done in the area of self-checkout technology, or in the way of controlling stock," Cheshire says. "These are all things that we face in daily retail life, and instead of broadcasting *best* practices, we're saying, 'There is a lot of *good* practice out there that may be more or less applicable in your area, and you can discover it in this shopping mode.' That's incredibly powerful."

The Marketplace session played upon the intuitive link between commerce and conversation—between the exchange of goods or services and the exchange of ideas. Every commercial trade begins with an act of communication between a seller and a buyer: The seller conveys information about what's for sale; the buyer asks questions about this product or that service. Many transactions then proceed to the chatty, back-and-forth process known as negotiation. Finally, just as any productive conversation entails an effort to close the loop on the topic of discussion, so any commercial endeavor has as its goal the closing of a sale. For people at Kingfisher, as we've noted, that connection between selling (or buying) merchandise and providing (or gathering) information runs deep. "Since we're retailers, going shopping for good ideas is naturally in our DNA," Cheshire says.

Nonetheless, as Kingfisher leaders were planning a retail-inspired experience for attendees of the Barcelona conference, they had cause for worry. The same quality that drew them to the idea of hosting the Marketplace session—its fluid and unscripted nature—raised the possibility that it would be a flop. "The people are the actors," Benenati says of the format that he and his colleagues developed for the event. "It's like a theater performance. Until the very end, you don't know if it will work or not." That said, once the show began, there were early signs that it would be a hit: "You could feel the energy, and people started really enjoying it," Benenati says. "People are keen to talk. It's just a matter of creating the right environment, and giving them permission to do it."

Open for Business

Intimate in spirit, interactive in style, and inclusive in structure, the Marketplace had the effect of opening up lines of communication between people who hailed from disparate quarters of the Kingfisher organization. Changing "the methodology or the technology of communication," Cheshire says, "changed the experience of sharing ideas." No longer did that process need to start with a summons from above—with, as he puts it, "me standing on a soapbox, saying, 'Will you please share that best practice?'" Instead, he and his team allowed conference attendees to take the lead in talking up what they had achieved in their part of the company. The essence of the Marketplace, Benenati notes, was "the peer-to-peer sharing of good practice in a completely informal, messy, and noisy environment." Enabling direct interaction between peers increases the likelihood that cross-organizational collaboration will become a matter of long-term habit, or so Kingfisher leaders believe. "If you get them to do it, it gets progressively more rooted," Cheshire argues.

The fact that the Marketplace was "noisy" and "messy, " Benenati argues, accounted for much of its power and much of its appeal. "Noise is a very important ingredient in communication," he says. "It's a paradox: During a plenary presentation, if the speaker says, 'Are there any questions?' nobody dares to ask a question in front of two hundred people. But if you put them in a noisy environment, people feel more comfortable. It's quite empowering." The messiness that characterized the event was evident not just in its bazaar-like aura, but also in its reliance on face-to-face talk—and in its avoidance of high-tech communication tools. Over time, Benenati suggests, the people who attended the conference will come to interact through media such as a company blog or an online networking platform. But they must "establish a human connection" up front and "test it physically," he says, before "that connection can continue on a more virtual basis." By way of explaining the outlook that governed the design of the Marketplace, Benenati offers a motto of sorts: "The real new medium is the human conversation."

Alongside this emphasis on informality, however, there was also a keen focus on intentionality. People at Kingfisher, after all, hardly leave much to chance whenever they create a retail experience for their home-improvement customers. Likewise, a considerable amount of advance planning and ambitious thinking—a big commitment to *conversational strategy*, as we would say—lay behind the creation of the Marketplace. Benenati, in close consultation with Cheshire, designed the event with two goals in mind: to bring buyers and sellers together in an efficient and useful manner, and to give participants ample scope for free and open interaction. To support the first of those aims, meeting organizers provided buyers with a booklet that contained brief summaries of the practices that were figuratively available at each supplier's stall. The booklet was "like an à la carte menu," Benenati says. "Everybody could cherry-pick who they wanted to visit." To support the second aim, meanwhile, he and his team worked to develop an atmosphere of casual intimacy that would encourage participants to speak without inhibition. In that spirit, Cheshire and other members of the group executive committee put on floppy straw hats that served to neutralize the air of top-down command that they might otherwise carry. They wore these "ridiculous hats," Benenati explains, "to show everybody that they were not there to judge their colleagues. They were there to play the role of sponsor and facilitator."

Yet, while the Marketplace exemplified the pursuit of conversational strategy, it also signaled a broader investment by Kingfisher leaders in promoting *strategic conversation*. Opening up a new mode of employee communication is, for them, only part of the conversational equation. The other part, and ultimately the more important part, involves closing the loop organizationally. It involves tightening the process by which the various units of Kingfisher coordinate their operations with one another, and by which they integrate those operations into an overarching corporate strategy. The entire One Team Leaders Meeting, in fact, grew out of an ongoing effort by Cheshire and his colleagues to improve strategic alignment by means of organizational conversation. Through the prism of that event—as we will demonstrate below—it's possible to observe the practice of conversational intentionality in a particularly robust form.

Journey to the Center of a Company

The One Team Leaders Meeting occurred at a crucial moment in the history of Kingfisher. The company had its origins in a conglomerate that encompassed a variety of retail businesses, including the Woolworth drugstore chain, a beauty-supply chain, and a small home-improvement retailer called B&Q. In the late 1990s, Kingfisher began to acquire other companies in the home-improvement sector, and in 2000 its leaders resolved to consolidate its operations around that sector alone. By 2003, it had sold off all unrelated businesses, and by the end of the decade, it was the number one home-improvement retailer in Europe and Asia (world-wide, it trailed only The Home Depot and Lowe's), with more than £10 billion ($16 billion) in annual revenue. It employed nearly eighty thousand people in more than eight hundred stores, and it operated in eight countries. Yet it remained a consortium of separately run, sepa-rately branded units. There was B&Q, for example, a chain with stores in the United Kingdom and Ireland (and with a foothold in China), and there was Castorama, which operates stores in France, Poland, and Russia. In addition, there were units with responsibility for outlets in Spain and Turkey. Each unit had its own culture, its own product line, its own set of supplier and customer relationships. Starting in 2008, however, Kingfisher leaders moved to change that situation. That year, a new executive team came on board, with Cheshire at the helm and with a mandate not only to make Kingfisher grow, but to make it grow under the auspices of a unified strategic vision.

"We've had a very decentralized, holding-company-type model, which has shifted since I've been CEO," Cheshire explains. "We're on a journey toward becoming a business that will be far more integrated, and run as a single retail entity." That journey will unfold over the course of five to ten years, he says, and ideally it will culminate in the creation of "a truly international retailer that unlocks the value of being a £10 billion business, as opposed to a series of small pockets of uncon-nected volume." Cheshire and his team, in short, aim to build a strategic core within an institution where no such organizing factor has previ-ously existed. Ultimately, Benenati explains, their goal is to transform Kingfisher into "the world's leading local home-improvement retailer."

Kingfisher leaders recognize that they must manage a fundamental tension that lies at the crux of their ambitious strategy. "The real chal-lenge for us," Cheshire says, "is to unlock the potential in two attributes that we have—our scale and our diversity." On the one hand, the King-fisher group will clearly benefit from the efficiencies that come with align-ing an entire transcontinental organization with a set of shared systems, shared products, and shared best practices. On the other hand, the group already benefits from the capacity of its country-level business units to respond adaptively and at least somewhat autonomously to the specific needs of their home markets. "About eighty percent of our customers are within twenty minutes of our nearest store," Cheshire notes. "We cannot get too cookie-cutter about this. We have to address this paradox of being global and yet local at the same time." To accommodate both sides of that paradox, he and his colleagues formulated the idea that Kingfisher and its people are *one team*. It's an idea that incorporates a sense of unity and centralization, while also evoking the way that the parts of a whole can remain distinct (much as members of a team can retain separate identities). Company leaders, according to Benenati, adopted One Team as an official term in order to "highlight that we are one group, made of different individual operating companies, and that we are also one team of people who share the same kind of global citizenship."

In practical terms, the current strategy depends upon an effort that Cheshire calls "the One Team rewiring of our business." Since the legacy condition of Kingfisher is one of organizational diversity, much of that effort focuses on implementing shared systems that leverage economies of scale. In one case—a move to develop a single e-commerce platform for all operating units—the "rewiring" process has been quite literal. More notably, the company has begun to adopt a common-sourcing system whereby stores all across the Kingfisher group will stock more and more of the same products, and more and more of those products will originate in the group's centralized sourcing operation. As of 2010, only about 5 percent of the items sold through Kingfisher outlets fell into the category of common products that come from a common supplier. (The term *common*, in this context, refers to any resource that multiple Kingfisher brands share.) "We are, effectively, not using the benefit of our scale at all," Cheshire says. He and his colleagues aim, in the coming years, to increase that common-product share to 50 percent. To further that goal, Kingfisher in 2011 started to roll out a series of own-label brands (the Colours line of home decor items, the Blooma line of garden products, and so on) that will eventually form the core of its in-store merchandise selection.

An effort of this magnitude won't succeed by mere executive fiat, as Kingfisher executives well know. Aligning each unit of the company around a shared product line will require the active cooperation of unit-level employees. "A lot of people aren't really aware that they belong to a group of eighty thousand people," Cheshire notes. "They look at the world through the lens of their own op co [operating company]." To counter employees' natural bent toward parochialism—to raise their group consciousness, as it were—the leaders of Kingfisher must rewire not just the company's systems, but also its culture. "We have to get people signed on to the idea that we are fundamentally one team," Cheshire says. The bid to gain that kind of buy-in from employees hinges on assuring them that the company can preserve the advantages of diversity even as it pursues the advantages of scale, that it can serve customers locally even as it sources products globally. "When you start from being very decentralized, any move that you make toward being more global feels like you're centralizing everything," Cheshire says. "What we want to get across is: No, we can get this balance right." The One Team vision thus puts a strong emphasis on fostering trust among employees, and Cheshire likens that quality of trust to a "sort of glue." Without it, he says, "nothing really can happen, because everyone will default to their previous operating style, which was completely independent." Building an integrated Kingfisher culture, he argues, "is absolutely core to strategy." It is also largely (if not absolutely) a matter of communication.

"Welding Job"

For the first year or more after becoming CEO, Cheshire concentrated on executing a recovery plan for Kingfisher. "Our priority was to get our debt paid off, to get our house in order," he recalls. Then he shifted his attention from turning things around to moving forward—to addressing the challenges and opportunities that would shape the company's longer-term strategic position. "It was clearer and clearer to me that the fundamental issue that we had to tackle was this: How do we weld together these disparate, decentralized businesses? And the more I thought about that welding job, the more obvious it was to me that it was all about communication," he says. To change the way that Kingfisher and its branded units compete in the marketplace, Cheshire and his fellow executives would need to change the way that its people talk (or don't talk) with one another. "We're in a phase of redefining exactly what we mean by 'internal communication.' It's part of trying to wire up the enterprise," he explains.

Hiring a new director of internal communication was a pivotal step in the "welding" project that Cheshire set in motion. "We had to demonstrate that we were doing something different from the old Kingfisher," he says. And in Benenati, who joined the company in early 2010, Cheshire found a different kind of communication professional. Yet Benenati, notwithstanding his official title, doesn't view himself as a communicator per se. "I see myself more as an architect, or an instigator, or a designer, or an enabler," he says. To that role (or set of roles), Benenati brings a wide range of experience. He served as a director of organizational development at the French food-products company Danone and as a knowledge manager at Marconi Communications. For two years, he worked at an Internet start-up that created digital communities, with the goal of helping businesspeople to connect with their customers. "I have a personal theory that there is one big issue," he says. "I've had many different job titles—leadership development, a bit of HR—but the real, fundamental topic that I've been focusing on over the last eighteen years is *connecting people*." Cheshire, similarly, describes Benenati's role at Kingfisher in a way that departs from the long-standing model of how leaders communicate with employees: "There is a very strong tendency for people to say, 'I've got to do some communication. Write me some internal communication. Go and do that stuff.' Instead of asking Benedikt to 'do the communication,' we're asking him to be—as he says—the architect, and to help *us* figure out how to do it."

True to his architectural role, Benenati began his tenure at Kingfisher by making a survey of the terrain on which any new structures of organizational conversation would arise. "I believe in storytelling as a management discipline," he says. "In the first weeks that I was here, I started gathering stories of people who had a problem and then solved that problem by connecting with colleagues from another store or another country. There were plenty of such stories, but people had never thought it was important to tell them." Those stories were "like gold in a mine," he says. One nugget that he unearthed, for instance, concerned a problem with managing energy use at a store in China. People at that store, by communicating with people based in the United Kingdom, had gathered information that resulted in a 7 percent reduction in the store's energy consumption. "I didn't start my career here by liaising with the IT department," Benenati recalls. "I started by making a lot of phone calls and looking for stories, so that people would realize that communication is good for business. And once they realized that, I was able to provide them with solutions to optimize and accelerate and multiply those connections."

Together, Cheshire and Benenati are remaking their company's entire approach to communicating with employees. "Historically, internal communication here has been (a) very country- or brand-specific and (b) very much in a command-and-control mode," Cheshire explains. As it turns out, changing the first of those qualities goes hand in hand with changing the second quality. To build what he calls a "transnational one-company ethos," he and his team are moving away from a reliance on one-way, top-down forms of communication. "Instead of being in broadcast mode—where we transmit a message from 'the great leader' at three minutes past two on a Friday—we're trying to create networks all around the business," he says. Kingfisher continues to deploy traditional media (newsletters, intranet sites) to convey basic company information. But it now supplements the use of those channels with practices that enable and encourage people to interact on their own with colleagues outside their business unit. The Marketplace session at the One Team Leaders Meeting, of course, offers a prime example of what lateral, network-based employee communication looks like.

"We're on a journey," Cheshire says, echoing the language that he uses to describe the company's shift in organizational strategy. "The point is to create real conversations. It's not to transmit stuff." That journey from transmission to conversation—from a broadcast model to a network model—involves a major restructuring of the roles that executives and others play in organizational communication. In a traditional leader-centric framework, Cheshire argues, "you don't actually tap into the talent of your people." By dispersing responsibility for carrying on a company-wide conversation to all eighty thousand of Kingfisher's employees, he and his colleagues aspire to bring fresh talent to the fore. "When you get a team going that really is talking amongst themselves, the energy levels are simply extraordinary," he says. "It very much starts with trust, with the belief that you will be listened to, the belief that conversation is worthwhile and that we encourage it. If people believe that, they bring so much more to the workplace than if they're just going through the motions."

Leadership still matters, however. Indeed, within the conversational architecture that Cheshire and Benenati have begun to build, active participation by leaders at all levels becomes indispensable. "It's all about managerial style," Benenati says. Too often, he contends, the existence of professional communication departments and advanced communication technologies provides "a kind of alibi for managers"—an excuse that lets them "delegate their role in giving purpose to their team." Frontline managers must instead function as what he calls "proximity communicators": They must communicate regularly with those who report to them and, more important, empower those direct reports to communicate with one another via cross-company networks. Such leadership is a critical prerequisite to aligning (or "wiring," or "welding") Kingfisher into the integrated group operation that Cheshire envisions. "What we're trying to do," he says, "is to structure processes in which people have to talk to their teams and engage with their teams. That's the heart of the matter, particularly in a retail business, which is so fundamentally about people."

Store of Value

The vision posited by Cheshire and Benenati, of a One Team company wired together by a certain kind of organizational conversation, is basically a wholesale idea. Conceived on a grand, group-level scale, that idea depends for its ultimate success on the ability of other Kingfisher leaders to retail it among the company's consumer-facing employees—to translate it into practices that make sense at a local level. Of necessity, the real work of organizational alignment will take place in country-based business units and in actual stores, and that work starts with measures to include employees more fully in the life of their store, in the fate of their brand, and in the future of Kingfisher as a whole. "We're trying to create engagement through better communication," Cheshire says. "We want to help people understand how they can contribute, how they can help us co-build this business." As he and his colleagues embarked on that effort, they could point to innovative and inclusive practices that were already under way in the frontline units of Kingfisher.

Take the example of Castoramoa, an intranet platform that serves the roughly twelve thousand people who work for the France-based Castorama unit. The name of the site plays upon *moi*, the French word for "me," and thus evokes the personal, customizable attributes of an online social network. In true social media fashion, Castoramoa goes beyond mere information delivery, enabling users to interact and collaborate with each other via blogging, discussion forums, and video capability. One feature allows employees to tag store products for inclusion in the chain's Do It Smart merchandising strategy. Most interestingly, perhaps, Castorama leaders used the platform to engage employees in developing a new look for the in-store uniform that staff members wear. "People were refining and debating over a whole series of options," Cheshire explains. "As a result, they are really proud of the uniform. They're attached to it, because they helped design it." For Kingfisher leaders, the popularity of that online design process—about 75 percent of Castorama employees took part in it—makes it a model that bears close attention. "It's a paradigm in terms of the mechanics of organizing a conversation," Cheshire says.

In Spain as in France, unit-level leaders are taking decisive steps to promote alignment by means of engagement. An initiative called Progression, launched in January 2009 by the Spanish division of the Brico Dépôt unit, stands out as a venture that holds high promise in the eyes of Kingfisher executives. Progression is an employee profit-sharing plan, but it goes beyond simply dispensing a certain number of euros to employees who meet a certain set of benchmarks. It embodies a "social model of how we want to work with our people," says Pascal Gil, deputy CEO of Brico Dépôt Spain, which employs nearly one thousand people in seventeen stores. Simply put, the Progression initiative yokes together a program of "hard" financial incentives and a "soft" commitment to open communication. "With this system, we share all the information, and we share the profits, too," says Albert Aranda, human resource officer for the Spanish division. Indeed, without the sharing of information, the policy of sharing profits would fail to meets its goals.

"We wanted to have one thousand CEOs in the company," Gil says, by way of explaining how he and his colleagues came to start Progression. The overriding goal behind the program, Aranda explains, is to "implicate" employees as deeply as possible in the operational and strategic realities of the place where they work: "We want to have stakeholders—people interested in the life of their store, people who know all the figures of the store, people who will take action to improve their store, people who will act like a manager of their store." By instilling a sense of ownership that is at once financial and attitudinal, leaders at Brico Dépôt Spain seek to widen the scope of what employees care about. Ideally, employees will be alert to developments not just in their section of a store, but in all parts of the store, and they will act on what they see. Consider the problem of inventory shrinkage, a category that includes (in particular) theft by employees. With a system like Progression in place, "people are more responsible and more involved in the management of their store," Gil argues. "If one of your colleagues in the store steals something, you'll say, 'What are you doing, guy? This is *my* money.'"

The core financial component of the Progression system is straightforward enough. "It's an obligation that our people feel and understand: If you want to get a bonus, you have to develop the profitability of the store," Gil says. Each quarter at each store, employees receive a share of a bonus pool that includes a certain portion (say, 3 percent) of the profits earned in that store over the preceding three months. In addition, that pool includes a portion (it might be as much as 50 percent) of the "progression"—that is, the amount by which store profits increased over the same quarter in the previous year. What truly sets Progression apart from other programs of its kind, though, is the organizational structure that Gil, Aranda, and their colleagues have built around it. For each store, there is a Progression committee with members drawn from people throughout the store, and with a president who comes from the middle or lower level of the store hierarchy. Significantly, the manager of the store doesn't sit on this committee. "We wanted to develop another power in the store," Gil explains. Empowering a group of salespeople, cashiers, and other rank-and-file employees to help administer the bonus program bolsters their sense of engagement, and it encourages other employees to engage in the program as well.

The Progression committee serves in effect as a parallel communication system, providing a stream of information about store performance that exists apart from the company's formal management hierarchy. "The communication of this system is down-to-up. It isn't up-to-down," Aranda says. Committee members gather financial data about their store, analyze the data with respect to relevant profit-sharing formulas, and present that information to their fellow employees at a monthly meeting. That meeting is the real cornerstone of the program. For a couple of hours every month, each store closes its doors so that committee members can set forth recent results—a breakdown of sales, costs, and profits—to the sixty-odd people who work there. Assembled employees also help the committee to set performance targets for the store and to develop an action plan to meet them. The monthly meeting, Gil notes, offers "a way to implicate everybody at the same moment" in a common understanding of the store's challenges and opportunities. "Progression is the best internal communication tool that we have invented," Aranda says. "We can talk about everything."

The Progression practice was among the ideas for sale at the Marketplace session in Barcelona, and it generated a lot of interest among "buyers" from other units of Kingfisher. "There is a whole stream of activity around the idea of employee alignment and ownership: How do we get people to behave as if they're owners of the business?" Cheshire says. "Progression is probably the nearest model that we've got" to a system that addresses that challenge. The next step, he adds, is to develop similar models for use elsewhere in the company: "We're now beginning to work with all of the businesses. We're saying to them, 'Take the principle—alignment, ownership, getting people engaged— and figure out how to tweak it to fit your local situation.'"

Design for Talking

The One Team Leaders Meeting, to be held in late June 2010, would bring together about 210 of the senior-most people in the Kingfisher organization—CEOs and other C-level executives from country-level branded units, regional directors, and the like. The purpose of the conference, as its title clearly indicates, was to align the company's crucially important unit-level leaders with the One Team vision that Cheshire and his group-level colleagues had begun to chart. "We're trying to involve them in the process of creating a strategy for the next five to ten years and to use that as a way to connect them," Cheshire said in advance of the conference. The event would thus constitute both a means to an end and an end in itself: It would further the long-term goal of building an integrated, transnational retail operation, and it would help to nurture cross-organizational relationships in the here and now. With its focus on reaching top-tier leaders, the meeting in Barcelona would be a key early step along the path toward organizational alignment. Later, according to Cheshire, he and his colleagues would "start building out from there to show our eighty thousand people that we are really capable of operating as one team." Another aim of the conference was to reinforce the message that pursuing efficiencies of scale wouldn't entail a serious erosion of unit-level diversity. Using an analogy from the world of soccer (football) competition, Cheshire spoke of working to convince attendees that "they can play for their local team, and they can also play for the national or international side."

Achieving the goals that Cheshire set for the conference required creative and careful planning. Toward that end, he asked Benenati to take responsibility for designing the event. "Ian Cheshire said, 'I want to create the right conditions. So, Benedikt, you have a blank piece of paper.' He put complete trust in me," Benenati recalls. The upshot of Benenati's design efforts was an ambitious feat of conversational strategy—a lineup of roughly fifteen sessions, or "experiences" (to use his term), whose collective purpose was to recalibrate how people throughout Kingfisher talk with one another. Benenati went so far as to classify each of those experiences according to the mode of communication that it would follow. On one conference-planning document, he color-coded each session: Informal gatherings and networking opportunities were purple. Top-down events, in which one or a few executives addressed everyone else, were dark blue. And structured occasions for "interactive, peer-to-peer" engagement were light blue, Benenati explains. "It was important to have the right balance among those three dimensions," he says. "Very often, we have too much 'dark blue' in our meetings." The Marketplace was one of the "light-blue" sessions, and sessions of that type formed the innovative core of the strategy that Cheshire and

Benenati developed to transform unit-level leaders into One Team leaders. "We really want to surprise them and to get them to have real conversations," Benenati said shortly before the conference took place. "It will be very much a laboratory."

In designing the physical look and feel of that "laboratory," Benenati opted to abandon the spatial form that's traditionally used at large-group event. "I have decided to destroy the stage," he said beforehand. "The room will be completely round." Instead of a raised stage of the kind that divides participants into speakers and listeners, there would be a theater-in-the-round space in the middle of the room, and surrounding it there would be an area called the One Team Lounge. In the lounge area, participants would gather in preassigned groups of five. "They will sit with colleagues from different countries. They will not sit with friends from their own national silos," Benenati explained. "That way, we create the conditions for connections to happen." Overall, he strove in his meeting-design work to achieve a balance between what he calls "permission" and what he calls "process"—or (as we would say) between openness and closure. "In Barcelona, people need to feel that there is permission to have real conversations," he said. "And at the same time, those real conversations must follow some process rules. It's not about just having conversation for the sake of it. It's about having conversation to generate engagement and performance." The essential challenge that Benenati faced was the classic one of planning for spontaneity. Regarding one of the "light-blue" sessions that he designed for the conference, he said: "The script is not really written. We have a very clear idea of what the process will be, but then it will be about the energy in the room."

While there would be no script for the conversations that were to occur in Barcelona, there would be an agenda. A few weeks before the conference, Kingfisher sent to invited participants a list of thirteen questions about various issues that they might address when they convened. "The questionnaire was a perfect opportunity to gather insight on their expectations, and on what they believed were the really hot topics," Benenati says. Responses to the questionnaire were anonymous, and he and his team compiled them into what he calls an "opinion book." From that document, Cheshire and Benenati derived a set of three broad issues that would be the focus of discussion at the conference. One topic was "customer happiness, or the way we deliver what the customer needs, which is different from what the customer wants," Benenati explains. A second topic involved the previously mentioned push to implement common sourcing of common products. The third topic was the all-important matter of Kingfisher's evolving organizational structure. "There was a strategy, and there was a process," Benenati says of this agenda-setting advance work. "It was a democratic, bottom-up identification of topics for conversation." Meanwhile, every attendee received a copy of the opinion book as well. Among the opinions included in the book, there were a number of critical comments about Kingfisher and its current strategic path, so distributing the document in a raw and uncensored form was a risky move. "It was a message of transparency: We have nothing to hide," Benenati says.

Heading into the conference, Pascal Gil certainly expected that an openness of spirit would be one of its main features. "We can change if we have an open mind," he said. He also noted that Barcelona would be a "great place for making this change": "It is open to the sea, to the world. It's an open town." Albert Aranda, his colleague at Brico Dépôt Spain, anticipated that the meeting would be "a good opportunity to share with people and to understand the whole strategy of Kingfisher." Gil, echoing that view, suggested that the key to grasping the Kingfisher strategy whole would be for "everybody to forget where we are coming from—forget that we are coming from Spain, from the U.K., from anywhere—and to think about where we want to go."

"Imagine, Create, Dare!"

In Barcelona, the work of conversational strategy culminated in a display of group-wide strategic conversation. The conference began on a Tuesday afternoon and ended on a Thursday afternoon; it lasted forty-eight hours but spanned three days. For each of those days, Cheshire and Benenati chose a one-word theme that corresponded to one phase of a conversational process. The keyword for the first day was *Imagine*. The meeting started with Cheshire calling on attendees to open their eyes and ears, and their minds, to what colleagues all across Kingfisher had to say. Benenati summarizes the spirit and purpose of that day's activity: "Let's avoid rushing into an action plan. Let's spend the afternoon discovering our diversity." On day two, the keyword was *Create*. Here, the emphasis was on "knowledge management and knowledge creation," Benenati explains—on turning provocative thoughts into action-ready ideas. The Marketplace session, for example, with its focus on sharing best-practice stories, reflected that day's theme of creative exploration. Finally, the keyword for day three (complete with an exclamation point) was *Dare!* As Benenati puts it, "the flow of energy in the room" now shifted toward a mode of commitment, with attendees resolving to take certain post-Barcelona action steps. "We started by discussing topics. We continued by creating ideas that we could make concrete. And we ended by selecting the ideas that we liked," he says. In sum, the conference followed an arc (from discovery to resolution) that resembles the arc (from opening a conversation to closing the loop on that conversation) that we associate with intentionality.

Running like a linked chain across all three days was a series of conversational experiences ("light-blue" experiences, according to Benenati's color scheme) that allowed attendees to engage directly with core issues raised by Kingfisher's evolving One Team strategy. On the first afternoon, in a session called Real Conversations, attendees convened in the One Team Lounge to talk about the three topics—customer happiness, common sourcing of products, and organizational structure—that Cheshire and Benenati had pinpointed before the conference. "We told them, 'It's not about agreeing with each other today. It's about listening to each other, and debating, and discovering our diversity, and getting these topics on the table in the most transparent way possible.' This was a crucial preliminary step in co-building one team, and of course it was all about trust," Benenati says. For each topic, there were three rounds of discussion. First, in what Benenati calls a "feeding" round, selected participants fed the conversation by offering their pulling-no-punches thoughts on the topic in question. "People agreed before the meeting to share their frank opinion," Benenati explains. In the next round, all 200-plus attendees were able to discuss the topic in an up-close, back-and-forth debate with other members of their five-person group. "That's the right number to have a really good conversation. If you have more than five, it's not intimate enough," Benenati says. Finally, in a feedback round, people from various groups of five reported to the whole assembly on salient points that emerged during their debate round.

The same topics provided an agenda for the Megastorm experience, which took place on day two. Attendees got together in their five-person groups, and conference planners charged each group with the task of generating innovative ideas related to one of those three subject areas. "It was a brainstorming session," Benenati says. (Hence the term Megastorm.) At this point, he explains, the focus of conversation grew more tangible: "How, concretely, are we going to make customers happy? How, concretely, can we organize ourselves to become the world's leading local home-improvement retailer?" Over the course of four hours, the five-person teams collectively generated a mighty storm of Post-it notes—2,500 of them, by Benenati's estimate—and then sifted through that flow of ideas to produce eighty-six clearly defined business recommendations. (There were forty-three teams, and they created two recommendations apiece.) On day three, in a session called the Gallery, conference organizers presented those eighty-six recommendations on a series of posters. Attendees, while touring this exhibition of ideas that their colleagues had developed, could cast their vote on which ideas merited further investment by the company. In addition, there was a session labeled Close Your Deal, in which participants signaled their willingness to invest their own time and energy into continuing the One Team journey.

Toward the very end of the conference, attendees took one other step to close the loop on their forty-eight-hour Barcelona experience: They arranged, in effect, to send a message to their near-future selves. "We gave everyone a postcard and said, 'Write down at least three things that you're going to do after this event. We'll post it to you ten days after the conference, so it will arrive just as you're beginning to forget what you've said here. And this way, you actually remember it.' It was a very helpful little device," Cheshire says. Even the best conversation, as Cheshire and his colleagues well know, is only as strategically effective as the follow-up work that occurs in its wake.

Immediately following the conference, in fact, participants found ways to continue the group-wide organizational conversation that they had set in motion in Barcelona. A subset of sixteen attendees formed a team that would work to create a comprehensive ten-year strategy for the Kingfisher group. In addition, Benenati notes, attendees "were invited to integrate all of this energy and all of these ideas into their local strategic plans." Unit-level leaders also started to borrow practices such as the One Team Lounge and the Megastorm for use in regional and national meetings. "This approach to communication is now being embedded in the way we work," Benenati says. During the conference, for example, leaders from one of Kingfisher's operating companies in France announced their intent to host a Marketplace-like event for several hundred of their employees. One regional director even voiced an interest in sponsoring a kind of Marketplace road show, in which three or four "suppliers" from the Marketplace session in Barcelona would visit stores in his region and describe their best-practice ideas to local managers. "That's very important, because it means giving permission to people down in the organization to break the silos and to have direct connections between stores," Benenati says. "It's internal communication done the warm way, not the cold way. That was a fantastic surprise. I didn't expect that impact to happen so soon."

Group Therapy

The cumulative experience of the Barcelona meeting reaffirmed the view among Kingfisher leaders that, as Benenati says, "communication is the enabler for building the strategy." From that experience, they also took some enduring lessons on how to leverage the power of organizational conversation.

HOW YOU TALK DEPENDS ON WHERE YOU SIT. In any conversation, the position occupied by each of its participants matters a great deal. One goal behind the Real Conversations session was to give attendees a chance to think like group-level executives—to trade their unit-level outlook for a Kingfisher-wide outlook. Conference planners asked attendees to communicate within their five-person teams as if they were members of the company's five-person group executive team, and to analyze issues from that vantage point. "Ian and other group executives told me, 'We want them to walk in our shoes and to experience some of the paradox of being a real leader,' such as managing short-term and long-term goals," Benenati explains. That tactic paid off handsomely, Cheshire says: "It put people in a completely different position.

They were debating issues from my perspective." Opening up the conference floor to unfiltered conversation required him to give up "the illusion of control," he concedes. Yet the opportunity to watch as attendees turned his vision into *their* vision easily made up for that loss. "That was actually creating alignment," he argues.

TALKING TOGETHER MAKES IT EASIER TO WORK TOGETHER. "People had enough time to discover other people and other ideas, and they did it at their own pace, as opposed to us telling them how to do it," Cheshire says, referring to the design and structure of the conference. Bringing together people from all walks of company life—through conversation, in groups of five—yielded "a change in the quality of relationships" that was "more emotional than rational," he suggests. "That was very much because of the fact that *they* were doing the work. It was the complete antithesis of the traditional death-by-PowerPoint piece." Early signs that attendees were following up on the connections that they had formed in Barcelona gave him confidence that Kingfisher was making headway in its push to build a cross-organizational One Team spirit. "It's turned into a series of organic connections that we are not having to run," he says.

REAL TALK CAN BE REALLY DIFFICULT, AND THAT'S OKAY. Not everybody in the Kingfisher organization eagerly embraces the notion of aligning the company more tightly at the group level. "People aren't entirely happy about it. They're worried about it," Cheshire acknowledges. But a chief aim of the Barcelona event was to give a full airing to such concerns, no matter how uneasy it might make people feel to talk about them. "There was a great desire for people to jump straight into action," Cheshire recalls. Instead, he explains, he and his fellow group-level executives insisted on "holding people to the question and saying, 'Let's talk about this. Let's face up to some uncomfortable things.'" Thus, during the discussion of organizational structure that was part of the Real Conversations experience, attendees had to reckon with their anxieties about the company's move toward greater centralization. "Some guys were saying, 'Well, does this mean that it's all going to be effectively run out of London or Southampton?' And I was able to say that I think it would be really bad for our organization if we overcentralized or overstandardized, because then we'd lose our focus on the customer," Cheshire says. Being up-front about the matter, he adds, is far better than a situation in which "people pretend to toe the party line" while working to subvert the new strategy. Benenati, for his part, worried beforehand that the open and frank conversational forum that he had designed simply might not work. What if no one was willing to speak up? Indeed, as the conversation on day one got under way, "there was some silence and some discomfort," he recalls. Soon enough, though, the mood shifted and the conversation began in earnest. "People realized that it was necessary, if not enjoyable, to be confronted with different points of view," he says. "It was a genuine collective moment."

UNDERLYING THESE LESSONS is a recognition of the strategic value of moving people beyond their comfort zone. Which partly explains why Cheshire, in bringing the Barcelona conference to a close, decided to step outside *his* comfort zone. At the end of day three, he stood in front of the entire gathering, and he got personal. Drawing upon details from his background, he offered an intimate glimpse into what drives his quest to build a strategically aligned yet regionally diverse organization. "It was just me walking around, talking with a clip-mike and referring to a series of photos that I was clicking through," he says. Among those photos was one of him "at age six months, apparently drinking beer," he notes. "It was the most embarrassing baby picture that I could find." An openness to embarrassment—a willingness to let down his guard—helped make the presentation work. "Technically, I was in control," he observes. "But I was at the same time *not* in control, and that allowed me to connect more effectively, I think, with my top two hundred managers."

The core message that Cheshire delivered to attendees was that a desire to pursue integration across diverse geographical entities, or across diverse national identities, comes naturally to him. He recounted his early life story, from his birth in Borneo (he recalls speaking Malay before learning to speak English) to a later period when he lived in Nigeria during the 1966 civil war in that country. His father worked for Shell, the multinational oil company, and as an adult, he too worked for Shell. "I grew up inside a one-team Anglo-Dutch culture," he says. "I'm just used to going anywhere in the world and finding interesting people." Yet he also received what he calls a "very traditional" and rigorously classical British education. "A background that is very international but very structured gives me a basis to say, 'I believe we can create something analogous to that—a truly global One Team company,'" he argues. "This isn't just lip service, or some sort of management theory. This is something that I am fundamentally wired to believe in."

WITH THAT SINGLE THREE-DAY conference in Barcelona, Kingfisher leaders evinced a keen interest in all four elements in our model of organizational conversation. In sessions that depended on sustained employee involvement, such as the Real Conversations event and the Marketplace, they proved their commitment to *inclusion*. By structuring many conference sessions around dynamic, back-and-forth discussion within compact five-person groups, they indicated their appreciation for the value of *interactivity*. Ian Cheshire, through his readiness to talk personally about the motive forces behind his One Team vision, made plain that he and his team prize *intimacy*. And, of course, the meeting as a whole—designed explicitly to promote the strategic goal of organizational alignment—embodied a commitment to *intentionality*.

Other current practices at Kingfisher reflect an investment in the building blocks of organizational conversation. The use of the Castoramoa intranet platform—in particular, its use by employees to design a new in-store uniform—exemplifies a forward-leaning approach to both inclusion and interactivity. The Progression initiative at Brico Dépôt Spain, meanwhile, shows how ready Kingfisher leaders are to pursue modes of communication that involve intimacy as well as inclusion. In that case, too, the company's emphasis on conversational intentionality looms as a highly salient factor.

CHAPTER TWELVE

Talk, Inc., Points (TIPs)

A Sense of Direction

A GOOD CONVERSATION WILL occasionally meander. It will go this way and then that way, as its participants talk about one topic before shifting to another topic, or as they fasten upon one idea before changing course to consider a wholly different idea. But in a *really* good conversation, those who talk together share a sense that they're moving forward together. They understand that their talk is taking them somewhere, however circuitous the route toward that destination might be. In an organizational setting, conversation will be good—it will be effective and sustainable—only to the extent that it embodies a sense of direction. That phrase, *a sense of direction,* has two meanings in this context. First, it means that one person or one group of people will take responsibility for managing (that is, *directing*) the overall flow of discussion within a company. Second, it means that such discussion will follow a trajectory that culminates in a well-defined end point (as with the direction *due north*). Crucially, moreover, a sense of direction is what enables communication to become a strategically critical, value-adding endeavor. Here, to help leaders maintain their bearings as they pursue conversational intentionality, we offer a few points for them to keep in mind.

Take Stock

Forward-looking leaders, when they decide to chart a new conversational strategy, often begin by looking backward—by taking stock of what they and their colleagues have done thus far to support communication to, from, and among employees. Being intentional, in other words, typically involves a willingness to be introspective. Whether they call it an audit or an assessment or something else, leaders who conduct a formal, top-to-bottom evaluation of their communication practices usually find that it yields sharp lessons on how to improve their organizational conversation.

A thorough survey of internal communication at General Motors in 2008 led company leaders to recognize that they needed to streamline that operation, just as they might need to streamline their automotive assembly lines (or, for that matter, some of the cars in their product line). "We did a complete assessment of how effective our communication system was—what was working, what wasn't," says Kim Carpenter, who was then manager of global internal communications at GM. "The big thing that we learned from it was that generating a lot of content is not necessarily effective." Before, the company followed a "cafeteria approach," she explains. "We'd put information in twenty different places, and you could get the information in whichever place you liked. But that generated a lot of waste and repetitiveness, and it required a lot of resources." After the assessment, Carpenter and other GM leaders opted to restrict their use of communication vehicles to just four areas: Web- and intranet-based content, video programming, "push" e-mail messaging, and face-to-face interaction.

Saying less, or saying something less frequently, isn't the same thing as communicating less. The management of GM's internal television outlet offers a case in point. When company leaders rolled out the GM video channel, it initially featured new content each working day. One upshot of the 2008 communication assessment, however, was a decision to update video programming weekly instead of daily. "We didn't want to lose the power of video, the ability to tell a story visually. But we also realized that we were creating information overload by producing five shows a week," Carpenter says.

Create a "Bucket" List

Just because leaders *can* talk about a given topic doesn't mean that they *should* talk about it. Just because they can undertake a communication initiative doesn't mean that they should undertake it. And just because they can deploy a particular tool to communicate with employees doesn't mean that they should deploy it. Before they take any of those steps, they do well to think about the purpose that they're trying to serve. Conversationally adept leaders, therefore, analyze each communication effort to see whether it matches up with certain key priorities.

At the utility holding company Exelon, those in charge of employee communication used to organize that function around a loose-knit set of traditional messaging vehicles—a newsletter here, a Web site there. "The internal communications group, by the time I got here, was seen by large parts of the organization as reactive," Howard N. Karesh says. In 2008, Exelon leaders hired Karesh to lead that group and to remake its operations from the ground up. Before long, he adopted a conversational strategy that organizes all communication activity not according to the channels that he and his colleagues use, but according to the objectives that they seek to promote. He decided to "focus on three specific buckets," he explains. First, there is *leadership connectivity,* which involves the quality of interaction between leaders and employees. Second, there is *strategy and business acumen,* which refers to the goal of educating employees about the competitive environment that Exelon faces today. And third, there is *workplace and culture,* which encompasses corporate values and employee engagement.

"The idea is that no matter what we do—an intranet site, a newsletter, a campaign, an executive message, whatever—it's going to clearly fit into at least one of those buckets, and probably more than one," Karesh says. Clarifying which communication efforts fall into which buckets, he notes, also enables Karesh and his team "to measure how successful we are at moving the needle in any one of those areas."

Go Wide, Go Deep

In any company that's grown to be large and complex, most employees necessarily devote most of their attention to what's happening in their narrow part of the organization. As a result, they fail to see what their colleagues in other departments and divisions are doing, and they lose sight of what their company as a whole aims to do. To counter that tendency, leaders need to give employees a chance to widen their perspective—and, just as important, a chance to deepen their knowledge of the company's big-picture strategy.

At McKesson, executives have turned part of a regular conference call with employees into a forum where people who work in one area of the company's health-care services business can learn about the ways and workings of other areas. Each quarter, top leaders host an hour-long call, and any employee can dial in to listen to it. During the first half of the call, participating executives discuss the kind of material that is standard fare for such events—financial results from the previous quarter, expectations for the next quarter. In the second half of the call, though, they focus on one aspect of the company's multifaceted operations. "We carve out half an hour for what we call a 'deep dive,' or a roundtable discussion, on a particular topic," says Andy Burtis, vice president of corporate marketing and communications. Over a period in 2009, for instance, McKesson leaders used a sequence of quarterly calls to talk in-depth about specific customer sectors: pharmacies, physician offices, hospitals, and so forth. Their aim, Burtis notes, was to educate employees on "how we serve those different segments, and how the work that we do in those segments aligns to our overall business goals."

Another venue where employees gain access to a broad view of their company and its place in the health-care marketplace is the McKesson Vision Center. "It's essentially an Epcot-like center that provides our vision for the future of health care," Burtis explains. "It brings together all of our technology, all of the products and services that we offer, and it shows how health care could function if all of those pieces were operating in perfect harmony." Designed and built to reach customers, policy makers, and other external audiences, the center has become a tool for engaging internal audiences as well. "We use it for new-employee orientation and for other employee events, to help people understand the full scope of what we do," Burtis says.

Make a Mark

No longer is branding for customers only. Employees, too, are more apt to become fully engaged with a company when that company displays a crisp, coherent sense of identity. For that reason, many leaders devote time, attention, and other resources—resources of the kind that external marketers typically deploy—to generating a strong internal brand message. A brand gives people a fixed, memorable understanding of what they're talking about when they talk about a company. For employees, it can serve as a tool that helps them to follow the thread of organizational conversation.

"Many people think that branding is just about having a logo. But it's clearly much more than that," says Kelly Lindenboom, vice president of corporate communications at Verenium, a biofuel-technology company based in San Diego. In 2009, after winding up a major external branding effort, she and other Verenium leaders turned their attention to enabling employees to see the company—its goals, its commitments, its culture—as a whole. They prepared a lean, polished marketing piece called *The Little Green Book: An Employee Guide to the Verenium Brand*. Between its covers (which are green, of course, partly in homage to the company's focus on developing sustainable sources of energy) are sections titled "What Is a Brand?" and "How the Verenium Brand Is Built." About the booklet, Lindenboom says: "It rolls out our core values and really explains to employees who we are and what we're trying to achieve."

Another highly intentional step that Verenium leaders have taken—one that draws upon the principles of branding—is the practice of adopting an annual organizational theme. Back in 2008, they branded the year (so to speak) with a simple message that had multiple ramifications: "Breakthrough to the Future." That phrase obviously had the potential to resonate with the scientists and technicians who work each day to develop breakthrough products at Verenium, but it also served as an "umbrella theme" that applied to all employees, Lindenboom notes: "We kept saying that we needed everybody to be making big and small breakthroughs. We wanted to hear from people in finance, or from the admin who was able to save money on catering." She and her team used the theme as a leitmotif in organizational messaging, and then-CEO Carlos Riva routinely cited "breakthrough" achievements at all-hands meetings. "It was a rallying point for the company," Lindenboom says.

Talk Together, Work Together

How does a company make sure that its left hand knows what its right hand is doing? The answer is simple, at least on one level: Those on the left-hand side of the organization must *talk* with those on the right-hand side. On the level of hard practicality, though, getting people to talk together requires a measure of intentionality on the part of those who manage the company's overall organizational conversation. Communication across departmental lines doesn't come naturally, and smart leaders thus work to make it a matter of carefully nurtured habit.

Rick Eno, CEO of the bioscience company Metabolix, keeps a fairly loose grip on the process of communication among his employees. "We've got some very bright people, so if we can outline where we want to go, they're going to help us get there," he says. "I don't want to overengineer how we get there." That approach, he adds, "has resulted in a lot of dialogue that's in alignment with the direction of the company." But a challenge arises when it comes to operationally aligning one part of the company with another. It is, to a large extent, the classic challenge faced by any organization that seeks to turn raw innovation into customer-ready products. The manufacturing group at Metabolix, for example, must keep in close contact with groups that come earlier or later in the company's value chain.

"As we move from pure science to commercialization, we migrate to a more cross-functional kind of communication," Eno notes. "We're trying to compensate for the natural breakdown of communication that occurs because of the pace at which technology is moving." Toward that end, he and his team have instituted practices that encourage people to talk outside the box, as it were. "We're doing some organizational training in which we look at points of integration between departments," he says. That training starts with getting employees to situate whatever they do within a larger context, he explains: "If you're pursuing something that's different, one of the first questions that you should ask is, 'Whose work does it affect other than my own? Who do I talk to about it?'"

Afterword

I's on the Prize

IN FASHIONING TERMS for the four elements that lie at the heart of this book, we chose words that begin with the letter *I*. That's an apt choice, we believe. As the saying goes, there is no *I* in *team*. Yet there is more than one *I* in organizational conversation. In fact, organizational conversation consists largely of bringing individuals *I*'s together for a shared purpose—of enabling them to see *I* to *I*, so to speak. It begins, as we've explained, by opening up new ways for employees from all parts of a company to put forth ideas and information, and it progresses by integrating their many voices and viewpoints into a common vision.

Let's review the terms of our discussion—the four parts of organizational speech, as we might call them—once more.

Intimacy, or Getting Close

Through conversational intimacy, leaders narrow the gap that otherwise yawns between the higher and lower levels of an organizational hierarchy. That's what the leaders of Hindustan Petroleum Corporation Ltd. (HPCL) did when they launched a series of vision workshops that allow employees at every level of HPCL to help chart the company's future. Along the way, these executives have shown how an organization can overhaul its entire approach to leadership.

Interactivity, or Promoting Dialogue

Using tools and techniques that support conversational interactivity, leaders ensure that organizational communication isn't a one-way proposition. Inside Cisco Systems, leaders have invested in advanced videoconferencing capabilities and in a robust collaboration platform. In doing so, and in working to build a highly interactive culture as well, they highlight the dynamic, social power of technology.

Inclusion, or Involving Employees

By engaging in conversational inclusion, leaders find new partners to assist them in telling their organizational story. At EMC Corporation, leaders invite employees of every stripe to create online communities, to maintain internal and external blog sites—even, in one notable case, to undertake a company-sponsored book project. The upshot of those efforts is a potentially transformative method for developing content.

Intentionality, or Pursuing an Agenda

From the practice of conversational intentionality, leaders derive a renewed ability to achieve operational closure and organizational cohesion. Thus, leaders at Kingfisher PLC have designed novel forms of internal communication—a radically different kind of business conference, for example—as a means to instill an ethos of cross-company alignment in their employees. In the process, these leaders have demonstrated that conversation can become a vehicle for driving strategy.

THE PROMISE OF *TALK, INC.*, is that there's a new and better way to lead an organization, now that the command-and-control way has ceased to work. As we noted previously, you don't need to dot all four of these *I*'s to start powering your organization along the lines of this new model. How you adapt the model to your own company is, of course, open for discussion.

So let that conversation begin.

NOTES

CHAPTER ONE

1. For this discussion of Rogers's leadership practice, we have drawn upon Boris Groysberg, Nitin Nohria, Colleen Kaftan, and Geoff Marietta, "Leadership in Energy: Jim Rogers at Cinergy," Case 9-408-097 (Boston: Harvard Business School, 2007, 2008), 11–12.

2. Ibid.

3. Ibid.

4. Ibid.

5. Exelon Corporation, "D&I Discussions: Ian McLean," video, provided to the authors by Howard N. Karesh, November 2009.

CHAPTER TWO

1. Hindustan Petroleum Corporation Limited, "We Believe," company mission statement, available at www.hindustanpetroleum.com/En/UI/WeBelieve.aspx.

CHAPTER FOUR

1. John Chambers, quoted in Bronwyn Fryer and Thomas A. Stewart, "Cisco Sees the Future," *Harvard Business Review,* November 2008, 76.

CHAPTER FIVE

1. John Chambers, quoted in James Manyika, "McKinsey Conversations with Global Leaders: John Chambers," *McKinsey Quarterly* 4 (2009).

2. Ibid.

3. John Chambers, quoted in Bronwyn Fryer and Thomas A. Stewart, "Cisco Sees the Future," *Harvard Business Review,* November 2008, 78.

4. John Chambers, quoted in Richard M. Smith, "'Know What You Don't Know': The CEO of Cisco Systems on the Future of Leadership," *Newsweek,* June 14, 2010.

5. Fryer and Stewart, "Cisco Sees the Future," 78.

6. John Chambers, in ibid.

CHAPTER EIGHT

1. EMC Corporation, "World's Data More Than Doubling Every Two Years—Driving Big Data Opportunity, New IT Roles," press release, June 28, 2011, http://www.emc.com/about/news/press/2011/20110628-01.htm.

CHAPTER TEN

1. See Boris Groysberg, Nitin Nohria, Colleen Kaftan, and Geoff Marietta, "Leadership in Energy: Jim Rogers at Cinergy," Case 9-408-097 (Boston: Harvard Business School Publishing, 2007, 2008), 10–11.

ACKNOWLEDGMENTS

Talk, Inc. is the product of a great many conversations. It started with a conversation between the two of us about the current state of play in the field known traditionally as *corporate communication*. We knew that organizational life, along with the competitive environment that surrounds it, has undergone wave after wave of disruptive change in recent years. We also knew that the apparatus of communication—the tools, the channels—have been changing just as quickly and no less disruptively. But we wondered: Have organizational leaders responded to those changes by significantly altering the way they manage communication to, from, and among their people? And if so, how has that shift affected the way these leaders run (or *power*) their organizations?

Further conversations between us followed, and they resulted in a plan to undertake the long series of conversations that make up the foundation of this book. Using the language both of academic research and of journalism, we called these conversations *interviews*. Yet, while we structured our interviews around a clear agenda—while we approached them with intentionality, in other words—they weren't entirely formal. As we talked with people in various roles at various organizations, we found that these discussions often exhibited the free-form, insight-rich dynamic of an informal chat. Thus, we'd like to acknowledge the scores of business leaders and communication professionals who spoke to us about their work, and who did so in a way that was intimate, interactive, and inclusive. We weren't able to cite all of these people by name in the pages of this book, but we greatly appreciate the contribution that each of them made to our project.

Overlapping that series of conversations were conversations with colleagues inside and outside Harvard Business School (HBS). Their apt comments and constructive questions helped us to develop a model for understanding the ideas and practices that we were gleaning from our interviews—a model of organizational leadership and organizational collaboration that we came to call *organizational conversation*. In that context, we wish to thank members of the administration and the faculty at HBS, who provided crucial institutional as well as intellectual support for our efforts. Equally crucial was the work of HBS's Kate Connolly, who supported our project in countless ways and at many a critical juncture.

The folks at Harvard Business Review Publishing, meanwhile, have allowed us to start a conversation with a much larger set of participants. Our editor, Tim Sullivan, not only supported this book from its early stages, but also took the notable (and notably risky) step of bringing it with him from one publisher to another. Along the way, he offered trenchant advice on the scope, structure, and voice we should use in transforming our research material into a cohesive, reader-friendly product. We also benefited from the shrewd minds and nimble editorial hands of other members of the HBR Press team, including Jennifer Waring, who led our manuscript through the book production process with sherpa-like resourcefulness, and Patricia Boyd, who rid the manuscript of numerous flaws and wrestled it into book-ready shape.

Conversations with our wives, Liliya Groysberg and Bina Patel, have provided each of us with an indispensable thread of support that has pulled us through each stage of this project. We mention Liliya and Bina last, but the foremost debt that we owe—regarding this project, and so much else—is to them.

ABOUT THE AUTHORS

BORIS GROYSBERG is a professor of business administration in the Organizational Behavior unit at Harvard Business School. Currently, he teaches courses on talent management and leadership in the school's MBA and Executive Education programs. He has won numerous awards for his research, which focuses on the challenge of managing human capital at small and large organizations across the world. His work focuses, in particular, on how firms can achieve a sustainable competitive advantage by engaging employees in the implementation of business strategy. Groysberg is the author of the award-winning book *Chasing Stars: The Myth of Talent and the Portability of Performance.* A frequent contributor to *Harvard Business Review,* he has written many articles and case studies on how firms hire, engage, develop, retain, and communicate with their employees. Before joining the Harvard Business School faculty, he worked at IBM. He lives in Boston.

MICHAEL SLIND is a writer, editor, and communication consultant. He served as managing editor and as a senior editor at *Fast Company* magazine. During his tenure as managing editor, *Fast Company* won a National Magazine Award for general excellence. Later, he worked at Harvard Business School, where he collaborated with faculty members to write widely used case studies on corporate strategy and entrepreneurial management. As a consultant, Slind focuses on developing creative and strategically relevant solutions that meet the communication needs of his clients. In that role, he has undertaken projects for Tom Peters and other business thought leaders. He lives in Palo Alto, California.